An Armful of Animals

Published by Midas Touch Books

Author's website
www.malcolmwelshman.co.uk

ISBN 978-1-72240-219-8

Also available as a Kindle ebook
ISBN 978-1-84396-514-5

A catalogue record for this
book is available from the British Library and
the American Library of Congress.

Pre-press production
eBook Versions
27 Old Gloucester Street
London WC1N 3AX
www.ebookversions.com

Praise for
An Armful of Animals

'A witty take on a young vet's life that pet lovers will find endearing.'
Bel Mooney, author and *Daily Mail* columnist

'A joyful read full of animals and fun. Guaranteed to delight, though there are some tearful moments.'
Celia Haddon, author and former *Daily Telegraph* columnist

'The author has an uncanny ability to paint human as well as animal characters. Any animal lover will adore this book, of that I am certain.'
Michael Smith, editor of *Green (Living) Review*

'Malcolm shares his everyday adventures that include encounters with creatures as diverse as a cow stuck in a tree and a red-footed booby. His human clients are as quirky as the pets he treats. This memoir is a must read.'
Sue Parslow, freelance writer and editor

'The writing is funny and full of character. This book deserves to be successful.'
Kate Nash, literary agent

'It was a pleasure to read. Malcolm's encounters with clients and creatures great and small, made me chuckle throughout. Highly recommended.'
Cathy Woodman, bestselling author of *Trust Me, I'm a Vet*

'Bursting with exotic creatures and eccentric characters, this touching memoir makes for a spellbinding read where the author's love of animals shines through.'
Jenny Itzcovitz, editor of Sixtyplusurfers.co.uk

'Malcolm's experiences, recounted in a most readable way, illustrate the interesting and challenging situations that can confront a vet. A most enjoyable insight into his fascinating life.'
Jim Wight, son of James Herriot, author of *The Real James Herriot*

*This memoir is dedicated
to all the animals that have
shaped my life as a vet*

An
Armful
of
Animals

Malcolm D. Welshman

Midas Touch Books

Contents

Prologue

My earliest recollection of communing with Mother Nature, attempting to find empathy for the animals we share our planet with, was when peering into a matchbox that contained the shrivelled remains of a newt called Nigel.

It was a special matchbox. One from my collection, the lid depicting three red dice. Lucky dice. Though not so lucky for the inmate inside – a common newt, *Triturus vulgaris*. Such a creature spent its days hiding under a stone. Sleeping under a log. But never in a matchbox.

I'd been up on the local golf course, near to a pond, poking through the rough verges, seeking out lost golf balls, when I discovered Nigel.

A book on British reptiles and amphibians, borrowed from the library, told me all I needed to know about Nigel's lifestyle. How, in the spring, he headed for the nearest pond to court females, sporting an impressive crest that ran from his head to his tail, complementing his black-spotted body – his equivalent of our tattoos. If that wasn't enough, Nigel would entice females to him with wafts of glandular secretions – guaranteed to make any nubile newt swoon with desire. Having done what was necessary to ensure the continuation of the species, Nigel would haul himself ashore to slump under a stone for the rest of the summer. Hopefully undisturbed. Unless the likes of me, a six-year-old, came along and winkled him out, took him home and plonked him in a converted aquarium, decked out with logs and rocks. There to remain for the rest of the summer, being fed a diet of worms and beetles.

One late September day, I discovered Nigel's body lifeless under a rock. It was then the matchbox made its appearance. Carefully chosen to be Nigel's coffin. A burial place was selected. Under a stone in the back garden. I even erected a little cross made of – yes, you've guessed – two matches. A week passed before it dawned on me that Nigel may not have died. Merely succumbed to the time of year when he was due to hibernate. Suddenly, I had this ghastly thought that I had buried him alive. I found myself digging up the matchbox and sliding it open to find out. I was saddened to look down on those desiccated remains, dried up beyond recognition. Poor Nigel.

If anything was to be learnt from that experience, it was the importance of being conversant with the characteristics of the creatures I would go on to care for. But even then, there would always be occasions where the unexpected could occur. Such is life with animals. Many challenges. Some joyous. Some sad. But the years threaded with those challenges has meant a rich tapestry of life for me – as the ensuing stories will demonstrate.

I relish this opportunity to share those stories with you.

1

For Love of Polly

'I'm sorry, Polly. But it's got to be done,' I murmured as the African grey squawked loudly from the muffled confines of the towel in which she was wrapped. With trembling hands, I extricated one of her legs, parted the feathers and injected the anaesthetic. The parrot slipped into unconsciousness, her frantic shrieks dying away. There was a growth, an ugly misshapen raspberry of tissue, pressing on her windpipe. If I didn't operate, she would slowly asphyxiate and I would lose 23 years of loyal companionship. Choice? There was none.

Polly and I were both fledglings when we first met. She, a mere bundle of grey down which growled and flapped within the confines of a rusty cage. I, a nine-year-old lad who had been living in Nigeria for just over a year, yearning to have a parrot like other army families had.

The meeting with Polly occurred one hot, dusty morning in

Ibadan's crowded market. The throng ebbed and flowed across the dusty roads. A parade of blue, crimson and yellow robes. Trays piled high with oranges, grapefruits, bananas. Battered enamel pots. Calabashes full of maize flour. Cackling chickens in palm-woven cages. The stench of urine from tethered goats.

Bored, trailing behind Father, I was scuffling through the sand, grains of it grating through my sandals, when a grizzled Housa trader in a grubby white robe waddled out of the crowd. In his hand swayed the cage from which the African grey parrot stared out, her pale grey eyes full of alarm, her beak open, hissing.

'Young master dum like this bird?' said the trader as he dangled the cage in front of me and gave a wide smile to expose a stump of red, betel nut-stained teeth.

'Oh please, Dad, please,' I implored.

'Dis is one fine bird,' coaxed the wily old man, darting between us.

Father made a determined effort to march on despite the throng of people. The trader clutched at his sleeve. 'Young master like bird.'

Father stopped, turned, thrust a hand into his khaki shorts.

I tried again. 'Oh, go on, Dad. Please.'

Father harrumphed, fiddled with his moustache. Then said, 'Five pounds.'

The trader laughed, his forehead creasing in a bunch of black wrinkles. 'Na ... Na ...' he replied with a shake of his head.

Father shrugged and turned away.

'Na ... Na ...' the trader repeated, this time more strident, echoed with alarm as he saw a potential sale slipping away. He hastily stretched out a dusty palm. The cage exchanged hands. The African grey parrot became ours.

For many months, Polly remained a frightened, nervous

youngster. Soon, though, her pale grey eyes matured to a golden yellow, her broken quills moulted one by one as strong, new, lighter grey flight feathers burst through on her wings; and her tail erupted into sea of vermilion.

I spent weeks trying to coax her out of her cage.

'Come on, Polly,' I'd whisper, placing a piece of banana just outside her open cage door. But she was never tempted; she merely opened her beak and hissed.

I didn't need convincing of the power of that beak, having seen her splinter a block of teak as if it were a matchbox. That power was normally directed at Father. Poor man. He was the one who fed and watered her and cleaned out her cage. Yet, whenever he went near, she'd lash out and several times managed to draw blood. He'd be walking round with bandaged fingers for days.

Her tongue was another tool but one used in a delicate, dextrous way. She'd grasp an unshelled peanut in one claw, crack it open to reveal the row of nuts inside, pick one out and then start to roll the nut round with the tip of her tongue, allowing her beak to skin it before it was swallowed.

But it was her beak that I feared. No way was I ever going to go near her in case she tried to bite me. Until the day I smashed the glass front of my aquarium. I was carrying it through the lounge when I knocked it against a door handle. The glass splintered. Out poured the fish, the weed, the snails. So too did my tears. They poured down my face. I dropped the shattered aquarium on the settee and, howling with all the force a nine-year-old could muster, ran across to Polly's cage. For a moment she looked startled, backing away. Then she waddled forward, putting her head down against the bars as if asking for a scratch. Still blubbering, I didn't stop to think and poked my finger through the bars. Polly's head whipped up. Her beak caught the tip of my finger. But no bite. Just the gentle feel of her tongue over my skin as she kissed me before she too burst out sobbing.

From that moment on we were firm friends and no further encouragement was needed for her to scramble out of her cage. Whenever I entered the room she would fly over to me with a friendly squawk. Sometimes, I would arrive home from school to find a dusty parrot strutting down the drive to greet me.

'It's no good, Malcolm,' Father finally declared. 'I'll have to clip her wings otherwise she'll be flying off. And that wouldn't do, would it?' There was twitch of his moustache. A raised eyebrow.

'No, Dad,' I murmured dutifully.

'Right. Let's get cracking then.'

A towel appeared. Polly was bundled into it with muffled screeches of alarm. Each wing, in turn, was extricated from the folds of the towel and the flight feathers trimmed back by a third. The avian equivalent of a military-style short back and sides.

'That should do the trick,' declared Father as he snipped through the last few barbs. With an indignant squawk, Polly wriggled free from the confines of the towel and attempted to fly up to her cage. Instead, she belly-flopped onto the polished red floor and skidded across it like a drunken ballerina to disappear under the sideboard. From that dark recess in Father's angry tone, she uttered her first word – 'Drat'.

She did look a bit bedraggled with her flight feathers cut back. It revealed the softer, lighter grey down round her tail. So she was not such a pretty Polly. But at least it allowed her freedom from her cage; and it meant we could let her sit on a specially constructed perch out on the veranda. There she'd spend most of the day, quite content, keeping a beady yellow eye on all that was going on. Though one morning it was almost the death of her. I was sitting on the veranda, alongside her perch, when there was the sudden whoosh of feathers. A blur of wings. A screech from Polly as she was knocked off her perch. A bird of prey, the size of a falcon, had decided the parrot might have made a tasty mid-morning snack and had swooped down, under the veranda's roof, with claws stretched out ready to snatch up Polly. But missed. Though only just. A few of her feathers had been grasped and released to float to the floor. A shaken parrot clambered back up onto her perch and a 'Bloody hell' echoed out from her.

Polly's vocabulary blossomed. The range of her repertoire was astonishing. Having mastered 'Good morning' in Father's bass voice, she embellished it with army slang so that at dawn we woke, bleary-eyed to a cheerful 'Wakey, wakey, rise and shine you shower.' One of her catchphrases was 'Wotcher mate!' usually directed at me and usually in my tone of voice. She'd take great delight in waddling up my arm, her wings lowered, crooning, and then once on my shoulder whisper, 'Wotcher mate!' before stuffing regurgitated peanuts in my ear. Apparently, it's a sign of love in parrots.

Mother invited the Colonel's wife for tea one afternoon – a tall, willowy lady with a touch of Grace Kelly about her.

'She certainly thinks she's the queen bee round these parts,' Mother once said of her, somewhat ungraciously. In swirled the lady, dressed in a white and red polka-dotted dress, flared and drawn in at the waist with a broad white belt. There was even a white bag, shoes, gloves and hat to match. I saw Mother's lips twitch, her hands smooth down the sides of her shapeless polyester flower-patterned frock. The Colonel's wife came to a halt in the middle of the lounge, spotted Polly's cage over in the corner and advanced towards it, stopping in another swirl of polka dots. By the look on Mother's face, I guessed she was seeing red dots as well. Polly greeted our illustrious visitor with a chirpy 'Hello' in Mother's tone of voice.

'Oh, hello. What a charming bird you have here,' replied the Colonel's wife, her voice brimming with plums. She turned to give Mother a dazzling smile. But the smile froze when from behind her came a very clear, 'You've got droopy drawers.' Backed up by a dirty cackle. The Colonel's wife's face turned as red as her polka dots. But worse was to follow.

Polly paused as if to take breath and then in Father's deep bass tone, shouted, 'How about it luv?' while bobbing her head up and down and wagging her tail suggestively. I was an innocent at nine years of age. How about what? I wondered. Though to judge from the tight lips on the Colonel's wife's face, she knew what only too well.

In those early days in West Africa, Polly and I became inseparable. I hadn't appreciated how close a bond one could develop with a pet. My relationship with her was to stand me in good stead in later years when dealing with owners and their pets, giving me a better understanding of the deep bonds of companionship that can develop. Polly's trust and loyalty made me even more determined to be a vet when I grew up. Little did I realise then how I'd eventually be the one who'd attempt to save her life.

When I reached the age of 11, Polly and I parted company as I had to return to England for further schooling. But the holidays always meant a welcome return to Nigeria and a reunion with my pet. 'Wotcher mate!' she'd exclaim as if I'd been gone only a day instead of three months. Partings though were a wrench. Her 'Bye-byes' would echo in my ears long after I had boarded the plane back to London.

All of a sudden it seemed Father's tour of duty was over. We were coming home for good – and so was Polly. Mother and Father flew back while Polly boarded a ship for a six-week cruise as part of her quarantine. When she arrived at Southampton, her cage had painted on it, in large red letters, 'I bite'. She was silent on the drive home from the docks where Father and I had gone to pick her up.

'Perhaps she's ill,' I said, anxiously, looking over my shoulder to Polly in her cage wedged on the back seat.

'Don't worry, son, I'm sure she's fine,' said Father, strumming on the steering wheel. But I detected a note of doubt in his voice. I knew he was as fond of Polly as me and wouldn't want anything to happen to her. I had expected her to look thinner, maybe have a few feathers missing. Not a bit of it. Plump and bright-eyed, she stared at us – but still not a word said. We needn't have worried though. When we reached home, Father swung the cage onto the pavement as Mother leaned from an upstairs window. Polly looked up, fixed her with a beady, golden eye, and in her voice yelled, 'Hello, Muriel.'

Polly was housed in the kitchen where she soon picked up and imitated the sounds of daily life. Only deafeningly magnified. Cutlery into a drawer was like scaffolding collapsing. Filling the kettle, Niagara Falls. She did a wonderful imitation of a beer bottle top being removed. Phish. A glass being filled. Glug ... glug. The beer drunk. Gump ... gump. To be followed by a hearty belch. Father's belch or Mother's belch? I could never tell as they both liked their beer.

We acquired a Maltese terrier that we named Yambo. He wasn't the sharpest knife in the drawer and became a source of delight for Polly. She'd imitate the back-door bell ringing. Yambo would skitter across the lino, barking. 'Go in your box, Yambo,' she'd command. The little fellow would meekly oblige. 'Sit, Yambo,' she'd order. The dog sat. Then she'd burst out laughing.

Polly had been taught the African word for food which is 'chop'. A portion of buttered toast was always on offer at breakfast time. Polly soon learnt the sequence for making the toast and would be waddling up and down her perch saying, 'Chop ... chop' sweetly in my tone of voice as soon as you took the bread out of the bin. One morning, I decided to tease her and not give her a titbit. Naughty. Naughty. Toast made, I sat down with my back to her cage and commenced eating. Polly had been saying 'Chop ... chop' over and over again. Realising it was to no avail, her tone of voice changed. A gruff, demanding 'Chop ... chop' in Father's military voice. Still no joy. I kept on crunching, ignoring her. She paused. Silent for a moment. And then, still in Father's voice, erupted a loud, emphatic, 'What's the ruddy matter with you?' I collapsed with laughter, choking on my toast. 'Serves you right,' she squawked as I went puce. What intelligence. Polly had never been taught those phrases, yet she had picked them up – no doubt having heard the occasional rows between my parents when Dad would have used such words. And here she was, using them in context because she was miffed that I hadn't let her have her morning titbit.

Another incident occurred which demonstrated Polly's intelligence and proved that African greys are the most intelligent parrots in the world. Father still kept Polly's flight feathers clipped back and had provided her with a similar perch to the one he'd constructed in Africa. Only now this was in the back garden of our bungalow in Bournemouth. Not quite such an exotic setting. Though less dangerous. The occasional wood louse crawling into the lounge replaced foot-long millipedes.

One hot June afternoon, Polly was enjoying a spot of sunbathing out on her perch in the right-hand corner of our small back lawn.

Right, I thought to myself. Now would be a good time to give her a shower. Just a dampening. Nothing too scary. Using the sprinkler attached to the garden hose which lay coiled over the other side of the lawn, one end attached to the outside tap. So, with that in mind, I walked out of the French windows, nodded at Polly who was watching me intently, and turned to cross the lawn, heading for that sprinkler. I was still yards from it, when suddenly Polly flapped down from her perch and waddled rapidly across the grass towards me, feathers ruffled, wings flapping; and in a very cross tone of voice screeched, 'Stop it, Malcolm. Stop it.' The inference was obvious. Polly had no desire to get sprayed no matter how gentle that shower might have been. It appeared she had read my mind and worked out what I intended to do. And had declared very distinctly her utter disapproval. Quite astonishing.

For 23 years, Polly provided marvellous entertainment – a much loved member of our family. So, you can imagine the emotions that swept over me when, having just qualified as a vet, Mother phoned me to say Polly was dying. A swelling had developed on her neck. The local vet had been called in. He'd said it was inoperable. Now married, my wife, Maxeen, turned to me as I put the phone down. The look on my face must have said it all.

'Bad news?' she said.

'Polly's got a growth on her neck. Can't eat. Can't talk.' My voice broke. 'Seems it can't be operated on.' I felt tears run down my cheeks.

'But you're going to try, aren't you?'

I hesitated. 'I'm really not sure I'm up to it. I haven't operated on a bird before. Perhaps we should seek a second opinion. Get advice from an avian specialist.'

'Oh, come off it. Your parents have already had an

experienced vet's advice. If you don't do anything, Polly's going to die anyway. And by the sound of it, that could be a long, lingering death.' Maxeen gave me a hard, penetrating stare. 'And you wouldn't want that to happen, would you?'

I shrugged and bit my lower lip.

'Course you wouldn't,' Maxeen went on. 'After all those wonderful stories you've told me about her. The "Wotcher mate" catchphrase that's special to both of you.' She shook her head vigorously. 'So borrow a set of instruments from the hospital and we'll go down to your parents tomorrow. Okay?'

'Well ...'

'Good, that's settled then.'

The next day, saw us down in Bournemouth, staring through the bars at a very poorly parrot. She was just about able to balance on her perch, huddled alongside her feed and water hoppers, both full, contents untouched. Her wings were dropped, her feathers ruffled up, standing out like those on a moth-eaten feather duster. Her head was tucked into her shoulder, her eyes closed. With her neck curved at an angle, I could see it looked swollen; and poking through the feathers was visible a raised, pink lump – the cancer.

'Hello, Polly,' I whispered, hoping for a response.

Momentarily, she pulled her head from under her wing, gave me a sleepy look, before tucking her beak back under again.

'So what do you think?' asked Mother, clasping and unclasping her hands. Father standing behind her, strangely silent, apprehensive. 'Can you operate?'

I'd no choice but to say, 'Yes.' After all, Maxeen was right. There was no way I could let 23 years of loyal companionship slip away. Watch the growth get bigger. Polly slowly and painfully be asphyxiated and unable to eat as the cancer pressed deep into her neck.

As instructed, I'd brought with me a pack of sterile operating instruments. The operating table was to be the kitchen table – a blue Formica-topped one at which I'd had countless meals during my schoolboy days. First, green drapes were laid across it. Then, instruments and swabs slid onto them. I drew up a dose of anaesthetic, conscious my hands were trembling. Was I really doing the right thing? Could the tumour be removed? Could I possibly save Polly? Questions. Questions. Questions. The doubts swam through my mind as they had done through the previous night's fitful sleep when memories of our lives together out in Nigeria came flooding back. The crooning. The 'Wotcher mates' whispered in my ear. Come on, Malcolm. Concentrate. You've got to give it your best shot. At least try to save Polly.

While Maxeen held the syringe, I opened the cage door and with a small towel winkled Polly out. There was no struggle. Barely a movement. Lifting her up, I found she was as light as a feather – almost to the point of emaciation. But she had the strength to squawk. Shrieks that were piercing. That tore through me as I extricated one of her legs from the towel and injected the ketamine into her thigh. Within seconds, she was limp in my hands. We stretched her out on the table and taped down her wings before I then carefully plucked the feathers from round her neck to reveal the tumour. It was a large, misshapen raspberry of tissue that covered half the length of her neck and stretched up through her pimply skin as a pointed, yellow necrotic mass. The success of its removal depended on how adherent it was to underlying vital organs such as the windpipe and oesophagus; and whether nerves would be damaged in my attempt to dissect it out.

I carefully cut the loose skin around the tumour, avoiding

the area that the cancer had eaten into; but aware I couldn't remove too much skin as there needed to be enough left to stretch across and stitch together. With forceps, I lifted the tumour and used eye surgery scissors to gently prise away the underlying connective tissues, tying off the tumour's blood supply when I finally managed to expose it. Then, with a final snip, the tumour was free and I lifted it out. Some blood welled up in the gaping hole left. But not as much as I had anticipated. A haemostatic degradable swab put a stop to that.

'Well done,' murmured Maxeen, as I plopped the tumour into a plastic food container Mother had provided. 'Seems to have shelled out all right.'

With the wound sutured and an antibiotic injection given, Polly was gently levered back into the bottom of her cage and laid on a wad of cotton wool to recover. Mother made some mugs of coffee and we sat round the table, anxiously waiting.

Within 15 minutes, the anaesthetic had started to wear off.

Polly kicked her legs and then rolled onto her side. Her claws made contact with the bars of the cage, whereupon she pulled herself over to grip one with her beak. Slowly – so slow it was painful to watch – she began to haul herself up the bars. At the first attempt, still woozy from the anaesthetic, she lost her grip and seesawed back down to the floor of the cage. But at her fifth attempt she managed to reach her perch and levered herself onto it. Here she sat, swaying alarmingly, her beak clamped to a bar in order to stop herself from toppling off.

There followed a desperate time. Daily, I caught her up to give her an antibiotic injection. There was no struggle. No squawk. She ate nothing for three days. On the third evening, I tried with a tiny portion of banana smeared on my finger.

'Come on, Polly,' I urged.

She tottered across her perch, looked at me with eyes

devoid of sparkle, but raised her head, opened her beak with difficulty and tweaked my finger. A little of the mashed banana slid onto her tongue.

'Go on, swallow it, girl,' I cajoled.

Polly closed her beak, paused a moment. Then swallowed. I felt a flicker of hope. Maybe, just maybe, she'd pull through.

The next morning, I went down to the kitchen and opened the door, my heart skipping a beat lest I was to see Polly huddled dead in the bottom of the cage. But no. She was still on her perch. As I approached, she slowly waddled across, pressed her head down against the bars of the cage and in a croaky voice, my voice, said, 'Wotcher mate!'

Choked, I replied, 'And the same to you, Polly,' while tears of relief rolled down my cheeks. I sensed then she was going to recover. And recover she did.

I have to confess that as a young vet still wet around the gills, it gave me a great sense of achievement, a boost to my confidence. Though full of self-doubt, I had successfully completed quite a tricky operation with all the emotional difficulties of operating on my own pet. Yes, I had done it. Polly had pulled through. It was the first step in building up my self-esteem to tackle similar operations in the future; and many did appear through the surgery doors over the years. I may have had lingering doubts as to my capabilities but I only had to hear that chirpy 'Wotcher mate!' in my head to urge me on. Then such doubts flew away. All thanks to you, Polly. My ever-loving friend.

2

Our African Bush Dog

'Just hope this is all worthwhile,' moaned Mother, as her shoulder hit the inside of the car door for the fifth time. Father's knuckles gleamed as he wrenched at the steering wheel spinning out of control, the wheels of the Land Rover locking into the ruts of the dusty African road we were driving along. As we ploughed into another sandy fissure, Mother and I were once again tossed around like a couple of trout that had just been landed.

Ahead, the track stretched in a straight, shimmering line, bordered by knobby-stemmed cassava, their leaves blotched yellow, withered by the scorching sun. In the far distance, a blur of red-tiled, white-washed buildings. Our destination.

It was the hand-written card, pinned to the noticeboard in the Club House, that had brought us on this trip. It said, 'I know I'm a bitch but I don't flirt. Please give me a new home as my master is returning to the UK.'

Below it was a name and Oyo telephone number.

This was when we were living in Ibadan, my father seconded to the Queen's Own Nigerian Regiment for a two-year placement as a quartermaster. I'd soon acquired an exotic menagerie of pets. Polly, our African grey parrot, topped the list of course. But there were other creatures vying for my attention. A hawk. A monkey. A baby duiker. Several tortoises. And a black cat with a very unoriginal name – Sooty. Yet despite this motley collection, I yearned for one particular pet. A dog. A canine who could be a loyal companion. To snuggle up with. Take for walks along the jungle tracks adjacent to our bungalow. Father also wanted a dog. But for different reasons. He rather fancied himself as a big game hunter stalking the savannah, rifle slung in the crook of his arm, gun dog at heel. Not that there was any big game to be bagged in those southern parts of Nigeria. But there were guinea fowl and the likes out on the plains to the north: so, he felt a retriever of such birds would be a useful addition to the family. That went against the grain with me; but I was comforted by the fact that Father was a rotten shot, so the likelihood of any dog being put to such use was minimal.

I was about to dive into the Club's pool when Father broached the subject.

'Like to go and see her?' he called up.

'Oh yes please, Dad,' I yelled from high up on the diving board.

Mother's voice groaned from the shadow of a sunshade by the pool's edge. 'Yet another mouth to feed.'

'Oh, come on, Mum. Don't be such a spoil-sport.' With that, I hurled myself off the edge of the board, tucked up my knees, and executed one of my better water bombs. Mother was thoroughly drenched. Her enthusiasm for a dog dampened even more. But Father and I continued to badger her the rest of the day and finally she relented. Father phoned the Oyo number that evening and arranged to travel up the following Sunday.

'It will mean an early start,' warned Mother, with a grimace.

'But at least it will be cool then,' I chipped in chirpily.

The sun, a molten fireball of orange, was rising rapidly above the rusty roofs of the shanty suburbs as we bumped and rattled out of Ibadan that Sunday morning. From red and white embers of charcoal, thin pencils of smoke spiralled up into the milky sky. Kids jumped and waved. Their mothers gave us sidelong glances as they continued to stir blackened pots over open fires.

The road took us north through mile after mile of cacao plantations, the ripening orange and brown coco pods like wrinkled rugby balls glued to the tree trunks. The plantations gradually gave way to scorched savannah rattling in the hot, dry wind blowing down from the Sahara, a wind that snaked and hissed through the open windows of our Land Rover. Grass stretched to the horizon, an undulating sea of yellow, the only relief, outcrops of granite – upturned cauldrons of glistening grey, stark against the cobalt sky.

We churned slowly through the town of Oyo, leaving a pall of laterite dust hanging in the air behind us. Our destination was a government veterinary field station two miles to the east. It was approached down a deeply rutted track, bone-dry.

'Almost there,' grunted Father, battling yet again to keep the Land Rover from plunging into the cassava fields.

'Just hope it's worth all the effort,' said Mother through gritted teeth.

The track swept us into a compound of patchy green-brown lawn, bathed in a rainbow mist of water squirting up from several sprinklers lined along the front of a white-washed bungalow.

Father braked and switched off the ignition.

'Thank God for that,' said Mother as the shuddering whine of the engine faded blissfully from our ears.

Stiff-limbed, we climbed out, aware we were being watched by a dog sitting up in the shade of the veranda ahead of us. She looked part-Labrador. Black with a white blaze on her chest and three white paws.

'That could be her,' I whispered excitedly as we approached.

The dog stood up, slipped from the deep shadow to pause on the top step of the veranda. She gave one dutiful bark. Then started wagging her tail.

As we climbed the steps, a man emerged from inside. Tall. Long-limbed. In khaki shorts and shirt. He introduced himself as Peter Stevenson, the local veterinary officer. 'And this, as you may have guessed, is who you've come to see.' Peter turned to the dog and patted her head. 'She's called Poucher. Now, girl, say "hello" to our visitors.'

The dog looked at us, her eyes deep pools of brown. Then raised a white paw.

Peter chuckled. 'It's her party trick. Shake-a-paw.' He looked at me. 'Feel free to oblige.' I reached down and shook her paw, instantly captivated.

Over cold lagers – lemonade for me – Peter explained the advert. 'She doesn't flirt because I've spayed her. So no worries about her having puppies. Often a problem with all the bush dogs round these parts.'

Up to then, Mother had been fairly quiet. Her mood difficult to determine. But now she suddenly perked up. 'You mean she won't come into heat?'

'Absolutely.'

'Oh, in that case … maybe …'

As if on cue, Poucher sidled up to Mother, pushed her nose under her hand, clearly wanting a stroke. You'd have to have been very hard-hearted for it to have failed. It didn't. Mother obliged. All three of us were now utterly beguiled; and Poucher became the newest member of our expanding household.

Poucher proved to have a sweet temperament. Adorable. Willing to make friends with everyone. Especially me. She followed me everywhere; and within a few days of arriving back at our bungalow, she took to sleeping in my room. Father disapproved of these sleeping arrangements and declared his disapproval over breakfast one morning.

'One of the reasons for getting Poucher was to help guard the gidah,' he declared as he sliced off the top of his boiled egg. 'No good if she's stuck in your bedroom all night. Much better if she has a kennel on the veranda. Then she can come and go as she pleases while giving the bungalow some night-time protection.'

'No, Dad. Please don't,' I said while toying with my bowl of cornflakes. 'She'd be really unhappy.'

'Nonsense. She'd soon get used to the idea.'

Mother interjected. 'I'm not so sure it is a good idea.'

I saw Father's moustache bristle as he swiped at it with his napkin. His eyes glared. 'And why's that?'

Unruffled, Mother continued. 'Remember what happened to Major Carr's dog?'

'Oh, yes, Dad. You remember, don't you? It was awful,' I added.

Major Carr, our immediate neighbour, had had intruders. Their dog, a thin, fox-like creature that could produce an astonishing deep-throated bark considering its size, used to roam freely round their compound. The intruders, on this occasion, had been carrying machetes. They had shown no mercy to the dog, hacking it to death with their long, sharp knives. The major was left to discover the decapitated corpse lying in a pool of blood on his veranda.

'We couldn't risk that happening to Poucher, could we, Dad?' I pleaded.

Mother reached across and gripped my hand. 'What a fearful ending for our dear, sweet Poucher that would be,' she said. She brought into play all the skills she had mastered from participating in the local amateur dramatic society. Her eyes rolled heavenward. Her head shook as she shuddered. 'It doesn't bear thinking about.' She released my hand and clutched her bosom.

Bravo, Mum, I thought. A class act.

Father almost choked on his toast. But he had no choice other than to capitulate. Poucher continued to sleep in my room.

An incident, a few weeks later, showed it was a wise decision.

My room was at the far end of the gidah, three rooms away from my parents' bedroom; and the most distant from the servants' quarters where Yusefu – my Father's batman – lived with his family.

It was a dark African night. Pitch-black. Not one of those full-mooned nights where everything is bathed in silvery-white. A muted growl from Poucher, lying in her wooden crate next to my bed, woke me. I pulled up the edge of the mosquito net and leaned over. 'What's the matter?' I whispered, my arm stretching down to her. I could just make out her raised head, ears pricked. Another growl rumbled in her throat. 'What is it?'

Poucher was looking across at the open window – an iron mesh with a square hole cut in each lower corner through which you could pull in the outer shutters. The window framed the night sky – an inky panorama of blazing stars. I followed the dog's gaze. Suddenly, a shadow blocked the stars. The only thing visible was the whites of two eyes staring in. With a savage bark, Poucher sprang out of her box and hurled herself at the window. At the same time, I let out a piercing scream. The shadow instantly melted away. Lights snapped on as my parents hurried from their room. Voices jabbered from the servants' quarters. Yusefu scurried along the veranda, a kerosene lamp waving in his hand.

'There was someone there …' I blubbered, pointing at the window. The evidence was on view. A pole with a hook in the end of it lay half-inserted through the lower corner of the window, ready to hook out anything worth stealing from inside. A pole dropped by the thief when Poucher started barking.

Father crossed over to her. 'That's what I like to see, my girl. Well done.' He gave her a pat as she settled down into her bed.

I settled down into mine as Mother gave me a similar reassuring pat and tucked in my mosquito net.

The rest of the household soon settled as well. And the question of where Poucher should sleep was settled for good.

At weekends, we often took a picnic to one of the local beauty spots. A favourite was the river Ogan, a half-day's travel from Ibadan and deep into jungle territory. Here, the river meandered through a tortuous series of bends carved through a gorge, lined with towering groves of teak and mahogany. Each tree so massive you could hack a tunnel through its trunk and drive a double-decker bus through it. I still have a Brownie-camera picture of Mother posed, one arm stretched out, leaning against a trunk – a pixie at the foot of a giant. Broad dinner plates of leaves crowded in a dense canopy high above us. Blotting out the glare of the sky, creating a muted emerald twilight. Humid. Dark. Foreboding. Occasionally, we were startled by a series of sharp, urgent squawks and glimpses of green and red as flocks of parrots screeched away down the gorge.

The rainy season transformed the river into a roaring torrent, spewing fountains of brown water between granite boulders. From a rusty, girder bridge, wooden-planked and hundreds of feet above the river bed, we'd scramble down to the bottom of the gorge. There to stand awestruck as the water pummelled past, sweeping with it rafts of dead grass, trunks of splintered trees and the occasional up-turned goat or dog, splay-legged, stomach bloated like a balloon.

On the return journey that day, we were driving along a section where the road and river ran alongside each other for several miles. We'd cut our picnic short as a heavy thunderstorm had erupted. Heavy rain was still pounding on the Land Rover roof, the wipers scarcely able to cope with the deluge. It was as if buckets of water were being thrown at the windscreen. Suddenly the rain stopped – like a tap had been turned off. The sun flashed into view. The road steamed. Myriads of rainbow drops plopped down through the trees. In the far distance, sheet lightning flashed against purple clouds. Gullies of water ran off the steep hillside above us, streaming across the road to cascade down into the ravine below.

'Cripes, this one looks a bit dodgy,' muttered Father, his hands clenching the steering wheel as he slowed down to negotiate a channel of water gouging a course across the tarmac, loosening chunks and pushing them over the edge.

Having just successfully manoeuvred through it, he was about to pick up speed when Mother declared, 'Oh, look up there. What beautiful flowers.' She was craning her neck as she spoke, pointing with her finger. I wound down the back window and looked up the hillside. High above us, framed in a halo of white mist, was a bush weighed down with large trumpets of cream lilies. 'You don't think we could ...'

'Stop and pick some?' Father finished her sentence.

'My dear, only if it's safe enough.' Mother's voice all sweetness and light.

Father braked and steered the Land Rover onto the side of the road below the hill. I didn't think it looked safe at all. A narrow road. Steep hill one side. Sheer drop the other. Water spewing across. Madness to stop.

'A few of those flowers would be delightful,' said Mother, turning to give me an encouraging smile. 'I'll stay in the car.'

Moments later, Father and I were scrambling up the hill, slipping and sliding in the steaming, wet undergrowth while Poucher raced up ahead of us.

The lilies certainly begged to be picked. Each trumpet was pale cream on its edge, deep buttery yellow in its throat. Each with a scarlet tongue. Each with scalloped borders lined with a delicate tracery of red that glittered with diamonds of dew. And the scent. Heavy. Cloying.

'What a perfume,' I said, sticking my nose into one trumpet I'd picked and breathing in deeply. Next, I was breathing in panic.

Poucher had suddenly started barking furiously and was zigzagging back down the hill.

'Hey, what's up?' I said, turning to look down over my shoulder.

'Christ,' swore Father, dropping his bunch of lilies. He scrabbled, slipped and slid down the wet tangle of grass. 'Muriel ... Muriel ...' he yelled, his voice ringing out across the gorge.

I too screamed, 'Mum ... Mum ...' and tumbled down the hill.

Mother appeared not to hear us. Her head was bent. She was busy filing her nails.

The cause of our concern was now swerving down the road at great speed. A red and yellow local bus, crammed full of passengers. Ebony heads packed every window. Bodies bobbed at the back, clinging to the tail gate. On the roof were mountains of baskets, chickens, stacks of bananas, piled high. The heads of small children peered out between them. The bus continued to speed down the road. No slowing down. There was probably room to pass our Land Rover. Just.

But to our horror, an identical bus loaded with locals was trundling up the hill from the opposite direction. The reputation of the bus drivers was notorious. Never willing to give way to oncoming traffic. And with the single-gauge bridges the outcome was often fatal. The evidence – the mangled wrecked lorries and buses strewn below many of those bridges.

A pile-up here was highly likely. No wonder Father and I were screaming as we hurtled down the hill, our arms flailing. Poucher reached the Land Rover while we were still only halfway down. Barking furiously, she leapt up at the front passenger door. Mother looked up, startled. She saw us gesticulating and shouting. She saw the buses converging on her. She saw the pending disaster and opened the door. Flung herself out. Sprawled in the mud as horns blared.

Neither bus slowed. In fact, both seemed to accelerate. Each determined to pass our Land Rover first. Neither did. There was the screech of brakes. The smell of burning rubber. Wheels locked. The buses slewed across the slippery road. One shot through the gap between our Land Rover and the ravine, its wheels spewing out mud and stones as it clung to the edge of the road. A basket of chickens, dislodged, burst open. In a flurry of feathers, the birds sailed over the ravine, squawking to their deaths. The bus to the inside swerved. It hit the bank. Bounced back onto the road. Glanced off the passing bus and went into a spin. With a deafening crunch of metal, it hammered into the back of our Land Rover and continuing its spin, pushed it across the road to the edge of the ravine. Our vehicle teetered – like a kayak on the lip of a waterfall – then gave a slow bow and plunged out of sight. The splintering of glass, the pounding of metal against rock, reverberated across the gorge. The bus came to a halt inches from the edge. The other bus shuddered to a halt yards up the road.

For a moment, there was an eerie silence. Then pandemonium erupted. Mothers, children, chickens and goats poured out of both buses. The two drivers, gabbling and gesticulating, leapt out and raced towards each other. Fists flew.

Father pulled Mother up the bank and put his arms round her quivering shoulders. We sat, too shocked to move, as a sea of yellow, red and blue robes surged back and forth across the road. The jabber of insults, accusations – an angry cacophony of voices – floated up to us.

'It's all right, you're safe,' Father reassured, giving Mother a hug.

Poucher crept up to her, sat and looked up, cocking her head. Then held out a paw. Mother burst into tears. So too did I.

Only when the nightmare was over and we had managed to get back to the barracks by means of a local taxi did the full impact of what had happened sink in. By racing down the hill and warning Mother, Poucher had saved her life. It made us realise what a truly remarkable dog she was. So, the time we nearly lost her is even more indelibly etched in my mind.

An evening stroll round the grounds of the gidah and beyond became a routine once we acquired Poucher. It was a time to relish the cool of the night. Mother would lead the way, closely followed by Poucher and me. Sooty, our black cat, made up the rear-guard, a silent, slinking shadow.

'It's heavenly, absolutely heavenly,' Mother would exclaim, taking in gulps of cool air as we gazed up into the night sky. Above us a myriad of stars blazed. The Milky Way twinkled like a diamond-studded necklace draped across an indigo throat. A scent-heavy breeze whispered through the frangipani trees and date palms that bordered our compound. Beyond, a dense, black tangle of elephant grass towered each side of the sandy track, seething with unseen creatures, rustling, rubbing, twitching. The ceaseless brittle click-click of cicadas. The muted whoo-whoo of an owl. The undulating rasp of a nightjar, its whirling tone like a clock mechanism about to strike the hour. Occasionally, we'd be startled by a shadowy figure slipping silently out from a narrow footpath in the elephant grass to one side; a local woman, swathed in dark blue, returning late from market, a bundle of firewood balanced on her head.

'*Jambo, jambo,*' she'd murmur, gliding across, before being swallowed by the grass on the other side.

One moonlit evening, the track had enticed us even further than usual along its silvery trail. I'd just bent down to watch a foot-long centipede churn across the sand – sand still warm from the day's heat. Like a mechanical toy, it moved in an undulating wave of legs. Precise. Direct. I was tempted to pick it up, place it back in the centre of the path and watch it skim forward again. But I didn't. Centipedes can sting.

Mother stopped to allow the centipede to lose itself in the undergrowth. As she waited, there was a rustle, the snapping of twigs. 'What's that?' Mother whispered.

Poucher gave a low growl. Another twig snapped. Mother stepped over the centipede, saying, 'Let's get back.'

I stood up. 'I'm sure it's nothing.'

Then there was a snarl.

'Nothing, my foot,' spluttered Mother, who turned and started to sprint back towards the gidah with the speed of a gazelle if not with its grace. I quickly followed. As did Sooty. I could see her reflected in the lights from the gidah, darting across the lawn.

'Hey, wait a minute. Where's Poucher?' I said, stopping to look for her.

''Don't worry, she'll soon be back,' replied Mother, as she scaled the veranda steps two at a time.

I hesitated. The drone of the cicadas was suddenly punctuated by a frenzy of barking, yowling, spitting. Beyond the compound, the undergrowth erupted in a maelstrom of snapping branches and tearing grass.

I fled across the compound towards the servants' quarters, wailing, 'Something's attacking Poucher. Quick. Help. Poucher's being attacked.' I could see Yusefu and his family preparing supper over a flickering fire. Yusefu jumped to his feet, joined by the cook.

I gesticulated wildly. 'Poucher,' I screamed.

'We dun look,' said Yusefu. And the two of them bravely trotted off into the darkness, the glint of machete knives in their hands.

Mother and I waited nervously on the veranda. I felt tears well up in my eyes. Mother gripped the sleeve of my shirt, pulled me to her and put an arm round my shoulder. 'Poucher can take care of herself,' she said. 'Don't worry.' But her faltering tone betrayed her fears.

I was convinced something terrible had happened. That Poucher had been harmed. Maybe killed. There was no stopping my tears. Hot and salty, they flowed down my cheeks.

The yowling stopped. An eerie silence ensued. Even the cicadas seemed momentarily to suspend their incessant drone. Straining my eyes into the darkness, I could just make out Yusefu and Cook padding back into the compound. They stepped into the circle of light fanning out from the veranda and shuffled from foot to foot, agitated.

It was Yusefu who spoke. 'No Poucher, master. She dun gone.'

At daybreak, we began the search.

The scene of the fight was found. Flattened grass. Blood. Poucher's blood I thought miserably. Of her there was no sign. Dragged away? Eaten? Father, who had been working late at the office the previous evening, was now very much in command.

'Now, pay attention,' he barked, gathering Yusefu, Cook and the houseboy round him. 'This is the scene of the crime, right?' He drew a cross in the sand with a stick. 'We need to make a systematic search. Understand?'

The boys' blank faces showed they clearly didn't.

Father's moustache twitched. 'Dat we go in der bush. Look for dat dog. Savvy?' he roared.

Three heads nodded vigorously.

Father drew a double line to indicate the railway line which ran along the northern border of our compound. A single line to show the road that took you back over the hill and down into the main army quarters. And a square to depict Major Carr's bungalow next to ours. The boys were dispatched according to arrows etched in the sand.

But it was a hopeless task.

The elephant grass was too high, too thick. An eight-foot yellow barrier in which Poucher could be lying only inches away and still be missed. The grass was beaten, hacked, thrashed. We trampled down vast patches of it, probing the paths tunnelling through it. But to no avail. By mid-morning, the heat forced us to retreat. My shoulders burned. My temples throbbed. Light-headed, I staggered back to the gidah and desperately guzzled several glasses of lemonade.

Later that day, we tried again. Criss-crossed the scrubland – the bush – between our compound and the railway line. Scoured every inch of the ground. Locals were stopped, questioned. 'Had they seen a dog? Black with white markings.'

Heads shaking, lips pursed, the answers were all the same. 'No dun seen dat dog.'

It seemed Poucher had vanished.

The third evening after her disappearance, saw me sitting morosely on the veranda. I was taking no heed of the advancing dusk – that transitory period when cerise mellows to pink, when the simmering orbit of the sun sinks with a rush of cool shadows that lengthen like distorted fingers, rapidly spreading across the hills, the palms, the ever-rustling grass. Fruit bats emerged. They flitted and wheeled like black umbrellas, hurling themselves into the indigo sky. Their high-pitched squeaks mingled with the rising drone of the cicadas.

My ears were accustomed to this twilight serenade. But I suddenly sensed another noise. Different. Not a squeal. More a whimper. The whimper of a dog. I leaned forward, the hairs on my neck tingling. My mouth dropped open as I strained to listen. To hear that sound again. My eyes searched the gloom. The red glow of the hibiscus blooms in the hedge at the bottom of the compound danced maddeningly in front of me, a blurred border melting into the night shadows. Then again, I heard it. A whimper. Legs trembling, I stood up. I took a step down from the veranda. 'Poucher?' I whispered, hardly daring to voice her name.

A blur of white moved in the darkness.

'Poucher,' I screamed. 'Poucher.' I leapt down the steps and raced across the drive, tore through the shrubs bordering the lawn with my feet scarcely touching the grass as I flung myself forward. I found her dragging herself through the hibiscus hedge. Her left hind leg trailed behind her, stuck out at an angle. 'Oh Poucher,' I cried and collapsed beside her, flinging my arms round her neck. 'You're alive.'

She gave a soft groan and pushed her head against my chest. Her nose, hot and dry, brushed my chin. I could feel her lungs heaving, her breath fetid. I patted her back. Her coat felt spiked, encrusted. I slipped my arm under her belly. She grunted. 'There, there, it will be all right,' I reassured her as I knelt and slowly got to my feet, lifting her up, trying not to jolt her.

I staggered back across the dark compound, the stench of rotting flesh filling my nostrils, a warm stickiness oozing down my arms.

Mother's hand flew to her mouth as we climbed onto the veranda. 'Oh, my God,' she exclaimed and sped indoors, yelling for Father.

I laid Poucher down, fighting hard to control the waves of nausea that threatened to explode from my stomach. Her wounds were horrendous. The skin had been ripped back from her midriff in a jagged tear. The muscles on the inside of her left thigh had been shredded to brown strings, exposing nerves, arteries and the pale grey glint of bone. The leg hung loose, caked in a thick purple crust of dried blood through which the torn flesh bubbled and glistened. Green-grey. Gangrenous.

Father was quick to assess the scene and the houseboy ordered to fetch a bowl of warm water and cloths. The two of us began the arduous task of gently soaking and lifting away the matted debris. The gaping wound we didn't dare touch. Far too painful. Poucher lifted her head. Licked her lips.

'She needs a drink,' exclaimed Mother who had been hovering in the background, hands still pressed to her nose and mouth. She hurried away and returned with Poucher's water bowl. It was placed near her muzzle and I supported her head as she took many long gulps before, with a rattling sigh, she flopped back and closed her eyes.

'I've rung Jock Campbell,' Mother informed us. 'He'll be over as soon as he can.'

The army doctor turned up minutes later in his Land Rover. He whistled when he gazed down at the stricken dog. 'My, oh my, you poor wee thing,' he said. 'Some beastie's certainly had a go at you and no mistake.'

'Can you save her?' I faltered.

'Now, laddie, don't you go worrying your wee head about that. Once we've got her down to the surgery, we'll soon have her patched up.' His warm Scottish brogue sounded reassuring. But I saw him shoot Father a warning glance. A sliver of fear shot down my spine. I suddenly wondered if I'd ever see Poucher again. As Father and Jock lifted Poucher onto a blanket, I ran down the steps and pulling out the bolts, dropped the flap at the back of the Land Rover.

As they slid Poucher in, I said, 'I'm coming with you.' My words hung uncomfortably in the air. There was an awkward silence.

Mother intervened. 'Now dear, I don't think that would be wise. Poucher's badly injured. It's going to take Jock a long time to patch that wound up.' The look in her eyes betrayed her feelings. I felt certain they all thought the task of repairing such an extensive wound impossible. It made me even more determined to stay with Poucher.

'I want to go,' I said simply.

'Malcolm, do as your mother says.' Father put out a restraining hand.

'Dad … please …'

Jock intervened. 'Och, let the laddie come along. We may save the dog yet.'

The army medical centre was no grand affair. It was comprised of a single-storey wooden building divided into two rooms. One a waiting room which doubled up as an office. The other an examination room which doubled up as an ops room for minor surgical procedures.

Poucher was laid out on the examination couch. Her eyes momentarily flickered open before she slipped back into semi-consciousness.

Jock paused a moment in front of a large glass medical cabinet, then opened its door and reached in for a brown bottle. From it he poured some thick, yellowish liquid onto a wad of cotton wool. Immediately a sickly, sweet smell permeated the room.

'Chloroform,' he explained.

The chloroform was wedged over Poucher's muzzle. Within minutes, her breathing became slower, deeper, more regular. Jock lifted one of her front paws. Let it go. It flopped back, limp.

'See?' he said. 'She's out for the count.'

Father and Jock then repositioned Poucher so that her injured leg rested on the couch, the torn groin exposed while her right leg was levered back to one side and strapped to the edge of the couch with bandage. Jock began to manipulate the mutilated limb. He moved it backwards and forwards. Lifted it up and down.

'Is it broken?' I asked.

He shook his head. 'No. She's been lucky there. The femur's intact.'

He reached across and pulled up a small metallic tray on which were piled scissors, needles and knifes. He selected a long, narrow handle that had a sharp looking blade attached to one end. 'A scalpel,' he explained, seeing me staring at it.

With a swab in his other hand, he began to scrape at Poucher's exposed flesh. Grit was poked out. Black, rotten muscle was cut away. Dead flaps of skin cut off. With forceps, he separated healthy skin from white underlying tissue. It made a sound like tearing of paper. I swallowed hard.

'This is a nerve,' said Jock, pointing to a glistening white thread that snaked through the muscles. Beads of blood began to well up. I gripped the edge of the couch.

'Are you all right?' asked Jock. 'You've gone very white.'

I nodded feebly.

He continued to clean the wound. It was the rasp of the scalpel blade against Poucher's exposed femur that did it. I felt the heat. Smelt the fumes. Saw the blood. And fainted.

When I came to, I was stretched out on the couch. Poucher, her leg heavily bandaged, was curled up fast asleep in a large open-sided crate, layered in blankets.

My first words were, 'Is she going to be okay?'

'Fine, laddie, fine.' Jock raised a tumbler half-full of whisky.

'Here's to a speedy recovery,' said Father, raising his. They clinked glasses and knocked back their drinks. I guessed the experience had been unnerving for them as well. As a rule, Father blanched at the merest pin-prick of blood. While the doctor's surgical abilities were usually confined to lancing boils, or ramming yellow fever vaccine into the buttocks of new recruits.

My next question was, 'Will she be able to walk?'

Jock was non-committal. He explained that one of the main thigh muscles had been severed along with several nerves. He'd done his best to stitch everything back together again and providing he could control the infection, there was a chance Poucher would regain the use of her leg. 'After all,' he said, 'she's tough old stick. Had to be to crawl home in that state.'

The next few days were touch and go. Poucher's temperature soared. Jock showed me how to take it, swivelling a greased thermometer gently up her bottom. I was soon adept at reading the temperature, praying each time that it would drop. But it continued to remain at 104 F – three degrees above normal.

I designed a medical card and carefully ruled out headings – dates, observations, temperature readings, food intake. I watched Jock change the dressing daily. Then plucked up courage to ask if I could have a go.

'Why not, laddie?' he chuckled.

He patiently showed me how to lay the penicillin gauze along the line of the wound – a long, neat row of blue stitches. There was a gap at one end from which yellow-green pus constantly oozed.

'Better out than in,' commented Jock, as he showed me how to compress one end with a thumb, and squeeze along the line of the wound to channel the infection out of the hole at the other end. The nozzle of a tube of antibiotic was then inserted into the hole and ointment squirted inside.

When it came to bandaging, I was all fingers and thumbs. At my first attempt, I was halfway through when I dropped the roll of bandage and watched it unravel itself across the lounge floor. Once I'd finally finished bandaging, I discovered it was too loose. Poucher stood up and the dressing slithered down her leg to end in a heap over her paw. Poucher turned to give it a sniff. But she was a model patient, never making a fuss, keeping perfectly still while I eventually mastered the art of bandaging her wound.

Jock showed me how to give her antibiotic tablets.

'Open her mouth and push the pill over the back of her tongue,' he instructed. 'Then hold her muzzle closed until she swallows.'

It was an easy task. But then Poucher was an easy patient and seemed to realise what was required of her. I soon discovered that by smearing the tablets with jam, Poucher readily took them from my hand with a deft lick of her tongue.

Gradually the infection subsided. How proud I felt when I was able to record a normal temperature on her medical card. I could hardly believe it and shoved the thermometer back up her bottom just to make sure. Poor Poucher. The reddened skin grew less angry. The bruising less severe. She began to use her leg. Hobbling cautiously at first. But soon trotting around with barely a limp.

A week later, Jock allowed me to remove the stitches. 'It's the least I can do, laddie. You've looked after her so well.'

Poucher lay on the doctor's couch.

'Lift the loose end of the stitch with the forceps,' instructed Jock. 'See the knot?'

I nodded.

'Now slide the scissors under it,' continued Jock. 'Then snip.'

I snipped.

'Now gently pull.'

I pulled. Out came the stitch.

With all the stitches removed, I took them home and laid them out on my desk. I counted them. Forty-eight in total. A lot of stitches.

As I stared at them, thinking of how they'd helped stitch Poucher's life back together again, I made a resolution. One that I'd be determined to keep if at all possible. I would train to be a vet.

When I reached the age of 11, I had to return to the UK for schooling. I missed Poucher and Polly, as much as I missed my parents. Dare I say it, even more so? School holidays saw me flying back out to Nigeria for joyful reunions.

Shrieks from Polly with a plethora of 'Wotcher mates.'

Excited woofs from Poucher who'd come bounding up, tail wagging so furiously, her hindquarters would roll from side to side. She'd then promptly sit and throw up a paw in a frenzy of shake-a-paws.

I knew sometime soon my Father's tour of duty in West Africa would end. That my parents would return to the UK. They'd already discussed taking Polly back. But Poucher? Nothing had been mentioned.

I finally plucked up courage to ask. 'Will you take her back, Dad?'

He shifted from one foot to another, hands stuffed deep in the pockets of his shorts.

'Well, will you, Dad?' I persisted.

He gave Mother a despairing look. A silent 'help'.

In that instant, I knew a decision had already been made. I bit my lower lip, determined not to cry. After all, it wasn't the done thing for a 13-year-old to blubber.

Father sat down next to me and put his hand on my knee. He was never one to show much affection so this must have been quite an effort for him. 'Malcolm, we've given this a lot of thought. We just wonder whether Poucher would be happy in England.'

'Of course, she would.' I cried. 'She'd be happy anywhere as long as she was with us.'

Mother interjected. 'But she'd have to stay in quarantine

kennels for six months. And it'll be the middle of winter. Poucher's used to Africa. She was born out here. This is her life.' She paused. 'Besides which, she is getting on a bit. Nearly 10 years old now. Don't you think it would be a bit unfair on her, making her travel all those thousands of miles?'

'You're just making excuses,' I said, grimly, looking up at Mother. 'And to think Poucher saved your life.'

That hit home. Mother averted her eyes, studied her nails.

Father cleared his throat as if to speak. Then seemed to think better of it.

I could contain my emotions no longer. I leapt to my feet with a howl and stormed off to my room, slamming the door furiously behind me.

But I was right. The decision had been made, however unfair I thought it was. Poucher was to stay. And in fact, a prospective new family had already been found.

After a weekend of coercion, I was persuaded to meet them. They were lecturers at the University of Ibadan. A couple with a boy of seven and a little girl of four. I confess to a stab of jealousy when Poucher trotted up to the children, wagging her tail; and followed it with her customary shake-a-paw. The kids squealed with delight and the parents patted and fussed over her. But that was Poucher for you. Friendly with everyone. A joy to be with. Without openly admitting it, I knew Poucher would soon settle down with her new owners. Just as she had done with us.

But when the time came, it didn't soften the wrench of parting. It didn't stop the tightening of the throat. The sting of tears fought back as I knelt down and stared into Poucher's trusting brown eyes for the last time.

'I'm going to miss you so much,' I sobbed, burying my head

in her neck. 'You've been such a great buddy.'

Her pink tongue lolled out to lick the tip of my nose. With a little grizzle, she cocked her head. And then for one last time raised her paw. I shook it not in greeting, but in farewell.

'Bye-bye, pet,' I whispered. Then jumped to my feet and ran to the awaiting Land Rover to hide the tears I could no longer control.

Mother did her best to console me. But even her eyes were moist, shiny. 'She'll be in good hands,' she said. 'And I bet you one thing.'

'What's that?' I sniffed.

'That Poucher looks after her new owners just as she looked after us.'

And she proved to be right.

Back in England, one frosty December morning, an air-mail letter arrived. It was from the Freemans – Poucher's new owners.

'There, what did I tell you,' exclaimed Mother, halfway through reading it.

'What's happened? What's happened?' I yelled, hopping up and down. 'Come on, Mum … tell me.'

'They say that their little boy was playing in the garden when he disturbed a spitting cobra. Poucher ran between the boy and snake, barking. The snake apparently spat at her.'

'But she was all right, wasn't she?' I knew the danger of those snakes. They could spit venom into your eyes with deadly accuracy.

'Well, she was partially blinded. But has recovered fully now. Here, why don't you read the letter for yourself?' She handed it to me.

I scanned its contents. Eagerly devouring every word describing Poucher's heroic action.

The letter ended with a P.S.

We can't thank you enough for giving us such a loyal and faithful companion. She's a much-loved member of the family.

Those words made my heart skip a beat. I smiled to myself. If Poucher was happy, then I, too, was happy. Happy with the memories I had of that wonderful dog. A dog that I'd helped back to life. A dog that put me on the road to becoming a vet. Little did I realise then what a cast of characters I would go on to meet during my future career.

3

Rampaging Rodents

Three years before our move to Nigeria, we were living in Bournemouth, on the south coast of England, in the rented first floor flat of a converted Edwardian house. Like so many youngsters of my age – five – I yearned to have a pet. But the owners, who lived downstairs, enforced a strict 'No Pets' policy. So a dog was out of the question however much I pleaded with Mother. And it was only Mother I could plead with, Father being away on a tour of duty in Germany at the time. She didn't wish to be caught sneaking down the stairs for poop-walks with a pooch. I lowered my sights. A cat then? Mother shook her head. 'Sorry, Malcolm, no.'

A house-bound moggy? Kept in the flat?

No chance.

I persevered, my list of possible pets reducing in size on

paper and in size physically – from rabbits, through to guinea pigs, down to hamsters. Each drew a blank, until Mother, worn down by my persistence, relented and agreed I could have a couple of white mice.

'But make sure they're two males or two females,' she warned.

I returned from the pet shop with two white mice which I cossetted in a cage in the kitchen. Three weeks later, they became 12 white mice. One day, while cleaning out their cage, I accidently left the door ajar. Overnight, the mice did what mice like doing best besides breeding. They moved house.

Mother was accosted as she came downstairs.

'We've seen mice scuttling round our living room,' she was told by the house's owner.

Mother showed due concern. 'Perhaps the local council pest control officer should be called out?' she suggested.

'These are white mice,' was the response. 'Is Malcolm keeping any as pets?'

Mother stood there, her face a picture of innocence – she could do 'innocence' very well – and shook her head. Well, the cage *was* empty now.

I was reminded of that tale 18 years on when a mouse popped its head up on the bedside table at Willow Wren, in Ashton, West Sussex – the cottage my wife, Maxeen, and I bought soon after we'd got married. Only the mouse in question this time wasn't a pet one. But a wild one. A wood mouse. Dark brown. Glossy coated. Rounded ears and pert nose. A nose which at that moment was wrinkling at the apple core I'd placed as bait. Not to snare it but to take a photograph with the camera I'd set up alongside.

I'd suspected something was afoot several days back when

my unsavoury habit of snacking in bed meant a plate of crumbs and the occasional apple core was left on the bedside cabinet last thing. Only the crumbs started to disappear. Then, the previous night, just as I was about to turn my light off, a mouse skipped onto the plate, sat up with whiskers all of a quiver, lifted the apple core between his paws, sank his teeth in it and dashed off. How sweet. Very picture-worthy.

So now with camera balanced on an adjacent chair, I was ready and waiting, sprawled across the bed in my boxer shorts.

'What on earth are you up to?' queried Maxeen, coming into the room. I suppose in my half-naked state with a camera angled at the bed it could all have looked a bit dodgy. As if I was waiting to take some steamy action shots of me and her rather than a mouse nibbling at an apple core. But, by now, she was used to my idiosyncrasies. After all, we'd known each other for over two years before getting married; and had travelled together across Africa in a truck for five months. A rodent on my bedside table was nothing in comparison.

I tried to explain. 'I'm hoping to get a pic of the wood mouse that's been stealing my apple cores.'

'You're nuts,' declared Maxeen, getting into the other side of the bed and switching her bedside light off. 'You should be trapping it not snapping it.' Ever the practical lady is my wife. Someone who doesn't stand for any nonsense. An attribute that had attracted me to her in the first place. That and her gamine appearance. The mass of auburn curls. The almond eyes with their long lashes. The impish smile.

Nevertheless, despite Maxeen's protestations, I got my picture. The mouse in our house. Actually, he was one of many mice in the house. It seemed Willow Wren had become a refuge for the local rodent population seeking to escape the ravages of a Sussex winter. What better than a tile-hung 18th century cottage, built on bare earth that sharp teeth and claws could bury under? Lath and plaster walls to tunnel through. And a labyrinth of nooks and crannies to nest in. A perfect des res for rodents. We were swamped. Something needed to be done.

'How about getting a cat?' suggested Maxeen.

I grimaced. 'You know I'm not particularly fond of cats.'

'Oh, for goodness sake. Don't be such a namby-pamby.' My wife glowered at me. 'We can't go on like this. We're being overrun.' She pointed across the room to where a couple of mice had started playing bowls with some peanuts under the TV one evening. She was right. Enough was enough.

Hence the arrival of Queenie. A very attractive-looking chocolate and cream long-haired Persian whose owners were going abroad. The cat required rehoming. But we soon found out that Queenie had no intention of decapitating a mouse or two for her dinner. Far from it. Any murine movements in the house were totally ignored by her.

She'd lie, stretched out along the back of the settee, and watch any cavorting mice without batting an eyelid. They were treated with utter distain. Clearly, she had no intention of swooping down to conquer. Not for her a Boudicca-style charge to snatch a rodent or two. Hence, the plague of mice continued to lead us a merry dance in Willow Wren.

As did other little furries, half an hour's drive away over the Downs at Prospect House, the veterinary hospital in Westcott-on-Sea, where I'd been working as a vet since graduation from Bristol University the previous year. Hamsters topped the list of those furries. Not that we had hordes of them descending on the hospital, pouring over from the Steppes of Siberia or from the deserts of Syria. But enough to make an impact on me.

There was one in particular. The one I was confronted with

on my first day in practice. Any first day is bound to be nerve wracking. But this day is indelibly etched in my memory. Never to be surpassed. It was a Monday morning, appointments were going to start in 20 minutes' time; and I was twitchy. Wrigglier than a bag of eels.

My nerves weren't helped when one of the two senior partners, Tony Sangster, sallied into reception, rubbing his hands together. He was a small man of wiry build. Arms and legs like flesh-painted pipe cleaners. Hair an untidy, bristly-brown thatch, thinning on top. Echoes of a weasel in his small white-pointed teeth. 'Well, Malcolm, ready for the off, are we?' he declared, baring those teeth in a sharp grin. 'Just hope you don't get savaged by your first patient. Can happen you know.' He sailed away, still rubbing his hands. 'Just be careful.'

'Don't take any notice of him,' said Jean, the receptionist. 'He's just winding you up.' Here was the anchor of the practice. Its backbone. A no-nonsense lady in her late 50s. Her looks defied her age: soft, dumpy with the smooth contours of a baby, dimpled cheeks, plum-like hands. Always immaculately turned out in pastel twin set and pearls. 'You'll be fine,' she continued. 'Don't worry. I've booked you in a hamster to start with. What could be easier?'

What indeed.

Fred, the hamster, turned out to be a very tenacious patient. His teeth sank into the finger I'd foolishly poked into his nest box in an attempt to get him out. He drew blood. My blood. Drops of it dripped down from my finger, splattering the cuff of my white coat. Eventually, I managed to catch him.

Once scruffed between finger and thumb, I turned him over so that his tan and white body rested in the palm of my hand. He looked up at me, his beady black eyes bulging like tiny currants. Whiskers twitched. Lips drew back in a demonic smile to reveal long curved incisors. Incisors that had overgrown and were making it difficult for him to eat.

Two snips with nail clippers and the problem was solved.

Afterwards, Jean thought it all a huge joke. ''First blood drawn,' she said. Her eyes, with their muddy hue like the deep silt of an estuary, lit up. In the two years since then, she'd continue to tease me whenever she booked in a hamster or similar small rodent for me to see. 'Just watch your fingers, Malcolm,' she'd warn, waving hers at me. I was sorely tempted to wave two of mine back at her. But didn't, of course. Too unprofessional.

But I did cross two when told I was due to see a hamster one September afternoon as one of my four to six o'clock appointments. Echoes of Fred? I sincerely hoped not.

The hamster was accompanied into my consulting room by four people. A mother, her daughter aged around 11, and two boys each a couple of years younger. Clearly this was an important family pet to have such an entourage. I felt slightly in awe of the four sets of eyes staring at me once the hamster cage had been slid onto the table.

'So, what seems to be the problem?' I said. There was an immediate barrage of voices out of which I heard the words 'Horace', 'hamster', 'bits of', and 'cheeks'.

'Shh …' said the mother, Mrs Nightingale. 'Don't talk all at once.'

It was one of the lads who spoke next. 'It's Horace. He's got...'

'Stuff stuck on him,' interrupted the other lad.

'He can't move,' said the girl.

'We came home to find Horace flattened up against the fridge,' explained Mrs Nightingale. 'With pins and tacks over his head. All very odd. As you can see.' Mrs Nightingale had opened the hamster cage and parted the pile of hay in one corner.

Pinned up against the bars was Horace, his face smothered in bits of metal. Several pins. A screw. Three paper clips. I gently levered him off the bars to which he appeared to be glued and eased him onto the table. The three children crowded round to see what I was doing. Which wasn't much – other than prise the objects off his face. Relieved of these obstacles, he perked up and started to scuttle across the table, weaving through the clips and pins I'd removed. They immediately sprang back on his cheeks. The girl cupped her hands round him to stop him running off while I removed the objects for a second time. Only then could I see that Horace's head was distorted. All due to his cheek pouches. Both swollen on each side.

'Keep him there,' I said to the girl. 'You're doing a grand job.' I crossed to the instrument trolley and unscrewed the metal cone of my auriscope. Returning to the table, I grasped Horace's head between my finger and thumb, conscious of the children's eyes almost level with mine. I levered the tip of the cone between the hamster's teeth and into his right cheek pouch. There was a tiny click. Extracting the cone, we all could see the remains of a magnet on it. Likewise, when I repeated the operation on the left pouch, more bits of a fridge magnet that had been chewed and stored by Horace were extracted. Problem solved.

I was chuffed. So too was the Nightingale family as they fussed and cooed over Horace. The happy hamster with a magnetic personality.

It did seem that many of my encounters with these furry fellows and their rodent cousins ended up with them escaping. As if they sensed I was a bit cack-handed. 'Hey, ho … I'll give him the slip' way of thinking as soon as the cage door was opened. Certainly, some hamsters seem very adept at making their escape. As if cunningly planned. The POWs of Stalag Luft 111 may well have been famous for their tunnelling techniques but paled into insignificance with the likes of these rodents. When in my hands – or more often than not, out of them – they had many 'Great Escapes'.

So I was a little alarmed when Josh Higgins, one of our neighbours down the road from us in Ashton, appeared on the back-door step of Willow Wren. Josh had his 11-year-old son in tow, carrying a hamster cage.

'We've brought round Odysseus,' said Josh.

I felt my eyebrows crease together in puzzlement.

'He's a Greek god,' said his son, Eddie. 'Homer wrote about him in *The Odyssey*.'

'Eddie's into Greek mythology at the moment,' explained Josh, as if that would allow my eyebrows to un-knot. But it was not the name that was puzzling me but why the rodent was here in the first place.

Maxeen provided the answer, appearing at my shoulder. 'Hi, Josh, Eddie. So this is our holidaying hamster is it?' She took the cage being proffered by the boy.

'Odysseus,' he said. 'It means he likes giving pain.'

Hearing that, my fingers gave an involuntary twitch. I now realised that Odysseus was going to stay with us for a while and just hoped he didn't live up to his name during that time. His stay remaining nip-less.

Once the two of them had left, Maxeen filled me in as I gazed into the hamster cage now deposited on the kitchen breakfast bar. Seems she'd bumped into Josh while in Ashton's Post Office and he'd asked the favour of her. Could we look after Odysseus for the week while they were away for the half-term?

'You didn't think to ask me?' I queried.

'Sorry, dear. I didn't think you'd mind. They seemed to be

in a bit of a fix. So, I said it wouldn't be a problem.' She looked at me. 'Well, it's not is it?'

'Could be if he escapes. You know what my track record with hamsters is like. All I can say is that if he does decide to go on his own odyssey, heaven help us if it's an epic one.' How prophetic those words turned out to be. Homer would have been delighted.

Odysseus didn't make an appearance until early evening, emerging from his nest of shredded paper towelling to sniff the air with a twitch of his snout, his button-black eyes gleaming – no doubt sizing up his escape routes. I had been expecting him to be of the standard golden variety, honey-coloured coat with white undercarriage. But as he tucked into a bowlful of mixed grain and sunflower seed topped with a sprinkling of peanuts – Eddie had provided a very comprehensive menu for Odysseus to savour – I found myself watching a very smart looking rodent with rich mahogany-red fur over-ticked with black guard hairs. Coat colouring that would blend very nicely with our carpet should he ever seize the opportunity to trek across it.

There was no sign of him the next day. I wasn't concerned. Hamsters are nocturnal, sleeping during daylight hours.

'No Odysseus then?' I remarked, glancing at my watch as Maxeen and I sat down for our supper. Just gone 7 o'clock. Meal finished, there was another glance at the cage. Still no appearance. All rather ominous. Surely Odysseus should be feeling hungry by now? Wanting his breakfast. Best take a look. Open cage door. Notice clip on door loose. Rising panic. Prod nest. Empty. 'Bugger, the sod's got out.' Search party time. I gazed round the living room, the endless hidey-holes from down the backs of the two settees to the hamster-sized gaps in the uneven skirting boards. In true heroic expeditionary-style,

Odysseus could already have mountaineered up the stairs to immerse himself in the subterranean depths of the overhead floorboards. Great.

'Could be anywhere,' said Maxeen, in what I considered to be a very unhelpful observation. But anywhere had to be somewhere. And we felt an obligation to at least mount a search party in an attempt to find him. Maxeen's head went under one settee. Nothing. Mine went under the other. No trace. Kitchen cupboards opened and closed without the slightest stirrings from within. Not the twitch of a whisker.

All the while, Queenie, our cat, looked on with a nonchalance that suggested she couldn't give a toss; and our two recently acquired rescue dogs, Judy and Winnie, having had their supper, were in full-bellied bliss stretched out asleep in front of the fire.

'I'll leave the cage door open and a bowl of food inside,' I said when eventually we decided to abandon the search and get some shut-eye ourselves.

The bowl was empty the next morning. Maybe there might be a curled-up Odysseus, fast asleep in his nest. I poked around inside it, hoping I might prod a warm furry body. But nope. Nothing. An empty nest. Odysseus had obviously chosen to slumber elsewhere.

'Well he's taken the food,' I said. 'So at least he must be around somewhere.'

'It might have been the mice,' said Maxeen.

Thanks, dear, that's cheered me up no end.

'I heard of one hamster that disappeared for three months,' she went on.

'And?'

'It was eventually found nesting in the vacuum cleaner.'

I wasn't sure of the point Maxeen was making. But I did

check the hoover bag later that morning; and rifled through the recycle bins. Just a load of rubbish. No hamster.

But my wife hadn't finished. 'There was also that case of a hamster that wasn't found until the people moved house. It then emerged from a pot plant. Apparently, it had burrowed down into it.'

I gazed round the living room, at the seven potted plants we had in there. Add to them, the cluster of pots in the hall and several more lining the windowsill in the kitchen and that equated to a sizable number of pots where Odysseus could have gone to ground. No way was I going to root through that lot in the remote chance I could unearth him.

'Tell you what,' I said. 'Let's see if the Internet has any suggestions on how to recapture a hamster.' So, I Googled 'fugitive hamsters' and was presented with several options. A fine dusting of flour round the food bowl. The next morning you pick up the trail of tiny, floury paw prints which leads to your escapee's hidey-hole. Or place the food bowl on a large sheet of tissue paper and then lie in wait with the lights off until you heard the tiny patter of feet rustling on the tissue. Or tie some string to a monkey nut. The hamster will pick up the nut and return to his hiding place, leaving the string trailing behind him.

All three were tried. All three didn't work.

Maxeen came up with the idea of a bucket trap. 'We make a staircase of books to the top of a plastic bucket with some food lying in the bottom of it. And entice Odysseus up the books by placing a sunflower seed on each step. He'll get to the top, see the food inside and jump in. But then find he can't jump out again.'

That was tried. That also didn't work.

We began to panic. Eddie and family were now due back the

following day. How could we face them with an empty hamster cage and tell them that Odysseus was missing presumed … well, just what was presumed? That one of our dogs or cats may have eaten the hamster? We didn't have the stomach for that even if our pets did.

With Odysseus due to be collected by Josh and Eddie later in the afternoon, I spent the last morning digging over the vegetable patch in preparation for some spring planting of onion sets and seed potatoes. At least it was a distraction from worrying about missing rodents. It had just gone midday when I heard Judy barking indoors. A furious series of excited yaps. Unusual for her. Then silence.

I had a sudden thought. Ahrr … She's spotted Odysseus. I gulped, imagining Judy doing the same as a hamster slid down her throat. I dropped my spade and raced up the garden path just as Judy came bounding out of the back door, tail wagging in a frenzy of excitement. She headed straight towards me down the path and as we met, she stopped and looked at me, Odysseus hanging from her jaws. I immediately dropped to my knees and extended my left hand towards her hand, palm up.

'Good girl,' I murmured. 'What a good girl.'

Judy gave a little grizzle, sidled up to my hand and dropped Odysseus in it. He immediately made to spring up and jump. 'Oh no you don't, matey,' I declared, clamping my right hand over him, cocooning him between my palms. 'You're not going anywhere other than back in your cage. Your wanderings are well and truly over.'

When Josh and Eddie turned up later that afternoon, the first question Eddie asked was, 'Is Odysseus okay?'

'Fine, yes,' I replied.

'Did you manage to let him out at all?'

'Well, actually …'

Maxeen butted in. 'He had the run of the place every day, didn't he, Malcolm?' She smiled sweetly up at me.

I nodded enthusiastically.

'Pleased to hear that,' said Josh. 'We didn't like the thought of him being cooped up all the time. Though of course it could have been a bit risky letting him out. But I'm sure you didn't allow your cat or dogs anywhere near him.'

I made sure my response was very cagey.

Jean thought it hilarious when I related the story to her. 'Lucky Judy didn't decide to make a snack of the hamster. Consider yourself fortunate that you've a very trustworthy spaniel there.'

I knew that only too well. Same went for Queenie. It would have been the instincts of most cats to have jumped on Odysseus during one of his scurryings across the kitchen. Little did I realise another test of such instincts was soon to come. This time in the hospital and via a gerbil. A gerbil brought in by his owner, Charlotte Hutchins, after she'd finished school for the day. She was a studious-looking young lady in smart maroon blazer and grey pleated skirt, hair scraped back from a high forehead in a My-Little-Pony Alice band.

In a serious voice which belied her 12 years, she said, 'I'd like you to take a look at Hermione, my gerbil. She's damaged her tail quite badly.' She paused and took a deep breath. 'I think you might have to chop it off.'

The gerbil at that point was hopping round the cage that Charlotte had placed on the consulting table. I went to open the door.

'You'll have to be careful,' warned Charlotte. 'Hermione's very clever at escaping.' Her warning came too late as a flash of brown and white fur sprang out of the half-opened door and ducked past my outstretched fingers. Minutes later, I was staring at a pair of eyes blinking and a set of whiskers twitching from behind a shelf full of medicine bottles. Proof of just how clever she was. I moved one in an attempt to catch her. There was another blur of fur as the gerbil sprang down onto the instrument trolley, scattering scissors and forceps onto the floor.

'Got 'er,' I cried triumphantly as I finally managed to corner her under a roll of cotton wool into which she had tunnelled. Once I'd bundled her back into the cage, I leaned against the consulting table to catch my breath. What was it with all these pesky rodents that I encountered? Seems they took one look at me and whoosh … they were off as fast as their little legs would carry them.

'Hermione's always getting out,' said Charlotte. 'Daddy tried to catch her when she got into the airing cupboard. That's when it happened. Her tail got trapped in the door.'

And I could see the result of that mishap without having to catch Hermione up again – with the inherent risk of another dash for freedom. The skin had been ripped back from the base of the tail, leaving an extensive length broken, red and looking very sore. As Charlotte had suspected, the tail would have to be amputated. I told her this.

'I read that gerbils use their tails for balance,' she said. 'Will she be wonky without her tail?'

'I'm sure she'll manage,' was my non-committal answer as I hadn't a clue.

Charlotte was happy to leave Hermione in the hospital overnight so that I could operate the following morning.

'And just make sure you stay in your cage, matey,' I muttered as I took the gerbil down to the ward. Carol, the senior nurse, was on duty that afternoon. She was a rather unattractive young lady, with a complexion akin to a trout seen underwater.

I warned her of Hermione's capabilities for doing a Houdini on us.

I was rewarded with one of Carol's 'You don't have to tell me' looks, flashed at me with fish-green eyes. It was an irritating trait of hers. A constant reminder that she was head nurse. She had been at the hospital far longer than me. She knew what she was doing. Whereas I being a newcomer ... It used to needle me considerably when I first started. But I'd become inured to it over the past two years and it didn't get under my skin quite so much these days. But even so, I could occasionally get a little prickly and today was one of those occasions.

'Okay, Carol, just letting you know,' I said, a little more brusquely than necessary, before returning to complete evening surgery.

I was just packing up, about to put my coat on and return home to Willow Wren, when Carol bustled into the office to stand, hands smoothing down her white apron. The look of concern on her face said it all. 'Sorry, Malcolm. Bad news I'm afraid. I've just found that gerbil's cage empty.'

I could feel a tic in my forehead start to throb. This was the last thing I wanted to hear. Especially as there were several cats currently hospitalised. They were housed in a bank of cages running down one side of the ward above larger pens used to accommodate dogs. None of them were so poorly that they wouldn't consider Hermione as a tasty snack. Crunch. Swallow. A lick of paws.

'Right. We'd better see if we can find her,' I snapped, wrenching my coat off and hurling it on a chair before stomping down to the ward, with Carol in tow. As we scoured the upper cages, I fervently prayed that Hermione lacked sufficient mountaineering skills to hoist herself up into the jaws of one of the felines. There was no sign of her up there; and no cat with a post-snack wiping of mouth or licking of paws.

In one of the lower pens was a bull mastiff, Freddie, admitted earlier in the day for observation following an epileptiform-type of seizure that morning. He was standing in one corner emitting short sharp whines, saliva pouring from his jowls, his attention rigidly fixed on a stainless-steel feed bowl which was over-turned, lying in the opposite corner.

'He looks as if he's about to have another fit,' said Carol, peering through the bars of the pen. 'Shouldn't we be doing something for him?' The inference was obvious. *I* should be doing something. Some dogs do exhibit such symptoms at the onset of a fit and so it certainly seemed possible that Carol was right. Grrr …

I watched Freddie pad across to the feed bowl and cautiously sniff at it. At that point the bowl suddenly took on a life of its own, jumping up in little jerks and then zigzagging across the concrete floor. I shot into the kennel, just in time to stop Freddie flipping the bowl over and having a helping of Hermione for his dinner. Carol didn't say a word as I popped the recaptured gerbil back in her cage.

Hermione escaped again the next morning. This time she sprang out of her cage and straight up the rubber cone of the facial mask due to deliver a waft of anaesthetic to her so that I could operate on her tail.

'That's very obliging of you,' I said, placing a hand over the cone to keep Hermione trapped inside while I turned the anaesthetic on. A few moments later, I was able to extract an unconscious gerbil and amputate her mangled tail.

A week later, Charlotte brought Hermione in to have her stitches removed. I made sure all the doors and windows were shut and checked I had a towel and stitch scissors at hand before attempting to catch the wily creature. She'd been jumping round her cage, standing on her hind legs, peering between the bars, no doubt planning the best escape route. It was on her second hop round the cage that I noticed something that made me sigh with relief.

'Hey, Charlotte,' I exclaimed. 'Would you believe it, but Hermione's nibbled her stitches out. And it looks as if the wound's healed fine. See?' I thanked my lucky stars that I now didn't need to catch the gerbil up and run the risk of her escaping yet again.

And thereby hangs a tale.

4

Going Bats

I'm not sure what woke me. The brush of wing tips against my cheek? Or maybe the high-pitched tic ... tic ...? But as I drowsily opened my eyes, I found a furry, little face with a scrunched-up snout, big ears and tiny, beady eyes staring at me, only inches away from my nose. Was it a dream? Like some sort of Halloween apparition brought on by too many swigs of cider over the pumpkins the night before? But as the little creature suddenly flapped its wings I was brought to my senses and realised I was sharing my pillow with a real live bat.

For many people this would have caused them to panic. To get in a flap. Rather like that little chap who had now taken flight and was winging its way back out of Willow Wren's open bedroom window. But not me. No way. I was more concerned as to why the bat was in the room. It should have been out with its mates on the hunt for food. His mates being one of the colony of bats that had decided to take up residence behind the tiles that hung on the upper walls of our neighbours' barn over at Ashton Manor.

It was Sandra Coles who had first noticed them, commenting one late spring evening, just before dusk, when I was crossing the field at the bottom of the Coles' property, intent on going for a walk with Judy and Winnie, over to the bluebell woods that lay beyond. She'd been out on her tractor mower giving their extensive lawns a cut. She stopped to have a chat as several bats dipped and swooped above us.

'There's been a great deal of scrabbling going on under the tiles of our barn recently. About this time of day. If you've a moment come and have a look for yourself.' She swung off the mower, pulling a loose strand of hair back under the green beanie she had rammed on her head.

I nodded, keen to take up her offer; and clipping the dogs on leads, followed her up the garden, meeting her husband, John, as we rounded the corner of Ashton Manor.

They made a good pair. Both short, solid-framed. She with mousy hair cut short, his of similar colour but receding. Both forever in their three acres of garden, constantly weeding hacking, chain sawing, mowing; which meant I seldom saw them out of green wellies and Barbour jackets.

Ashton Manor had originally been a five-bedroomed farmhouse – a classic white and black-timbered building with red-tiled roof. The farmyard had been paved over for parking with the adjacent hay barn converted to two garages. It was to the barn that Sandra and John led me, joined now by their two boisterous boxers, Henry and Heidi, who greeted Judy and Winnie with much stump-wagging and rear-sniffing.

'We won't have to stand here long,' said John as we came to

a halt in front of the garage. 'The bats come out from the tiles over the top of the doors. You can hear some of them now.'

He was right. All too clearly, one could hear scratching and scrabbling above us. Then suddenly a bat flipped out from under one of the tiles and shot into the air, whirling away. Another closely followed. Then a third.

'Wow. Sounds as if there could be quite a few in there,' I said, as the level of scratching increased, spreading out across the entire upper wall of tiles. 'Have you any idea how many there might be?'

'To be honest, never thought about it, have we, Sandra?' John turned to his wife.

'We just see large numbers flitting about over the orchard as it gets dark,' she said.

'Perhaps we should do a head count, eh? What could be nicer than sitting on the patio out here with a bottle of chilled white wine to watch them emerge as the sun sets. Wouldn't you agree, Malcolm?'

'Sounds an excellent idea.'

'In which case join us tomorrow. Let's say about 6.45 or thereabouts? Maxeen as well of course.'

The following evening proved perfect in every sense of the word. A beautiful warm, sunny spring day was slipping into an equally stunning sunset; the sun dipping down below the meadows to the east of Ashton, filaments of dark orange lighting the underbellies of pink clouds.

The four of us settled into patio chairs around a table which Sandra had laid out with plates of nibbles, while John had opened a couple of bottles of Prosecco. Seems he was anticipating we'd have a big count on our hands that might take some time.

'How many so far?' Maxeen asked me, as the first half hour

slipped by, during which the bats had been slipping out from between the tiles in a continuous stream.

I held up my glass. 'This is my fourth,' I said, my voice slightly slurred.

'I mean bats,' said Maxeen, crisply.

'Oh, bats ... yes. Lots and lots of little lovelies,' I replied, having lost count after 60.

'I've got to 72,' said John, draining his glass and refilling it.

'Oh, no, no. It's more than that. I make it 82 so far,' said Sandra, slightly sozzled.

By the time it was too dark to see any more and the two bottles of wine had been emptied, we decided to call it a day with a count of 90, give or take a bat or two. Or three. Or more. Who cared? No need to get in a flap about it. Even if the bats had to in order to hit the night sky.

Later, in more sober mood, we managed to identify those 'lovelies' as being Lesser Horseshoe bats, one of 17 species that are known to breed in the UK. And to think, 90 such creatures had taken up residence here. A real privilege.

'Yes, we are so lucky,' I murmured contently a few weeks later. This time out on our own little patio, the still warm rays of the sunset flushing my already flushed face, as I finished the first of my sundowners.

'In what way?' asked Maxeen, taking a small sip of her wine, as several bats swooped close over our heads.

'Mossies,' I replied, slapping my bare forearms as a mosquito attempted to sink its proboscis through my skin. 'Bats are great pest controllers. A small bat, like a Pipistrelle, can eat up to one half of its body weight on a given night. That's over 1000 mosquitos per day. So, with these Lesser Horseshoe bats, being bigger, say 5 grams, and us having 90 of them in the neighbourhood ... that means over ... uhm ...' I tried to make a calculation of the weight of mosquitoes that could be eaten by any one bat. 'Many mossies,' I eventually said and took another gulp of my Prosecco. 'Fascinating, eh?' I said, turning to find I was addressing an empty seat. Maxeen had slipped away.

I could have gone on to tell her that the onslaught on those mossies and other insects begins in earnest in May. Not only that, by that time, female bats have started forming maternity colonies and nursery sites. The large roost that we counted emerging from Sandra and John's tiles in early June was one such site. In such roosts, bats usually give birth to a single pup which they feed on their milk.

A day later, we were presented with one by Sandra who had walked over to Willow Wren carrying the baby bat cupped in her hand.

'Henry brought it indoors,' she said, handing the pup over to me.

I peered down at it. 'Must have lost its grip on its mum and slipped out from between the garage tiles.'

'Poor little thing,' murmured Maxeen.

It was certainly little. A real titch. Less than the size of a 50p piece. With a slight dusting of grey fur. Probably just a week or so old. It was alive but very sluggish. I doubted whether it would survive and said so.

'Trust you,' tutted Maxeen. 'Always the Jonah.'

'Worth trying to save though, surely?' said Sandra.

'Definitely. Especially when Malcolm's been droning on about them being a protected species and all that these past few weeks. I'll go online and see what needs to be done.'

Sandra smiled. 'I'll keep my fingers crossed for you.'

My wife wasted no time in tracking down the information required. The pup had to be kept warm and fed every few hours with a milk substitute.

'Until the pup recovers and seems more active,' she stated, busily making up some kitten milk formula which she then applied to the baby bat's lips with a syringe. 'Go on, take it,' she urged softly while I stood to one side, a sceptical look on my face.

'Perhaps it's too weak.'

'Well I made it up to the standard strength.'

'No, I meant the bat's too weak.' Words that prompted a withering look from Maxeen.

A few seconds passed while the drop of milk quivered on the pup's lower jaw. Then suddenly the lips parted. The drop vanished. Swallowed. 'There ... see?' said Maxeen, the implied 'I told you so' left unsaid. Through the day she continued to give the baby regular tiny feeds; and that coupled with being snuggled up in a ball of cotton wool made for a far more active and alert baby as evening approached.

'What now?' I queried, visualising a sleepless night ahead – my Jonah feelings coming to the fore. But Maxeen had consulted the Bat Helpline and had the answer.

'Providing the pup is strong enough, their bat rehabilitator has advised we put him back at dusk where he was found. Mum will hopefully pick him up.'

I pulled a face.

'We can keep watch.'

That could take ages I thought, the grimace still on my face.

'I'm sure John and Sandra would be happy to have a drink with us while we waited,' she added. 'Especially if we take a bottle over.'

My face lit up. That was more like it.

And so, with the tiny bat gently placed on the ground below the garage tiles, the four of us sat back with our glasses of wine. As the scrabbling above the garage doors started, the little creature flapped its wings and squeaked. Several bats flitted out, ignoring it. But a fourth emerged and swooped over us. It then returned to the tiles and fluttered down to the baby. There were several more squeaks as mother and pup were reunited before they vanished back up into the roost.

'Well that was a success,' declared Maxeen, beaming, raising her glass.

'Here's to the baby,' I said, raising mine.

'To the baby,' echoed Sandra and John, raising theirs.

Even Heidi and Henry sensed we were celebrating and each gave a bark of delight. 'No, we aren't forgetting you two,' said Sandra turning to reach across and pat Henry on the back. 'Especially you, sweetie. As you rescued the baby in the first place.'

'So here's to Henry,' I said, raising my glass again.

'To Henry,' said John, raising his.

'Henry,' said Sandra and Maxeen, raising theirs.

Heidi grizzled. 'Feeling left out?' queried Sandra.

'To Heidi then,' I said, my glass shooting up.

'To Heidi,' said the others, following me.

'What an evening,' I declared as another bottle of Prosecco got opened. 'All thanks to the bats.'

'To the bats,' we declared as one, glasses raised once more.

5

Winnie the Schipperke

It was one of those magical, early spring days. A crisp, bright, sunny one. And unseasonably warm too. Reaching nearly 20 C. Trees everywhere were bursting with new vigour, buds unfurling. Some already in bloom. Many magnolias now heavy with cusps of cream.

Not so the three sickly sycamores on Westcott's Green. Their spindly branches were still bare, devoid of any trace of green. The council had planted them as replacements for the oak that had crashed down in a storm a year back but had unimaginatively plonked them next to the roundabout. Here, they are subjected to a constant barrage of exhaust fumes which is now taking its toll. If ever a sycamore looked sick, that sorry trio does. They have a distinct lack of get up and grow.

Nevertheless, on a sunny day, the Green is still able to provide an open space for residents and workers during their lunch breaks.

Jean and I seized the chance that lovely spring day to escape the hospital and have one of our customary lunches on a park bench; savouring the delights of Bert's Bakery in the form of a baguette for me and a pizza slice for Jean. I was munching on a mouthful of my 'full English' – a baguette stuffed with rashers of bacon and two fried eggs – when I spotted the dog on the other side of the Green. He or she – I couldn't quite determine at that distance – was rummaging around a municipal bin overflowing with tin cans, plastic take-away cartons, and a scattering of left-over chips, the latter of which the little terrier was voraciously hoovering up.

'Looks like a stray if you ask me,' said Jean, as the dog trotted along a line of benches, being shooed away from each by people intent on keeping their packed lunches to themselves. Our turn eventually came. I could now see that with nothing to disturb the contours of the undercarriage, the dog was a female. She stopped, her tongue lolling out to one side: her hindquarters sank down slightly, her stumpy, tail-less rear end only inches off the ground. Clearly, she was apprehensive. Ready to bolt.

My 'Well, well, little lady, what are you up to?' seemed to reassure her and she edged forward, licking her lips. She was of stocky build, with a heavy, thick, tan coat which fanned out round her neck in a mane from which her foxy face peered out.

I confess I didn't recognise her as any particular breed.

Jean put me right. 'Looks like a Schipperke,' she said, adding, 'a Belgian Barge dog,' when she registered my blank look. I'm an expert at doing those. 'Mind you, they're usually black. So that's probably why you didn't recognise the breed.'

Ah, I was let off the hook.

I leaned forward and gave the terrier the end of my baguette. She wolfed it down and then gazed up at me, her eyes liquid-gold. Watering. Full of anticipation.

'No more. Finished!' I raised my hands. 'All gone.'

'You shouldn't be encouraging her, Malcolm. Shoo.'

The dog pattered back a few feet, her eyes still on me. With a final 'Shoo' from Jean, she gave a tiny whimper, turned and trotted off, her spindly little legs going at a rate of knots. No doubt she hoped to find another person willing to donate a portion of their Bert's baguette.

With the forecast set fair for the next couple of days, it seemed sensible to make the most of it. 'Over to the Green at lunchtime then, Jean,' I said, 'with a couple of Bert's best?'

The extensive choice of takeaway from Bert's Bakery means you can choose something different every day. Freshly prepared, his baguettes and baps are popular; and so he is always busy, often with a queue out onto the pavement. To avoid too long a wait, Jean would phone Bert in advance with our choice. Today it was a salami and feta cheese ciabatta for me. Local cured honey-roast ham and sliced pickled gherkins in a bap for her. I was halfway through mine when the dog appeared at my side, her tongue, as yesterday, lolling from her mouth. If she had a tail, she would have wagged it for sure. As it was, her docked stump wiggled furiously, making her back-end jig from side to side.

'Why, hello, Sunshine,' I said. 'Still around then?' The last of my baguette was proffered, taken and swallowed in one.

The next day's order included an extra item – a sausage roll. Jean raised her eyebrows.

'Just on the off-chance,' I said. The dog was waiting outside Bert's as we emerged with our order. She loved my choice.

On the fourth day, the dog was sitting patiently on the steps as we came out of the hospital.

'Seems you've acquired a new friend,' remarked Jean. 'Next thing you'll know, she'll be sitting in your car.'

And so, it proved, but not in the way one could have predicted.

I've never really got used to the phone ringing, wondering who would be at the end of it. Good news? Bad news? Whatever, I still get nervous, the palms going sweaty, my heart thumping that little bit harder.

I wonder if it is connected to when I was a teenager. That time when the Welshman family enjoyed the company of Polly, our African grey parrot. She was a great mimic and picked up many of the household sounds. Particularly the ring of the telephone. One day, she persistently kept imitating the phone, hour after hour. Very out of character as she normally only mimicked the phone if it actually rang first. Eleven o'clock in the evening it did eventually ring. Mother answered it to discover her brother had just died of a heart attack. Creepy. Definitely unsettling.

Now I was in practice, a night-duty call invariably set off a standard reaction in me. That particular late-evening call was typical. As the jangle of the bedside phone rang, I was instantly awake. Hand on receiver.

'Yes?' I said, no slur of sleep in my voice.

It was Carol, duty nurse on that night. 'Sorry, Malcolm. But there's an RTA on its way in. A couple ran over a dog.'

'Okay. I'll be over ASAP.'

I leapt from the bed and fumbled for my clothes in the dark. I always put them in an order-of-wear pile on a chair, pants on top, so as not to wake Maxeen should I have to dash out. But in my haste, I put both feet down one trouser leg and crashed over the chair, clothes scattering everywhere. Maxeen mumbled in her sleep and turned over to resume her gentle snoring. I rapidly tip-toed down the stairs and snatched up the car keys. I clipped five minutes off my usual time for driving over the Downs into Westcott and screeched into the gravel yard of the hospital as a Fiesta drew level with me and its two doors sprang open.

From one, a man raced round to me. 'The dog's in a really bad way,' he gasped, turning to help a woman struggling to get out of the passenger seat. 'You take her, Trevor,' said the woman, handing him a bundle of blanket.

The porch light of Prospect House suddenly flooded the carpark and the front door swung open. Carol appeared in full uniform despite the unearthly hour. 'Here, let me,' she said, as we tore up the steps. She levered the covered dog from the man and sped through reception, down to the theatre.

'You two, please wait in the waiting room,' I ordered. 'I'll be back shortly.'

I tore down to the theatre where I found Carol had already unwrapped the dog and had laid her out on the table. It was then that I recognised her. The Schipperke that had been roaming the Green.

A mounted sachet of saline on a drip stand was ready for me to insert intravenously. Standard procedure in cases of shock. And the little dog was very shocked. Her head had taken the full impact from the car. Her face obliterated by swelling, her eyes so puffy she couldn't open them. I wondered whether she'd smashed her jaw but remarkably it seemed intact. As did the rest of her body when I gave it a swift examination. I made a quick evaluation of her mucous membranes, pressing down on her gums to blanch them. They were pale but not deathly white. So her circulation was holding up well. Her feet were cool but she pulled them away when I pinched her toes. I gently ran my fingers down her spine gently pressing as I went. My actions elicited no grunts of pain.

'Lucky to have survived,' I murmured to Carol.

Having started the intravenous drip and given an anti-inflammatory injection, I returned to the worried couple.

'I think she'll pull through,' I said.

There was an audible sigh of relief from both of them.

There followed an anxious 12 hours before the little dog gradually came to and attempted to sit up. Over the ensuing days, she rallied well, the swelling of her head reducing rapidly. And, apart from her puffy eyes persisting for a few days, there were no neurological symptoms suggestive of brain damage. So after a further couple of days' recuperation in the hospital ward, she was ready to go home.

But that was the problem. Where was home? She had no collar. She wasn't microchipped. And the police, when we notified them, hadn't had any reports of a missing dog fitting her description.

Linda, the junior nurse, had now taken over from Carol to monitor the dog's progress and care for her on a daily basis.

'Quite a cute little lady, isn't she?' she remarked as I was doing a ward round one morning. I had to agree. She was never ruffled. Very laid back. Got on well with the other inpatients – cats as well as dogs. A real cutie. 'It's that look in her eyes,' added Linda. 'She's almost pleading with you to take her home.'

The little dog's golden eyes staring up at me did indeed have an imploring look to them. But more likely seeking a bit of a baguette rather than a slice of home life.

I turned to walk away.

The little dog grizzled. Just the merest of whimpers. A plaintive plea. But it was enough to grab my heart.

'Okay, sweetie-pie,' I murmured, turning back 'A slice of

home life with us it is.'

And so, the Schipperke's new home became Willow Wren.

On arrival there, having been lowered gently to the floor of the cottage – she was still a little unsteady on her legs – she promptly scooted around the corner into the kitchen and polished off the cat's dinner before diving into the refuse bin to seek out any further food.

'What a piglet,' exclaimed Maxeen, open-mouthed, the dog now having disappeared, head first, into the bin, only her back legs sticking out, waving up at us.

That piglet we named Winnie.

And I fell head over paws for her.

I should have known better really. I was past the excesses of adolescent human trysts, the free-love of my hippy, flared jeans, tie-dye T-shirted former self. And certainly, light years away from the shadowy flickering of senility with its Zimmer frames and circling, in red pen, the times for *Emmerdale* in my TV guide.

Yet there I was, in the throes of an affair with a frisky little bitch that required visits to the local dog-poo park where I hovered alongside my beloved with a jiffy bag at the ready.

I now tossed little bits of bacon on the floor at breakfast time. A chunk of cheese sliced off the pack in the fridge at coffee time. Winnie particularly enjoyed Wensleydale. All vacuumed up with relish.

I reasoned such titbits were a means to get her to obey commands. In return, she brought me her own gifts. Often in the form of a dying rabbit she'd found collapsed on the lawn in the final throes of myxomatosis, its eyes matted with pus. She'd deposit the putrid remains proudly on top of my slippers – the ones with bunny bobbles on them – so an appropriate place I suppose. Such love for Winnie was not just sentimentality. She was good for me.

Studies have shown that when you gaze into a dog's eyes, there is the release of oxytocin, the 'cuddle' hormone and brain chemical known for its role in love. So, as I cuddled Winnie on the sofa, staring into her eyes as I gave her a tummy tickle, oodles of love were pouring out into our respective eyes. That gaze mustn't be a hard stare. In the dog world, that's seen as a threat. Whereas between humans it's seen as a sign of sincerity. I often try to catch Maxeen's eye as she sits, hunched up, at the other end of the sofa from Winnie and me, muttering to herself, eyes glued to the TV. But I usually fail. Oh, dear.

It's been known for dogs to be cited as the reason for marriages breaking down.

I'd only been at Prospect House a couple of months when I met a client who subsequently always insisted on seeing me. She was a middle-aged lady, who doted on her elderly Cairn terrier, spending all her waking hours with him.

She would bring him for monthly check-ups, even though they weren't really necessary. At each consultation I learned a little more about her rapidly disintegrating relationship with her husband. It got to the stage that when I suggested the Cairn could benefit from a bit more exercise as he was getting overweight, the lady left the marital home for an apartment on Westcott's seafront.

'It's so Bertie can get plenty of walkies,' she informed me. 'We'll both feel so much better with strolls along the prom. All that sea air,' she added, cuddling the Cairn. Her husband was never mentioned again.

Winnie was certainly a sharp, little dog.

Besides being her besotted owner, I was also her vet. So there were occasions when I had to do things to her which were definitely not to her liking. Examples being vaccinations, flea drop applications, clipping nails. She always sensed something amiss before it happened. People experiencing fear and many other emotions give off distinct odours which can be detected by super-sensitive pooches such as Winnie.

Take the day her right ear canal had become inflamed and she'd started shaking her head. Time for me to squirt in some ear drops. She was snoozing in her basket when I walked into the kitchen first thing, the bottle of ear drops curled up out-of-sight in my hand. I'd already decided to 'act normal'. So I greeted Winnie as usual.

'Morning, sweetie-pie.'

I then went across to fill the kettle for a cup of tea. Having switched it on, I turned around to find an empty basket. Winnie had fled out of the room and was a quivering heap at the far end of the corridor. The only explanation was that she'd picked up on my unease – the adrenalin pumping through me. Winnie had smelt trouble brewing besides the tea and had scarpered.

Maxeen commented scathingly one day, 'You do realise you're becoming obsessed with Winnie.' The 'at my expense' was left unsaid but hanging in the air. Funny that. I could have sworn she didn't know I'd used her best tweezers to remove a tick from Winnie's bottom.

But obsessed? Surely not.

Okay, the other evening when Maxeen came home exhausted after a long day visiting her aunt, I said, 'Ah look, Winnie's made a sad face for you.' My little sweetie's ears had flopped and so I'd dropped down by her bed to cuddle her rather than my wife. Whoops. Maxeen reached over both of us to open the fridge and snatch out a bottle of wine.

And it's true I couldn't wait to put on the diamante-studded designer collar with Winnie's name engraved on it which I'd ordered from Pampered Pooches only that morning.

But I stopped short of buying bone-shaped fairy lights to string round her basket. That was going to be a surprise for her next Christmas.

6

Judy the Springer Spaniel

I first met Judy as a patient, when she was a lively youngster, 18 months of age, typical of her breed – a Welsh springer spaniel – brown and white, with freckles on her face, floppy brown ears and a white-tipped stump of a tail forever wagging.

Jean had warned me the dog's owners were rather fussy, not easy to please. 'So, do be careful,' she said, having booked them in to see me.

Not an auspicious start to a consultation.

In the event, Jean proved to be right.

The Fitch-Williams were very Sloane-ranger types. Not the sort to be seen huddled on Westcott's promenade in pack-a-macs, sharing a polystyrene cup of chips. On asking what the problem was, I was told between 'Yahs' that Judy was constantly scratching and nibbling herself.

'Just doesn't stop does she, Charlotte?' drawled the husband.

'It's perfectly frightful,' the wife drawled back.

I ran my hands down Judy's back on the lookout for signs of fleas – black flea dirts, their droppings. The spaniel's skin was clear. But then it didn't need an abundance of fleas to get an allergic reaction. Just one flea bite could do that and lead to the itchiness we were seeing in Judy.

We turned her on her side. She stayed still, with Charlotte's restraining hand on her neck. I discovered some red wheals on the dog's flank, self-inflicted during her scratching sessions; and the hairless areas of her groin were slightly pink. I tickled her side. Her skin twitched strongly and her back leg shot forward in a vigorous scratch reflex. All symptomatic of an allergic reaction. But a reaction to what? I was a little mystified.

In the end, I plumped for a flea dermatitis with treatment directed at reducing the inflammation and tackling any possible flea problem. I could see the Fitch-Williams were unconvinced.

'Guess we'll give it a go, yah?' the husband finally said to his wife. 'But we'll be back soon enough if it doesn't work.'

And they were back soon enough as it didn't work.

During the next few consultations, I worked through a list of other possible causes of allergic dermatitis. And there was quite a list. Food. Contact with bedding and carpets. Feathers. Mixed moulds. House dust mites. Judy was admitted for allergen testing. All to no avail. She continued to scratch and nibble herself.

Finally, the Fitch-Williams presented me with a shattering resolution to the spaniel's condition.

'Difficult decision, I must admit,' said the husband, taking a deep breath. Judy gazed up at him, tail wagging. 'But we want her put down.' Judy's tail still wagged, her head cocked to one side, her eyes still full of trust.

Their decision simply floored me.

But nothing was going to dissuade the Fitch-Williams. The deed was to be done. Judy was to be put to sleep. My suggestion of rehoming was greeted with vigorous shakes of the head. Referral to a skin specialist likewise.

I slid a consent form across the table. The husband signed it with a flourish. 'That's it then, yah?' he said. I shrugged. The couple left with scarcely a 'Good bye' to Judy who strained at the lead I was now holding, tail wagging, attempting to follow them out.

I seethed with rage as I marched Judy down to the prep room, steeling myself to do the deed. But it never happened. And I have to thank Carol for that.

'Don't you dare,' she said when I told her what I was going to do.

'But Carol, her owners have signed the consent form.'

She shrugged and pointed out that it was only a bit of paper whereas we were talking about a young dog's life being destroyed.

'The Fitch-Williams were adamant that she was to be put down,' I went on.

'So? They're not going to know if you don't do it.'

'A new owner might ask questions. It could get back to the Fitch-Williams. Then, what? I'd be the one at fault for not carrying out their request.' I shook my head. 'I don't think it's really on.'

Carol gave me a cold stare with those fish-green eyes of hers, raised a beefy arm and clenched a fist. For a minute, I thought I was going to get a left hook. 'That's a load of rubbish, Malcolm, if you don't mind me saying.' She bent down and tickled Judy's ears. 'We're not going to let it happen are we pet?'

'How, then?' I looked puzzled.

Carol stood up. Her mouth nipped in at the corners in the semblance of a smile. 'Easy. You take her on.'

'Me?'

Carol nodded. 'You're always saying how much you like springers. Well, here's your chance to own one.'

I looked down at Judy. She looked up at me, her head cocked to one side, her big, brown eyes asking, 'Well, what about it?'

So that's how I came to have a Welsh springer spaniel with an itchy bum, scoot her butt across Willow Wren's living room carpet.

Much to my relief, and certainly to Judy's, her itchiness slowly subsided, the bum slides across the carpet lessening until they ceased. And within three months the itchiness had gone completely. I can only assume she'd been allergic to something in the Fitch-Williams' home environment. Yah?

'How's Judy settling in?' asked Jean a few days later.

'Not so well as we'd hoped,' I confessed.

Maxeen and I had expected the first meeting between Winnie and Judy to be a friendly one. Much rump wagging. Bottom sniffing. All the customary overtures made between two dogs of friendly disposition.

But it wasn't to be.

Judy was willing to become firm friends within minutes of meeting Winnie. But the Schipperke wasn't having any of it. Just snapped and growled at her every time.

'Such a shame,' I said. 'I really thought they'd hit it off.'

'Maybe Winnie feels threatened, it being her home territory,' said Jean. 'Or perhaps she's had a bad experience with a springer in the past.'

Actually, Jean had a point there. We didn't know anything

of Winnie's background. Maybe there had been a confrontation with a springer before. If so, then this might have accounted for her untypical behaviour.

Poor old Judy. Try as she might – and she did many times – Winnie's response was always the same. Snarls. Raised hackles. Bared teeth. 'Push off' signals galore. So, in the end, Judy did just that. She backed off. Kept her distance. Did nothing to antagonise the little dog.

'She's so good-natured,' remarked Maxeen, one evening. 'Not a bit jealous.' We were watching TV on the sofa, Winnie stretched out on my lap having her tummy tickled in the flickering glow, while Judy lay on the carpet a few feet away, head between her paws, her deep brown eyes fixed intently on me as if to say, 'When's it going to be my turn?'

The only time the situation changed was when it was time for a walk. Then the barriers miraculously fell away, all animosity on Winnie's part vanishing: the overriding factor now being the race round the rec, picking up the scents of other dogs or haring through the nearby woods picking up the scents of rabbits and roe deer.

Those woods are always exceptional in spring. An undulating carpet of bluebells, the virtues of which I can forever enthuse about. Just can't help it. The minute those fragrant blue heads start to unfurl beneath the soft green brush-strokes of beech, my heart unfurls with them. My spirits lift to float like silky spindles of gossamer, threading through the overhead branches.

Winnie and Judy enjoyed those woods as well. They'd dart backwards and forwards along the sappy green paths ahead of me; excited yaps ringing out, echoing between the tree trunks as they picked up another scent.

On one such evening walk, I'd traversed the wood, reaching

the far side where gorse, bramble and hawthorn had encroached from neighbouring scrubland to form an impenetrable barrier, several yards deep. The perfect place for a rabbit warren – to which the mounds of sandy soil dug out along its perimeter testified.

It was there, Winnie suddenly vanished. One minute she'd been ahead of us. The next, gone. No sign of her. Judy was still with me, a few yards to one side, head out of sight down a rabbit hole, her back end still visible, her stumpy tail wagging furiously.

I called. 'Winnie. Winnie. Come here, there's a good girl.'

I stood, hoping, just hoping for a response – the sight of a little tan dog hurtling towards me as fast as her paws could carry her. But no. Nothing. Judy looked up from the rabbit hole, cocked her head and bounded over to flop down next to me, panting heavily after all the chasing about she'd done.

'Where's the little toe-rag got to?' I said to her, reaching down to stroke her ears. I shouted again. Still no response. I began to get concerned. Had she sniffed out a rabbit like Judy had done, then tunnelled her way down and was now stuck underground, deep inside the warren?

The light was beginning to fade though the sun had not entirely disappeared: the sky to the east a radiant lilac, with the first shimmer of a half moon. My concern grew with the lengthening shadows. I strode over to the rabbit hole Judy had been sniffing down. I dropped onto my knees, a hand to the ground each side of the entrance and shouted, 'Winnie' down the hole.

I knew in my heart of hearts this was a futile exercise should Winnie be stuck down there. Though, maybe she'd have responded with a whimper. Letting me know where she was. But silence reigned. 'Where's she got to, Judy?' I said, as she pushed herself up against me and licked my face. 'You go find her, eh?' She sprang back and gave a bark. 'Yes, that's right. Where's Winnie?'

Judy gave another woof and turned to tear along the edge of the bramble patch, nose to the ground. I quickly got to my feet and followed her in the gathering gloom. 'Good girl, good girl. Find Winnie,' I said, running to catch up with her. She rounded the far end of the brambles and disappeared into the scrubland beyond, me floundering after her as best I could. But rounding the corner I lost her. Oh no, not her as well, I thought, the impending darkness making it difficult to discern anything ahead of me. Minutes passed as I stumbled on, the ground getting wetter and wetter. More and more boggy. Unknown terrain to me. But decidedly marshy. Then in the far gloom I saw the blur of Judy again. Only this time she was heading back towards me, definitely in my direction but with difficulty. Her paws sinking in the mud perhaps? Slowing her down? It was certainly now seeping into my shoes, its suction dragging me back.

'Good girl, good girl,' I called out, encouraging her forward. The nearer she got the more I was able to make her out. Very bedraggled. Very wet. Very muddy. And hanging by the scruff from her mouth a very bedraggled, very wet, very muddy Winnie.

I was jubilant. 'Oh, my goodness, what a clever girl,' I cried, as she dropped the little dog at my feet. I could only assume Winnie had got bogged down in the mud somewhere, unable to move and that Judy had tracked her down and pulled her out. Winnie gave a tiny whimper to indicate she was alive and another when I picked her up to carry her home. There, a warm bath and a cuddle at one end of the sofa eventually revived her. While Maxeen did that, I attended to Judy, hosing her down and drying her off, heaping her with praise. I then sat at the other end of the sofa, she on my lap, her head on my shoulder, my arms wrapped tightly round her, tears trickling down my face.

Despite Judy having found and brought back Winnie, the dynamics between the two dogs didn't really change. Winnie still wasn't comfortable in Judy's presence. Still gave the occasional growl, the occasional snap if she thought Judy was straying into her comfort zone. So poor old Judy continued to keep her distance. But eventually, that changed. And in a very dramatic fashion.

It was the result of Winnie's wandering instinct. She just couldn't help herself. She'd scoot off whenever the opportunity made itself available. Gate left open by the postman. A new hole in the hedge made by a visiting badger – we had them calling in occasionally. Whoosh. Gone. Despite our vigilance. And Judy's. She, bless her, did her best to warn us whenever Winnie managed to slip away and go AWOL. A whine. The cock of her head. Signals to alert us.

'Probably why she ended up on the Green in the first place,' said Maxeen, retrieving Winnie once again from next-door's front garden.

Fortunately, Willow Wren was situated some distance from the main road on a no-through lane, so Winnie was less likely to suffer a similar fate she'd met before as an RTA. Nevertheless, fate intervened in a no less dramatic fashion and with a far more devastating outcome.

The whine from Judy was the start of it.

'Oh no, here we go again,' I muttered, following her out into the back garden to discover the side gate ajar and no sign of Winnie. I called back to Maxeen, telling her I'd go and find the little oick and then strolled round to the front of the cottage, Judy bounding ahead. I was expecting to discover Winnie in Rita's front garden, pottering through her perennials, or over the drive in St Mary's pottering through the gravestones. But no sign of her in either place. Seemed today, she'd decided to potter further afield.

'So, Judy, where do you reckon, eh?'

She nosed the drive, zigzagging from side to side: and then headed on down it towards the entrance to Ashton Manor. 'Ah, so you think she's gone off to visit Henry and Heidi, do you?' I crunched up the Manor's drive to the front door and rang the bell. The bellow of barks from inside told me where the boxers were. Sandra opened the door, cautiously levering it ajar sufficient to see who was there, while stopping the dogs from trying to scrabble past her.

I'd put Judy on her lead just in case they got out. On previous occasions, the boxers' encounters with Judy and Winnie had been – let's say – rather exuberant. To the point the four dogs hurtled around in a madcap game of chase all through Sandra's carefully tended herbaceous borders. Not a popular pastime. After an exchange of 'Good mornings' I asked Sandra, 'You haven't seen Winnie around here by any chance?'

'No, sorry, Malcolm, I haven't. But you're welcome to check round the back if you wish.' I saw her glance down at Judy. 'And you can let her off the lead if you like. I'll keep Henry and Heidi indoors.'

Both the Coles were fanatic gardeners. Their garden always immaculate especially at the back, where a magnificent manicured lawn swept down from their sunken rock garden with its swimming pool to the edge of the field and the path that led across to the bluebell woods.

It was to that sunken garden that Judy headed, streaking

away in front of me. And that's where I discovered Winnie.

I saw her little body floating in one corner of the pool, head bobbing just below the surface, tan mane and coat fanning out in the still water.

'Winnie,' I screamed, scrabbling down the path to the edge of the pool.

I reached out and pulled Winnie's body to the edge, hauling her onto the side. I prised open her sodden jaws. Pulled out her tongue. Pumped her chest. Her eyes remained watery and glazed. Her tongue blue.

'Winnie, come on, please.' I pumped her chest some more. Still nothing. I swung her round and bent down, raising her foxy face up to me. Then, taking a deep breath, put my lips round her muzzle and blew. Her rib cage expanded. Then collapsed. I blew again. Another rise and fall. Then another as I blew more air into her. 'Winnie, Winnie,' I cried, massaging her little body, pressing her ribcage between my finger and thumb, hoping to feel a heartbeat. Nothing. 'Please … Please …' I took another breath and pumped it into her. Her chest rose again. Fell. There was a judder. A twitch. Her chest expanded. I felt the flicker of a heartbeat. Then another. Her eyes blinked. Her tongue curled out. 'Thank God, Winnie … Thank God,' I sobbed, as her heartbeat got stronger and stronger beneath my finger and thumb.

From that moment on, it was if Winnie sensed that Judy had saved her life. She became far more amenable. No raised hackles. Just the occasional little growl if she thought Judy was going to snaffle the lump of cheese I'd dropped on the floor, thinking it should be hers.

'Winnie now sleeps with Judy in her basket. Something she never ever used to do,' I told Jean when she asked after the dogs.

'And you should see her sunning herself out on the patio,

paw to paw with Judy, as if butter wouldn't melt in her mouth.'

'Well, there you go,' Jean said. 'Glad to hear it's all worked out for the best.'

It certainly had, all thanks to dear Judy. Bless her.

7

So You're a Vet

There is often a problem when people ask what I do for a living and I tell them I'm a vet. It's as if suddenly I am there to advise them as to why their Fido is rubbing his bottom across the carpet. Or is the eczema on Auntie Mable's thighs due to an allergy to Tibbles' fur; and if so should they get rid of her? I'd be tempted to say, 'Shove her in a nursing home. That should do the trick.' But of course, I don't.

If it isn't questions, it's photographs. The wallet taken out, a picture slipped from a fold within. Fido, a panting distant dot on the beach. Kitty, curled up on the sofa looking at the camera as the flash goes off, giving her the demonic look associated with red eye. Cute. Pretty. Sweet. Those platitudes roll off my tongue. Fat. Slobbery. Ugly beast. They stay unsaid.

I was once sitting opposite a farmer and his wife at a Rotary

Club dinner. The talk inevitably turned to animals and what pets we each had. The moment arrived when the farmer pulled his phone out of his pocket.

'Here's pic of my pet,' he said, handing the phone across to me.

I found myself staring at a head, shoulders and horns shot of a Jersey heifer. A pretty picture indeed. And I said so.

The farmer nodded enthusiastically. 'Certainly, better than the old cow sitting next to me.'

The look his wife gave him could have curdled a pint of that Jersey's milk within seconds.

I suppose doctors get subjected to similar lines of discussion. Though not why one would be scooting on one's backside across the carpet. Even if piles were the problem.

What about if they discover you are an undertaker? I did have the weird experience of walking down Westcott's high street alongside the local funeral director. We'd just been to a charity lunch where he'd taken photos of the cheque being handed over by the Rotary Club's president for the money raised in a recent fund-raising event. The undertaker was on his way to Boots to have the pics downloaded as prints.

'Let me show you them,' he said, as we walked along the pavement. 'Here.' He was about to let me have a look. 'Ah, no, not that one. Nor that.' He kept pressing the button on the camera, flicking from one pic to the next. 'Nope. Nor that.' He looked across at me apologetically. 'These are of the deceased we've been working on this week. In their coffins,' he explained before finally finding the required picture. It was unfortunately underexposed – too dark – making us look like death warmed up. Together with our fixed grimaces we probably didn't look much different to those he'd recently laid to rest.

There were times when I met someone who had their pet

with them. That could have led to a tricky situation if they'd been brazen enough to hint at getting a free consultation there and then on the spot. Of course, I could have always said, 'No.' Or 'Very happy to see Rover. Just phone up for an appointment.'

That was one of the hazards of exercising the dogs over on Ashton's rec.

I often took Judy and Winnie to the rec for their constitutionals. Handy as only a couple of minutes' walk away from Willow Wren. And when time was short, it was preferable to heading across the adjacent fields to the bluebell woods. That was saved for after work – if it was still light – or at the weekends. On the rec I'd meet other residents of Ashton exercising their dogs, poo bags discreetly tucked in their pockets.

Seeing my two mutts scoot round, sniffing the lampposts, the ends of the benches, the corner of the cricket pavilion – a particular favourite place to cock a leg – did remind me of the importance of smell for canines.

I was discussing this with Steve Roberts one morning, as we watched our respective dogs sniff each other's bums.

'Good job we don't go around doing that,' he commented.

I readily concurred.

Steve was the proud owner of a miniature pinscher. 'My min pin' he'd said when I first bumped into him on the rec. Or rather when Winnie had first bumped into the min pin's bum. That was before the acquisition of Judy.

The standard questions of any dog owner were asked. So, I quickly discovered he was called Klaus. Three years old. His grandfather had been a Crufts champion. On further rec encounters, I was to learn that though the min pin looks like a miniature Dobermann, the breed predates the Dobermann by some 200 years. This information imparted while Judy's and

Klaus's noses were under each other's tails, discovering what each had had for breakfast. Over poo bag shovel-ups, I was told there's the suggestion that during the 19th century dachshunds and Italian greyhounds might have been used to improve the quality and reduce the size of min pins.

'Of course, that could be just be a load of old crap,' said Steve, dropping Klaus's fresh load in the poo bin.

Whatever might have been used in breeding programmes, the result was certainly a fine-looking dog; and Klaus was a fine-looking example. Blue-black coat with rich tan markings. A short muzzle and slender lower legs.

'And note how he moves,' Steve pointed out. 'That high stepping gait of his. Each paw lifted like a little Hackney horse.' Klaus at that precise moment had his left-hind paw held high, leg cocked up against the pavilion corner, giving it a good squirt. Something a Hackney horse could never have managed.

Klaus's virtues were extolled during other rec encounters. 'He's a gutsy little fellow,' remarked Steve. 'No surprise, as they were trained to be ratters. If needs be, Klaus will challenge anyone – and any dog – snapping first and asking questions later.'

I should have heeded that warning.

'I've a favour to ask if at all possible,' said Steve, one morning.

Uh … Uh … I had an inkling of what was coming. I braced myself.

'Klaus needs his claws cutting. Any chance you could do it for me?'

I should have told him to bring the miniature pinscher into surgery. But I was in an affable frame of mind. It was a pleasant late spring day, the sun was shining. What the heck.

'No problem. Pop him round this evening when I'm back from surgery.' Turns out that was a mistake. A very big mistake.

Maxeen certainly thought so. 'For heaven's sake, Malcolm,' she warned, 'It's not a good idea. Much better if Steve took him over to the hospital.'

'Nonsense,' I declared. 'It's only for nail clipping. It shouldn't be a problem.'

'Ah, but you did have that difficult corgi once, remember? Carl. That was just for nails. But he nearly snuffed it.'

Yes, well, thank you for reminding me, dear. That had certainly been a horrendous experience; and the poor dog did nearly die. But as a rule, nail trimming isn't difficult. And Klaus seemed amiable enough. Should be a doddle. It wasn't. I realised that as soon as a healthy set of teeth were bared once Klaus was lowered onto our kitchen table. Added to which, Steve warned, 'I'm afraid you'll have to watch him. He can be a little temperamental. Bit the last vet who tried to trim his nails.'

Now he tells me. Great.

As if to emphasise the point, Klaus emitted a surprisingly deep, threatening growl for such a small dog. The hand with which I was about to pat him was hastily withdrawn. 'Mmm … yes I see,' I muttered. I circled the table, tapping my nail scissors pensively against my chin. 'Well, I'm sure we can manage to cut Klaus's nails without too much of a battle. After all, it's not as if he's an Alsatian or bull mastiff.' As soon as I uttered the words, I realised how pathetic they sounded.

Steve shook his head. 'Sorry, if there's going to be a tussle, don't involve me. Klaus is funny like that. He remembers everything. I'll never be forgiven and will live to regret it.' He gave a nervous little laugh.

I felt the tic of a vein throbbing in my forehead. A sure sign of mounting irritation. My professional mask slipped briefly. 'Well, if he's that difficult, how am I supposed to cope?'

Steve's face reddened. 'Can't you sedate him?' he huffed.

'What, just for nail clipping?' I huffed back.

'You won't manage any other way.' Steve steamed.

'Nonsense. I can tape his muzzle.'

At which point, Maxeen slipped between us two huffing, puffing billies, holding up a length of white cotton bandage. 'This should do the trick,' she said, quietly. And then proceeded to tie it in a loop.

Without moving a muscle, Klaus eyed the bandage until it was within inches of his muzzle. He then lashed out, teeth snapping like demonic castanets. I threw a hand over his back and swung the other over his head to clamp it down on his scruff, bunching the loose skin between my fingers. In the ensuing kerfuffle, the bandage was wrenched out of Maxeen's hand while I still attempted to restrain Klaus's head. And boy, did he fight. His head twisted from side to side. Mouth agape. Lips curled back like a grinning mask. Saliva poured from his jaws.

'Come on, Maxeen, try again,' I gasped, while Steve backed away, both hands over his mouth, horrified by the right royal battle that he was witnessing. Maxeen swiftly edged forward again with the retrieved loop of bandage and managed to work it over Klaus's nose, tightened it and tied a knot behind his ears.

With his mouth now clamped shut, I could get to work, cutting the min pin's nails. Throughout, his eyes continued to glare, the whites bulged with fury. From deep within, came a strangulated growl, rising and falling like a lumberjack's saw.

Once finished, I yanked off the bandage.

'There, matey, that wasn't so bad,' I spluttered, jumping back as Klaus, now free, made another lunge at me, shredding the cuff of my jacket.

Steve was quite right about what he'd said earlier.

Klaus remembers how I'd treated him. I'm constantly made

aware of the fact whenever I encounter him over on the rec. As soon as he spots me, up goes his lip, a deep growl thunders out of his throat and his hackles rise.

Clearly it had been a hair-raising experience for him. And for me.

There was another client who would confront me with veterinary problems. Only in this case there was never ever a means of escape since I would be trapped in a barber's chair, rubber bib round my neck and scissors flashing across my scalp. Yes, my local hairdresser.

When I first started work at Prospect House, I asked Tony if he knew of a decent barber.

'Not much point asking me,' he said, with a chuckle, running his hand through the remaining fringe of his thinning hair.

For a while I did use a barber's across the Green. Handy, as I could nip over there of a lunch time. But I was never that happy with the result. Too much cut off the front. Too short or too long at the back. Not enough left over the ears. Too much taken off. A bit lopsided, surely? Always something not quite right. But then I must confess, I am a bit of a prima donna about my hair. A little bit touchy. I reckon it stems back to when I was about six years old. My mother decided that I might suit a crew cut. I was dragged off to the nearest barber's to where we lived in Bournemouth. No salubrious premises this. A very seedy-looking back-street joint, tucked behind a pawnbroker's and a shop with blacked-out windows and door, a red light flashing over the entrance night and day. A shop I was hustled past very quickly when I asked what it sold.

The crewcut was an unmitigated disaster. With my head shorn, it emphasised my facial features. The high forehead. A sign of intelligence – so said Mother. The big ears. Well, Prince

Charles has the same – Mother again. Ah, but so did Big Ears and Dumbo – that was Father. Just joking, son, he added. And my long, sharply pointed, prominent nose? Both parents fell silent.

So, in trying to portray a professional image with good grooming that included a well styled head of hair, I was still looking for the place that could provide it to my exacting standards.

'What about Alma?' Jean suggested. 'She's a client of ours. Owns two Lhasa apsos. Taken over the barber's in central Westcott. Sweeny Todd's I think it's called.'

'Careful if you do try Alma, Malcolm,' warned Tony. 'Sweeny Todd's got nothing on her. She's demonic. Mad as a Hatter.'

'Well I've heard she does a good cut,' said Jean.

'And possibly a slash at the same time,' said Tony, wagging a finger at me. 'Don't say I didn't warn you.'

Not the best of recommendations. But nevertheless, I decided to give it a go.

If any warning signs were needed, then the two barber's poles, one each side of the plate glass entrance, spelt them out: their bandages of red and white suggestive of a blood bath to be experienced within. Hey, what the heck. Sweeney Todd wasn't real whereas this Alma … I stepped inside to meet her.

Kneeling over a tray laid on a low glass table was a woman in her forties. Black T-shirt and black jeans clothed a heavy builder's body. Greasy blonde hair fell to her shoulders and fringed eyes that were encrusted with black mascara. She saw me looking at the tray and got to her feet. 'Just sorting through my gear,' she said.

The gear in question seemed to consist of some steel-toothed thinning scissors, a pair of electric clippers, two combs and a black brush. All items were enmeshed in a tangled weave of grey, brown, black and blond strands of hair.

'It's a cut you want then,' said Alma, guiding me to the one black barber's chair. 'It's gone a bit quiet,' she added, as I hunkered down. 'But there were quite a few in earlier.'

I gulped. The evidence was everywhere. Clumps of hair encircled the chair. And a flurry of short clippings flew into the air when Alma shook out a black cotton cover and knotted it round my throat before slipping a rubber bib under my chin. I wondered where she had stored the scalps as she started to tackle mine.

I did survive that session; and it gave me the courage to return on a regular basis. In doing so, I eventually met two of her other regulars. Her Lhasa apsos – Su Li and one of her sons, Ming.

'My lazy apsos,' Alma would exclaim, referring to the fact that the two dogs, whenever present, would commandeer the large sofa that stretched along the back of the salon, spreading themselves out, leaving any waiting client squashed at one end.

They should have been a smart-looking pair of dogs. Bicoloured. Long hair parted down the back, falling each side in bands of black and white to almost touch the ground. Likewise, the silky white hair on their heads parted to sweep down over their eyes and line up level with their beards. Well, in theory, that's how they would have looked had it not been for Alma's constant tinkering with her scissors. She might have had the skills to style a man's hair. But in the case of Su Li and Ming, her skills sadly fell short, leaving them looking like a day's worth of barbering that had been swept into two piles.

Visits to her salon were fun more than fearful. There was the occasion when I found her pounding along a portable running track while watching a Jane Fonda DVD. 'Trying to get fit,' she gasped. 'Doing a sponsored dog walk this Sunday.'

I looked across to the sofa where Su Li and Ming were stretched out, fast asleep and snoring. I wondered if she'd try getting them on the machine. 'Do you want a go?' she said, stumbling off.

I shook my head. 'Just a haircut, thanks.'

Inevitably, there were times when Alma sought veterinary advice from me. I'd be tied down in her chair, with no escape from the scissors waving in my face, as she asked about worming, vaccinations, the fleas she'd found on Su Li.

I once found her rummaging through a huge pile of toenail cutters. At least 12 pairs. 'It's a new venture,' she explained. 'Chiropody. I've got three nursing homes on my books already. And more to come.' Alma stood up and reached for a calculator. 'Now, let's see. There's 40 old dears in each of those three homes. So that's 120 times two feet. 240. Times 10 toes. 2400. Every month.' She paused to peer at the calculator screen more closely. 'Hey, I make that 28,800 toenails a year. That's a lot of nails. Talking of which, Su Li's are getting long. Any chance of you trimming them before I do your hair?'

Her scissors were snipping away at top speed one afternoon, when she asked, 'Do you think I should have Ming doctored?'

At that precise moment, Ming was under my cotton cover, his front legs wrapped tightly round my left one, humping vigorously. I shook my leg free and nodded. Definitely snip … snip … time for him. And on that occasion, I'd be the one holding the scissors.

8

I See the Light

I have to admit there were occasions when the rigours of a busy practice did get to me. I'd drive over the Downs to Westcott from Willow Wren, wondering what was in store for me that day. The bottleneck of traffic at the roundabout before turning onto the main road which would take me to Prospect House only fuelling my mood. Come on Malcolm, this isn't right I'd think to myself. You should be looking forward to the day. Wondering what the challenges would be. Not dreading turning up, fearing the worst.

But there we go. We all have our ups and downs.

I just needed to find ways to make sure that when the downs occurred, they didn't get the better of me.

One of the ways I tried was on the advice of a Chinese client of ours. When I think about it, it was a crazy idea but I was willing to give it a go.

It found me standing naked in front of a small bonfire at the bottom of Willow Wren's garden on a mild, if rather damp, January morning. But despite the flames, it was still too cold to be hanging round in the buff – with rather less hanging than usual due to shrinkage. I tried standing in closer to get some warmth: but think 'roasting chestnuts' and you'll appreciate why I eventually had to step back. I might have felt the fire on my belly but there was certainly none in it. Something which had been noticed by that Chinese client, Mrs Choo Ning.

'Forgive me for saying, Mr Welshman, but I can't help feeling you've lost your chi,' she said as I gave her shar pei its annual booster.

I was a little perturbed. I always thought I managed to keep my feelings well under control in front of clients. But Mrs Choo Ning had been very perceptive. I was indeed feeling a bit under the weather. A touch of the January blues. In her words, my chi had been lost. Done a bunk. My life force was out of kilter. She promptly compiled a 10-page dossier on how to get my chi back. How to get re-energised.

She handed in a large Manilla envelope at reception a couple of days later.

Jean brought it down at tea break and gave it to me.

'It's from Mrs Choo Ning,' she explained. 'How to get your chi back.'

'What's this ... what's this?' queried Tony, looking up from the newspaper he was reading. 'Someone lost their chi? Well make another cup then.' He chuckled. 'Only joking.'

'Yes, Tony, quite ...' said Jean, shaking her head and tutting loudly.

'Sorry.' Tony glanced across at me with an apologetic look. 'But I can't say I'm really convinced all that sort of stuff is any use. Wouldn't be doing with it myself.'

Willow Wren's back garden is long and narrow with a huddle of outbuildings halfway down, before continuing as our vegetable patch and composting area. By siting the bonfire at an angle to the cottage, behind one of the wooden sheds, I was confident that our neighbour, Rita Cussins, would be unable to peer from her bedroom window and witness the re-emergence of my chi as I disrobed.

Having managed to stoke up a reasonable bonfire and stoke up enough courage to strip off, I watched the flames curl round the shirt I'd just removed and tossed onto the burning wood. Old trainers and socks followed. Then my jeans, almost overbalancing as I hopped around trying to pull them off each ankle. Onto the fire they went. I was now just in boxer shorts. They swiftly followed.

It was at that point, I heard a horse snort. Another loud snort made me look across to the bridle path that ran down the side of the cottage. Over the top of the hedgerow peered another neighbour, Sally, a rambunctious country girl, out for a morning ride on her horse. It wasn't just her horse that had a bit between its teeth.

'Morning, Malcolm,' was all she said. The leer on her face said the rest.

I rapidly dashed indoors, my chi even more shrivelled, my life force now at a dangerously low ebb.

I did consider trying a bit of feng shui – that ancient Chinese art of creating a harmonious environment. Make some moves in the cottage. Alter things round. Get some positive energy generated indoors. Feel the flow and go with it. It had been Jean's idea in the first place.

'It's called acupuncture of the home,' she'd explained. 'It benefits your health through releasing channels in your environment where energy can flow.'

'Just open a few more windows,' was Maxeen's comment. Ever the practical one is my wife.

But I persisted.

First there were the ions in the house to deal with.

'The what?' questioned Maxeen.

I explained. They are electrically charged particles – negative ions and positive ions. It seems we need a correct balance of the two, with more of the negative ones to keep us healthy.

So I bought an ioniser – a small plastic pyramid-shaped machine – which I plugged in next to my side of the bed. When discharging negative ions, a little red pilot light comes on.

I found it extremely useful. When I staggered through to the bathroom for a pee in the middle of the night, that little red light was a beacon to guide me back to bed instead of sleepily wandering into the wardrobe.

Green plants had already been tried. They're also supposed to increase negative ions and make you feel better. To be most effective, nine are required, purchased fresh. And they should be placed near particular irregularities in the room. Our main one happened to be the corner on the tiny landing we have to negotiate round to go through to the bathroom. I hurried down to B&Q and bought nine potted plants and returned to place them round that protruding corner.

I spent a couple of nights blundering into dumb canes, mother-in-law's tongues and philodendrons, and stubbing my toe on a prayer plant in my attempts to get to the loo in the dark.

'Told you it wouldn't work,' said Maxeen, as I re-housed the plants downstairs.

But I was still keen to boost my yin-yang in the bedroom where it had been flagging of late. Hence the purchase of the painting. Feng shui suggests you buy bedroom art of images that you want to see happening in your life. Goals you want to achieve. I did try Homebase. But there didn't seem to be anything there that fitted my requirements. The piece of artwork I eventually bought off the Internet did; but it didn't go down too well with Maxeen.

She peered at the Karma Sutra coupling on the canvas, flexing her head from side to side. 'Not sure I want this hanging over our bed.'

The picture showed a turbaned gentleman in the process of inserting his lingam into a willing courtesan's yoni. 'You're not suggesting we try this,' she said. 'Impossible.' She twisted her head at 90 degrees and frowned.

'You're looking at it upside down,' I said, turning the painting round. The correct way up, the gentleman's lingam seemed in a better position: the lady's yoni not quite so insurmountable.

My idea had been to stimulate a bit more chi under the duvet by having the picture over the bed-head. But Maxeen was having none of it.

'No way,' she said. 'Especially in the manner depicted in the painting, upside down or otherwise.'

It was rapidly wrapped in brown paper and despatched to our local Age Concern charity shop where it was bought within 30 minutes of being hung in the window.

I did wonder about the use of a mirror. It would certainly have lightened up the room. But would it have lit up our sex life? If I were to have used one, then I needed to be careful as to where I placed it, since according to feng shui, mirrors should not face the end of the bed because the spirit leaves the body in the night and might get upset at seeing itself in the mirror. I know I'd have been scared stiff if I'd caught sight of myself tottering across to the loo, black eye-shade flattened on my forehead, wax earplugs sticking out each side. Enough to give any roaming spirit the willies.

I decided, instead, to concentrate on our bed. Perhaps that way I could re-discover my chi which up to then had been very unwilling to make an appearance.

'*Now* what are you doing?' complained Maxeen as she walked in and found me shunting the bed across the room.

'It's in the wrong position,' I explained. 'According to the feng shui school of thought, the foot of the bed shouldn't be in a direct line with the door and should be as far from it as possible.' Having heaved the bed into what I considered the best placement, I retired that night hoping to get a good night's sleep. Only I was completely disorientated when I sallied forth for my nocturnal toilet visit, returning, befuddled, to find myself crawling into Maxeen's side of the bed and attempting to cover myself with her nightdress. I was dispatched to my side with a sharp dig in the ribs and a sleepy, 'Bugger off.' Not the sort of sexual charisma I'd hoped to engender.

So I abandoned any further attempts at feng shui to restore my energy lines. Too stressful.

But there had to be other ways of getting to grips with my chi.

And, thus, see the light.

Trouble is, January is a bad time of year to lighten up, metaphorically speaking or otherwise. Grey dismal days. A mere glimpse of the sun if you are lucky. Getting dark at five o' clock. Talk about feeling under the weather.

There was a distinct lack of sympathy from Maxeen. 'Lucky you don't live in Iceland then,' she said one evening when I was bemoaning having to cope with another leaden-sky day. 'They barely get five hours of daylight this time of year.'

Thanks, love.

I went on the Internet that evening and diagnosed myself as having Seasonal Affective Disorder – SAD. One of those people who becomes very grouchy during the winter due to a lack of sun to the eyeballs.

I slumped back on the settee where Maxeen was watching TV and informed her I was a SAD person.

'You said it,' she replied, without taking her eyes off the TV.

My spirits sank even lower the next day. Another dreary one. Waves of drizzle swept across the pencil-grey Downs as I drove over to Westcott.

Jean noticed as soon as I walked into the hospital, her antennae always on the alert for mood swings. 'Bit under the weather, are we?' she queried.

Tony breezed in, cheerful as ever. 'Down in the dumps, eh?' He slapped me on the back. 'Can affect us all.' Then, off he went, whistling 'Singing in the Rain'.

My spirits plummeted to even deeper depths on dealing with my first client of the day. Talk about a grumpy old man with one foot in the grave. He had both of his well and truly interred. Hooked nose. Hunched shoulders. Permanent scowl. His crustiness would have outdone the topping on a steak and kidney pie.

I unwisely mentioned the weather as he entered the consulting room.

'Worse to come,' he muttered.

'Really?'

'Storm Justine. Tail end of a hurricane.'

'Oh dear.'

'Force nine gale.'

'Ah.'

'And severe flooding along the south coast.'

I didn't know about the south coast, but here, in my consulting room, it felt as if Storm Justine had already decided to tip its entire contents upon us. The word 'Noah' had nothing on this client. I wondered where he had moored his ark.

Even his surname, Dearth, sounded lifeless.

'So, Mr Dearth, what can I do for you?' I said, trying to instil some warmth into my voice.

'It's not me. It's them,' he said gloomily, wagging a skeletal finger at the three basset hounds lined up alongside him, looking as miserable as sin. Their dejected look was compounded by three sets of pendulous ears that flopped forlornly and three sets of downcast eyes.

'Ah, yes, your hounds.' I peered at the computer screen. 'Darcy. Percy. And Neville. Interesting names.' I tried a cheerful smile.

'Uhm,' grunted Mr Dearth. 'Them three got beheaded by Henry VIII.' My smile got the chop instantly.

Trying to keep the conversation afloat, I sailed on. 'See they're due for their annual boosters.'

'That's why we're here.'

'Yes, quite.' I scrolled down their case histories. Over the years, Percy had suffered a couple of ear infections. Dudley a broken dew claw. Neville a tick bite abscess. Otherwise for 12-year olds they were in remarkably good condition. I mentioned the fact.

'They're not at death's door yet,' growled Mr Dearth.

'No, not at all. Not at all.' I quickly turned to concentrate on preparing the vaccines. As I gave their boosters, I did wonder about attempting a pun along the lines of them being at Dearth's door instead. But thought better of it.

Driving back to Willow Wren that evening, I continued to feel as low as the clouds that were still banked over the top of the Downs. The precursors of Storm Justine no doubt. I was thankful Maxeen hadn't been witness to my moodiness. She certainly wouldn't have been sympathetic if last night was anything to go by.

I swung onto the small concrete parking bay in front of the cottage, surprised to see the curtains weren't drawn and the tiny front window ablaze with flickering lights. Walking round to the side gate, the porch window was also glinting.

I unlocked the front door and stepped into a living room bursting with light. Dozens of candles were lit on every available surface. Their flickering flames cast a soft warm glow especially on the person who glided forward to hug and give me a kiss.

'Thought they might lift your spirits,' murmured Maxeen.

'They do indeed,' I replied, beaming from ear to ear as I enfolded her in my arms. 'But you're the true light of my life.'

However successful I am in tackling my bouts of depression, they still occur albeit it just for brief periods. Hence, there were days at the hospital when it felt I was in the middle of some violent sandstorm. Not that I imagined myself as Lawrence of Arabia, mounted on a camel, charging through the sand dunes on a mission to save a distressed pet. If anything, I was more likely to be the dromedary. A depressed dromedary. One with a perpetual hump.

So whenever Jean booked a slot for me to go over to Badgers Holt, I relished the prospect. It was always uplifting. An oasis of calm beckoning. Its centre was a circular log cabin with a turf roof, standing in a patch of broadleaf woodland. Its owners were Nesta and Callum Summers, who had ditched the day job and the stresses of a consumerist society for the tranquillity of this woodland wonder. Sharing that retreat and its three acres were Primrose the goat, Bluebell, a Shetland pony, two wheaten terriers – Petal and Blossom – and a deerhound by the name of Willow.

As soon as I hit the chalky track that wound down to Badgers Holt, I could feel the tensions of the day also winding away. None more so than one sunny March morning. The beech and birches through which I drove were coated in soft mantles of green. The steep banks of the track swathed with yellow celandines and clumps of primroses. I found myself plunging through shaded tunnels peppered with sunlight. Intoxicating. Then to emerge, blinking, from the last tunnel, into the sun-dappled glade carpeted in yellow daffodils that surrounded Badgers Holt. Sheer magic.

Today, the Summers' stock was due for its annual check-up. Annual booster vaccinations given; and allow me a chance to relish some time, however short, in this wondrous place.

Nesta was a lady of medium stature, ruddy complexion, hair a tangle of heavy curls. Nothing striking in her appearance. Not so her partner, Callum. He had a frizz of black and grey hair that cascaded to his waist, matched by a beard of equal length. Both he and Nesta exuded an air of tranquillity. Calm. Unruffled. Never rushed.

They approached as I got out of the car. Nesta embraced me and smiled. 'So, Malcolm, how are you?'

'No doubt stressed as ever,' said Callum, also giving me a hug. But one that was more bear-like.

Was it that obvious? I wondered as I snatched my black bag out of the car boot and followed them round to their collection of sheds and pens, feeling with every step I took, a lessening in my tension, Badger Holt beginning to exert its effect. Before we'd reached the yard, Blossom, Petal and Willow had joined us, quietly trotting alongside, as calm as their owners. The magic of Badger Holt had long since permeated their paws.

'The hounds look fine,' I commented.

'Touch wood, yes,' said Callum reaching out to run his hand across the trunk of an oak that we were passing.

Once in the yard, Nesta went to put a head-collar on Bluebell while Callum knelt down with the three dogs and quietly ordered them to sit. Without a murmur, they obliged and continued to sit there, their eyes on Callum, while I gave each of them their booster. Bluebell too was very obliging when Nesta returned with him. Placidly, he stood there while I checked him over and gave him his flu and tetanus jab. 'Good lad,' I remarked as I withdrew the needle from his neck. There'd been not been a flinch from him.

Marigold, the Nubian goat, had been watching proceedings from inside the paddock fence, front hooves up on the first rail.

'Your turn,' said Callum quietly, and reached through to gently grasp one of her horns before leading her along to the paddock gate for me to examine her.

'She did have a touch of mastitis last autumn,' Nesta informed me. 'But we stripped the milk off the affected side for a few days and she seemed to get better.' Her udder was certainly fine now as she calmly let me feel it. Again, no flinching. No sign of stress.

'Now, have you time for coffee?' said Nesta when I'd finished.

I always made sure I had time for coffee with the Summers. Today no different. Time to soak up the scene. Their woodland glade amber-dappled with warm, yellow sun. Blackbird's song ringing out in the treetops. A robin chiming in. Then, from a patch of brambles, a delightful burbling tune, sweet and soft. A willow warbler, one of the first of our summer visitors to arrive. Its arrival a reminder of my departure.

As I drove back through the tunnels of hazel, I was conscious

I was taking with me a slice of the Summers' serenity. I knew it wouldn't last when back in the hurly-burly of life at Prospect House. But maybe the camel that I'd revert to once back would have less of a hump – less down in the dumps – than previously.

9

Antics in Africa

I blame the painting by David Shepherd depicting a line of elephants in front of some acacia trees while behind towered the peak of Kilimanjaro, its summit covered in a cap of snow. It's a scene that I often yearned to see for real, during the winter months in our flat in London – where I lived with Maxeen, my girlfriend at that time, before moving down to West Sussex and Westcott. I'd gaze up at the reproduction of his painting while shivering in front of a popping gas fire.

'Well, why don't you?' queried Maxeen, stretched out on the settee, next to me.

'Sorry?'

'See it for yourself. Ourselves, actually, as I wouldn't mind a trip to Kenya as well.'

By coincidence, in the following Sunday's adverts in *The Sunday Times*, I spotted one asking for volunteers to join a lorry-load of travellers crossing the Sahara and on down to Kenya. Five months rattling through Africa in a truck. Not quite the package holiday Maxeen had originally intended us taking.

My girlfriend shrugged when I suggested it. 'Don't mind giving it a go.'

So, we packed in our respective jobs – mine as assistant clinician at London Zoo, Maxeen's as an agency nurse – and duly gave it a go.

Little did I realise then what challenging things I'd end up doing to an ostrich let alone a camel.

David Shepherd would have a lot to answer for.

The camel flickered his long eyelashes at me and spat.

'Yes,' I muttered, 'you're angry all right.'

My veterinary training wasn't necessary to realise that. But the animal was lame and needed treatment, so I edged forward again. He bared his broken, yellow teeth and made another determined lunge at me from his crouched position. Having heard that a camel goes for the belly, and not wishing him to go for mine, I stepped back smartly.

That camel was a fighter. Male, heavy, weighing around half a tonne, the scars of many skirmishes etched into his thick, brown hide. He was part of a large caravan train heading from the southern Sahara to Agadez in Niger.

Our expedition group, which Maxeen and I had joined two months back in Putney, consisted of a motley bunch of 12 youngsters, none of us experienced in the hazards of crossing Africa in an ex-army truck. But we were surviving. Just.

That morning, we were lurching along the same dirt track as those camels. An old slave trading route that stretched from Tripoli on the Mediterranean coast down to Kano in northern

Nigeria. Yellow, laterite dust, churned up by our wheels, billowed across the string of a hundred beasts, a mixture of baggage and riding camels. Astride their humps, feet resting on the camels' napes, were Tuareg traders swathed in dark blue.

It was a sight that could scarcely have changed since their predecessors followed the same route in the 16th century, though I did notice one camel sported a bright blue plastic bucket.

'Oh, look, a baby,' exclaimed Maxeen, pointing as we bumped and swayed past the line of camels.

A curly-haired little fellow, barely waist-high, trotted gamely ahead of his mother, a graceful white female ridden by a young Tuareg, unveiled, in a stained white robe. Behind, hobbled a dusty, brown baggage camel, covered in sores, foaming at the mouth and lame. My patient-to-be.

We jolted on. The camels dropping away, merging with the acacia scrubland – thorn trees which the short rains had cloaked in soft lace-green.

By midday, we'd reached Agadez, a bustling market town where we made a welcome stop to rest and buy provisions.

Here was a lively crossroads of ethnic groups. Ebony-faced Housas. Lighter-skinned Fulanis. Berbers. Arabs. And distinctive among them, the Tuaregs. Tall and graceful, these 'Men of Allah' mingled with the crowds, their light-blue *gandourahs* billowing above white baggy cotton trousers; their heads buried beneath yards of tightly-wrapped indigo cloth, leaving only their dark, almond eyes to stare haughtily at you.

Maxeen and I were exploring the market, picking our way through the tiny piles of spices, charcoal, millet and red-brown kola nuts spread out on the ground, when a guttural bellow thundered from the market's edge.

'Streuth. What on earth was that?' said Maxeen, her

eyebrows arching, her forehead creasing.

I shrugged. 'Sounds like some poor beast in agony. Let's go and find out.'

It meant squeezing through lines of mules, donkeys and camels being loaded up with bags of sorghum flour, red calabash pots and bundles of thatching straw. Dust swirled. Traders gesticulated and shouted, waving their arms as they bartered with one another. Animals stamped and grunted as they were herded up.

Into this melee had arrived the caravan train we'd passed that morning. Surrounded at a safe distance by a small group of bemused onlookers, the lame camel I'd spotted earlier, was now lying exhausted and very bad-tempered.

'Maybe, I should take a look,' I said.

'You sure?' said Maxeen. 'He looks pretty grumpy to me.'

I hesitated. Half a tonne of distressed camel was a daunting sight. And besides, my knowledge of such beasts was very limited.

'But you know what will happen otherwise,' I said.

Maxeen nodded.

If I didn't do anything, the Tuaregs certainly would. Considering the camel no longer fit for service, they'd slaughter him. Like the emaciated female we'd seen the previous week, throat slit, skinned and quartered within minutes. Piles of her flesh went on sale, each swamped in a seething, black mass of flies.

As I stood there, a Tuareg – who I assumed was the owner of the camel – glided over and stopped in front of me.

I raised my left leg and twisted my foot round to point at the sole of my sandal. 'Your camel,' I said, 'bad foot.'

Between the folds of his turban, the Tuareg's dark eyes narrowed.

'Lame,' I added, before hopping round in a circle.

The eyes narrowed even further. Clearly, I was nuts. Had a screw loose. There was the shake of a head. The shrug of shoulders. Then the owner darted across to the camel, snatched up his headrope and yanked the animal's head round.

'Ah, he must have understood after all,' I said to Maxeen. 'Well, here goes then.'

'For goodness sake, do be careful,' she warned.

'Don't worry. I will,' I said, the reassuring smile I gave her belying the unease I felt.

I cautiously approached the camel's hindquarters. The air was rancid with sweat. That of the camel. And mine – beads of it ran down my face and dark pools soaked my armpits. His tail twitched. A flurry of urine-splattered dust was flicked in my face. Warily, I bent down to examine his feet.

Fortunately, when a camel's couched, the knees rest on the ground with the hind feet splayed out behind, soles uppermost. Each foot has two toes. Between the toes of this animal's right foot the skin was red and swollen.

It was then I made my first mistake. I reached forward and prodded the area. A stupid move. Very foolish. With an agonised roar, the camel shot out his leg, catching me on my right shin. Like a skittle, I toppled over.

'Stupid fool,' I cursed, levering myself up from the sand. I'd forgotten the first principle of examination – adequate restraint.

While still muttering to myself, two young lads slipped out from the circle of onlookers who had gathered, curious to know what on earth this white man was up to. The boys straddled the camel's leg as if mounting a seesaw, their fingers digging into the camel's hide.

The owner waved a hand at me. The inference was obvious. I was to try again. So I did. Cautiously, I scraped away the caked dust between the two claws. The camel roared. His thigh muscles trembled and bulged. The lads rocked violently from side to side. But they hung on, allowing me to determine exactly was the problem was.

The sole of the camel's foot had been pierced – most likely by an acacia thorn. Infection had tracked in and an abscess had formed. It needed lancing.

By now, it seemed, half the market had moved in to watch. A ripple of anticipation swept through the crowd as I unbuttoned my sheath knife. A hush descended.

'Here goes,' I warned the two boys. 'Hold on tight.'

Taking a deep breath, I jabbed the blade between the camel's toes. A green and red fountain of pus exploded into the air. The camel shrieked. He wrenched his head round, burning the headrope through the owner's fingers. With a thrash of his hind legs, the camel toppled the two boys. They plunged into the dust, rolling over and over. He threw himself on his side, still bellowing, and flailed sand and blood into the crowd. Jabbering excitedly, the crowd reeled back as he lurched to his feet.

But I hadn't finished yet.

Maxeen had gone back to the truck to fetch our medical box and from it I now extracted a needle and syringe – my intention to give the camel a shot of antibiotic.

The camel's owner took the syringe and rolled it in his chafed hand.

'Na … Na …' he muttered, handing it back with a shake of his head.

Undeterred, I filled the syringe, the thick, white penicillin trickling into the barrel. Injecting such a large amount I knew would be difficult. But I had to give it my best shot. Literally.

Half a dozen traders formed a circle round the camel. They started to jig up and down on the spot. They flapped their hands, stretching their arms high in the air, waving them from side to side.

'Yip … yip,' they cried.

A drum started to pound. The crowd clapped to the infectious beat.

'Yip … yip,' they roared. 'Yip … yip.'

The camel staggered round, distracted by the commotion. It was enough.

In a flash, the headrope had been winkled from under his nose. It was yanked. Stretched. With a resounding thud, the camel plummeted into the dust once more.

I leapt forward, plunged the needle through the thick hide and attached the syringeful of penicillin. I felt perspiration bead my forehead as I rammed the antibiotic into his thigh. Half the dose. Three quarters. Nearly there. Then splat. The needle blocked. The syringe jumped off in a spray of white. Still, the camel had got most of it. Snatching out the bent needle, I retreated rapidly. But it proved an unnecessary move. The camel didn't stir. He lay there, prostrate, quietly groaning.

And he was still lying there when our lorry rumbled out of Agadez. I glanced back. Several traders were forlornly prodding him, tugging at his headrope. But, to no avail. I wondered uneasily if he'd ever get up again.

The next morning, as the heat of an orange sunrise began to filter through our tent, I was woken by the thundering of hooves.

I crawled to the tent flap, pushed it aside, and gazed out.

The caravan train was striding by. Way down the line, hobbling, but keeping up with the rest, I spotted my lame friend.

The cheery wave from his owner told me all I needed to know.

*   *   *

The lure of Kilimanjaro and those elephants pulled us on. Though not before a gored ostrich crossed our path.

At that stage of our trans-African expedition, we had reached Kano in northern Nigeria.

It had been a typical start to the day. Early rays of sun, already as strong as those of a British summer, had picked out our orange and blue tents. Fly sheets, drenched in heavy dew, steamed in the steadily increasing warmth. The whoops and squawks of an African dawn chorus heralded the arrival of another vibrant day.

Lying alongside a softly snoring Maxeen, I turned over, hoping to snatch a few more moments of sleep. It was then I felt something hot and hairy slide slowly up my thigh. A hand maybe? In my sleepy state, I thought it could have been Maxeen. But hang on a sec. She might have had hot hands. But hairy ones? No way. I was brought rapidly to my senses as the hairiness reached my crotch and started to explore my credentials. Startled, I sat up. A young chimp backed down the tent and paused to gaze at me with soft, amber eyes. I hastily retracted my legs.

'Susie!' A bright, bubbling voice pierced the tent, and a freckled face, fringed with curls, peered in through the mosquito net. 'Oh, I'm so sorry.'

My naked predicament had been spotted. Her head withdrew discreetly and Susie loped out after her.

'What's going on?' said a sleepy Maxeen, rubbing her eyes as she came to.

'There's been a chimp in the tent,' I replied, struggling to pull on my shorts.

'Oh, really?' Maxeen yawned, her voice full of disbelief.

I shuffled towards the tent flap. 'Yes, really. You'll see for yourself when you get up.'

'I'm terribly sorry if Susie frightened you,' exclaimed the chimp's owner, as I emerged.

Considering my vulnerability, it could have been a painful experience, and the chimp could have been wild. We had often camped in remote areas teeming with game. But at that particular moment, we were pitched on some waste ground behind the main hotel in Kano. The only game we were likely to disturb was the local football match.

As Maxeen crawled out of our tent to join me, Susie's owner introduced herself as Gillian, the wife of the district veterinary officer.

'I heard you were a vet,' she went on. 'And as my husband's away up north at present, I was wondering if you could have a look at an ostrich for me at the local zoo.'

I hesitated, hands spread out, about to confess my lack of knowledge of such birds. The nearest avian equivalent I'd ever treated was a budgie whose beak and claws I'd clipped. That, and the carving of a turkey at Christmas.

'Malcolm will be delighted to help out if he can,' said Maxeen, challenging me with raised dark eyebrows. 'Isn't that so?'

'Er ... well ... yes ... of course,' I stuttered.

So while Maxeen stayed behind to catch up on some badly needed washing, I found myself climbing aboard a Land Rover in which Susie was already eagerly bouncing up and down. As the vehicle roared into life, she swung over, throwing herself in my lap while Gillian expertly manoeuvred across the muddy field on which we were camped. We slid from side to side, wheels churning in the sticky black soil so common in that part of Africa.

I was relieved when we reached the road where a marginally better surface at least allowed us to proceed in a straight line.

Though the multitude of potholes made it an excruciating drive. With every bump, Susie was thrown in the air, only to land forcibly back in my lap as we hit the next crater.

Gillian seemed oblivious to my anguish as she pushed the Land Rover on, scattering scrawny brown and white goats in our path.

'What's happened to the ostrich?' I gasped as Susie catapulted into my lap again.

'She's been gored by one of the antelopes in her paddock. Tommies have got quite vicious horns. Pity, as she'd been sitting on some eggs. We were hoping they'd hatch soon.'

Gillian swerved to avoid a wobbling cyclist, buried beneath a mountain of green bananas. I looked back anxiously but he was lost from view in a billowing cloud of dust.

A loud blast on the horn announced our arrival in the local market. But it made no difference to the throng that ebbed and flowed in front of us. A dazzling parade of gaudy printed robes – blues, reds, yellows. Ebony faces turned to stare with defiant eyes as we attempted to nudge our way through. Faces that broke into white, toothy grins as we battled in vain. Back and forth they surged. Trays piled high with oranges and grapefruits. Battered enamel pots. Calabashes dusted with maize flour. Even the occasional green beer bottle balanced precariously on top of a frizzy head.

Naked youngsters screamed with laughter as they chased us, their pale brown hands playing tag with the tailboard. Cackling chickens bounced across the bonnet in a welter of flying feathers. A startled sow, smeared with oil, shot from under us with loud snort, followed by a line of squealing piglets.

Emerging from that living maelstrom, we eventually swung off the road through a large entrance smothered in a heavy canopy of scarlet bougainvillea. A notice proclaiming 'Kano

Zoo' in faded black letters lay partially buried in a profusion of tangled blooms.

We plunged into a tunnel of giant creepers that turned the scorching sun into a twilight of cool, emerald green. Abruptly, we burst out again into the searing heat. Ahead lay our operating site. A large, open paddock where tiny tan and white antelopes with a black stripe along each flank advanced and receded in a haze of shimmering white light.

As we ground to a halt at the perimeter fence, a bevy of glistening black faces crowded in round the windows.

'Welcome, madam, welcome, master,' they chorused.

We were saluted by the head keeper – a tall, gangly figure, whose well-pressed but shiny khaki uniform flapped forlornly round his spindly legs.

Eager hands pushed and shoved to unload the medical equipment. Operating gowns and drapes made from local printed cottons. Instruments sealed in an old, olive-green ammunition box, steam-sterilised for emergencies such as this. A box of assorted drugs and dressings, needles and syringes; and the most important item of them all, the small glass vials of ketamine – the anaesthetic we were to use.

Amidst a babble of exuberant voices, Gillian and I were rapidly escorted into the enclosure. The ostrich lay in the far corner, resting in the dappled shade of a magnificent flame tree. However bad her injury, it didn't prevent her from getting to her feet as we approached. She gazed balefully at us from under long, dark eyelashes. It was only then could I appreciate the enormity of the task that lay ahead.

'She's quite a size,' I murmured softly, more for my own benefit than for Gillian's. As the ostrich stretched to her full height of about eight feet, I saw just how large she was – a good 300 pounds of solid flesh. Her long, supple neck carried her head into the lower branches of the tree, heavy with scarlet blooms; and from here she suspiciously peered out. Uncertain of us, her large, if functionless, brown wings were raised and partially outstretched.

But it was to her legs that my eye was drawn. Adapted for running, the thighs rippled with muscular power, blue-grey skin stretched tightly over them. I could see her tensing herself, ready to run or lash out if cornered. Her toes – there are two on an ostrich's foot – looked strong. Designed to bear all the strains of locomotion. Their strength was ably demonstrated by the way she effortlessly dug her claws into the ground.

I shivered, thinking how easily those claws could dig into me. And suddenly remembered what someone once had told me. 'You know, Malcolm, one kick from an ostrich could easily disembowel you.' The thought made my stomach lurch.

Gillian and I stopped in the middle of the enclosure, laying out the equipment on the hard-baked soil. This was to be my operating table.

The keepers glided swiftly forward. A large net stretched between three of them. As they converged, the ostrich took two gigantic strides in an attempt to break through the line. But the keepers were ready. With innate dexterity, they tossed the net up into the air. It ballooned over the ostrich. Sailed down. Enveloped her. The keepers pounced. Grabbed her wings. Pinned her legs. With a flurry of brown feathers, the ostrich spun to the ground in a whirlpool of dusty bodies.

'Well, Malcolm, now's the time.' Gillian gave me a reassuring smile as she handed me a syringe loaded with the roughly calculated dose of ketamine.

I approached the heaving bird, pinned to the ground by half a dozen keepers. One of them pulled back a wing to allow me easier access to the ostrich's chest.

'Here, master, it better now,' he said.

I parted the few remaining quills. They rattled like bamboo canes. Each the thickness of a pencil. Downy barbs dark and iridescent.

I took a deep breath. Felt my heart thumping. 'Here we go then,' I said as, with an area of pimply skin exposed, I slipped the needle into the bird's chest muscles. There was a slight twitch. Seconds later, the ostrich gave a sigh and gently relaxed.

Just how much damage had the antelope done? I wondered. It was easy to spot where the Tommie had gouged a hole. There was a gash on the left-hand side of the abdomen. Six inches or so in length. The skin folded over its edges. I gently plucked away the feathers and congealed blood. In doing so, the wound opened up to reveal a glistening layer of muscle. Muscle which had a rip in it.

'This doesn't look too good,' I said to Gillian. 'That horn has punctured the abdomen. I'll have to take a look inside. See if there's any internal damage.'

It meant working swiftly. The only sterility available was a bucket of water and soap. I scrubbed up rapidly, dropped to my knees beside the bird and set to work, slicing through the muscle to open the wound up further so that I could insert my hand inside the bird's abdomen.

Gingerly, I slid my hand in, moving in deeper and deeper until up to my forearm. I touched the slippery edges of the liver. The spleen bumped my hand. Warm coils of intestine slipped through my fingers. I felt the length of some gut. Then nothing.

'Shit!' I exclaimed. 'There's something wrong here.' I eased the piece of gut I'd been holding out through the incision. It flopped onto the drape, glistening. It was severed. Its jagged end oozed green fluid. That meant somewhere still inside the ostrich was the other end of that portion of gut.

'I'll have to go back in and see if I can find it,' I said. 'And try to stitch the ends together.' I warned Gillian it was going to be a mammoth task and unlikely to be successful, especially with such poor surgical conditions.

'But still worth a go,' she urged.

Perspiring freely, I set to work. Black faces craned over my shoulders, eager not to miss this white man's magic.

I managed to locate the other end of intestine and pulled it out.

Only then was the full extent of the damage revealed. The two ends didn't match. A large section was missing

I swore again and shook my head. 'You know what this means?' I looked up at Gillian from where I was kneeling beside the ostrich.

She nodded glumly. 'She's been disembowelled.'

The proof was suddenly slid across the ground to me. A battered box containing several feet of pulverised bowel. Unbeknown to us, a keeper had found them earlier, trampled in the dust, and had put them in the box for safe keeping. No doubt, they had slipped out when the ostrich had been gored. In her panic, she had trodden on them and gutted herself.

'Sorry, Gillian, but I don't think there's anything I can do to save her.'

My words were prophetic. A few seconds later, the ostrich gave a rattling gasp and died.

'Don't worry, you did your best,' Gillian said, patting my arm. 'It was a hopeless case anyway.'

But the sense of failure affected us all. As we silently trailed back to the Land Rover, a little boy darted towards us through the herd of antelope.

'Master … master …' he shrilled, racing up to me.

He was hugging a sticky bundle of feathers close to his

chest. The struggling mass gave a determined cheep. Small wings flapped and long legs kicked out resolutely. A beady eye peered at us, full of indignation.

Suddenly the mood changed. Spontaneous applause broke out from all the keepers and faces beamed once again.

Even I was forced to smile as the newly hatched chick jumped down and strutted proudly round us. The spitting image of mum.

Onwards we went. The snow-covered peak of Kilimanjaro, if still many hundreds of miles away, now nudging closer. When we finally made it to Nairobi, Maxeen's and my departure from the expedition was ignominious. The truck got bogged down in the middle of a carpark, churning wheels sinking down into the mud.

We looked at each other, with one thought in common. Time to leave.

We waved our goodbyes, wished the rest of the group an incident-free journey on down to Johannesburg: and with rucksacks slung over our backs, we trudged across the muddy carpark to find our own way down to the Amboseli Game Reserve and seek out that David Shepherd scene.

A hired clapped-out VW car became our means of transport. A little yellow beetle that blended in with the tall, dry grassland through which we bumped once in the reserve. The grass was so high in places that it made for difficult game viewing. We often had to rely on the zebra-striped safari trucks, packed with trippers, we could spot in the distance. A collection of those usually meant there was something worthy of seeing. One such cluster we tracked down, rattling along a narrow track in its direction, hemmed in by a towering tangle of grass each side. Suddenly, we burst out of the grass into a clearing around which a circle of safari trucks was lined; only to find ourselves smack bang in the middle of a dozing pride of lions.

But it was elephants, not lions, that we were really anxious to see.

I studied the reserve's map and pinpointed an area to the south, some way off the trail we were supposed to keep to.

'Are you sure we should?' queried Maxeen, when I suggested we drove down there.

'Can't see it doing any harm,' I replied, suppressing any doubts to the contrary. But those doubts surfaced when we found ourselves off-track, stuck in scrubland that had become slippery due to the November rains. Our trusty VW gave up on us, shuddering to a halt, its tyres unable to get any grip.

'So, now what?' grumbled Maxeen, her exasperation evident as I put my foot on the accelerator, only to have the engine whine, the tyres spin.

I switched off the engine, gazed out of the window, tried to strike an optimistic note. 'Well, if nothing else, the view's good.' In front of us, the acacia trees fronted a magnificent panorama of Mount Kilimanjaro, even though its peak was obscured by a blanket of cloud. 'Just needs a few elephants to complete the picture.'

'Well, there are some around,' said Maxeen. 'If all those piles of dung are anything to go by.' It was her observation that gave me the idea.

'Elephant dung, yes,' I exclaimed. 'That could be the answer.' Without explaining further, I jumped out of the car, instructing Maxeen to stay put. She watched, puzzled, as I scurried round picking up clumps of dry dung, bringing them back and ramming them under the VW's wheels with the sole of my sandal. The hope was that the dung would stop the tyres spinning. I was bending over the second back tyre when I heard a trumpeting. I looked up to see a young bull elephant had emerged from between the acacia trees and was standing, watching me, his ears slowly flapping, his trunk raised. I felt my mouth go dry, my pulse pound. This was potentially a dangerous situation. Especially, when four other elephants also appeared, and began to slowly advance towards me. Not a good sign. Were we in for an attack?

I backed against the side of the VW and slid forward to slip into the driver's seat and cautiously click the door closed. At that point, Maxeen suddenly reached across and clamped her hands over my eyes.

'What the heck?' I stuttered.

'Shush …' whispered Maxeen.

What on earth was she trying to do? Protect me from the sight of angry elephants charging our car? I felt her pull my head round so that I was facing directly out of the front windscreen.

'For heaven's sake, what are you doing?' I said.

'Quiet,' she commanded. Then, took her hands away. 'Now, look.'

I blinked and looked as instructed. There, ahead of us, stood a line of five elephants, the bull elephant his trunk still raised. Behind them a line of acacia trees. And the backdrop – Kilimanjaro. Only the veil of cloud had now lifted. The top was in view. A top capped with snow that gloriously glittered in the sun. Here was my painting. One that I'd travelled three thousand miles over five months to see.

I gulped. Felt my eyes brim with tears. 'Beautiful,' I murmured. 'Truly beautiful.'

I turned to Maxeen, looked into her dark brown eyes, sniffed and then smiled. 'And you've been with me all the way,' I said, my voice a little shaky. I paused. Reached over to take hold of her hand. 'So will you stay with me forever more?'

'You mean …?'

'Yes, marry me.'

'Of course I will, you silly sod.'

'Thank you,' I murmured and leaned over to kiss her.

Thank you too, David Shepherd.

10

Startled by a Starling

Mozart used to keep a starling as a pet; and apparently the close association the composer had with that bird helped to improve the composition of a piano concerto. While not sharing the musical mastery of Mozart, I did briefly share a similar bonding with a baby common starling – *Sturnus vulgaris* to give it its Latin name.

One June Sunday morning, whilst we were enjoying mugs of coffee and chocolate chip cookies on the patio at the back of Willow Wren, Judy and Winnie had been hoovering round our sun loungers, hoping that some crumbs might fall their way. Disappointed when the biscuits disappeared down our throats without any disappearing down hers, Judy wandered off to sniff the shrubs below the kitchen window, in search of any scraps that might have missed the recycle bin. Head out of sight in a Spotted Laurel, she began to whine. Her tail began to gather speed as it wagged more and more.

'Judy,' I called. Her head remained buried. 'Judy,' I repeated. Still no response.

'Looks like she's found something of interest,' said Maxeen.

Curiosity roused me from my sun lounger and I sauntered over.

'So what is it, Judy?' I enquired, bending down next to her. I parted the leaves and was just quick enough to grab her collar before she lunged at the baby starling. I scooped it up. Other than as a tasty morsel for Judy, it was far from appealing. Not a single feather on his body save for a few sparse quills on the wings. Translucent pink skin outlined his innards as if they were being displayed on an X-ray plate. His belly looked like a balloon pumped full of air. Above it, on a scrawny shoe-string neck, lay his flat head from which dark beady eyes peered out. Overhead, I could hear his nest mates chirruping as one of the parents delved into the loft with more food.

'Look what I've found,' I declared.

'Don't tell me it's one of the starling chicks,' said Maxeen, springing to her feet.

'Poor blighter's fallen out of the nest,' I said, craning my neck up to the gable. 'A long drop too.'

Maxeen took over holding Judy's collar, pulling her back from me. 'Any injuries?'

'Don't appear to be.' The chick had snuggled into my palm, his broad beak on my thumb, and closed his eyes. 'Cute little chap, isn't he? Guess I ought to try popping him back up in the loft.'

A while back, on one of my rare sorties up there, crawling across the joists, reminding myself that at some point I ought to get some boards laid for easier access, I'd spotted a hole in the eaves. A tiny circle of light ringed by blackness. It was where frost had penetrated the mortar, cracked it open and now allowed access to the roof space. Must get that filled in, I thought. Then promptly forgot about it. Not so a pair of starlings looking for a place to nest. What better than a cosy, warm spot, nestling between the rafters in a soft bed of fibreglass insulation? I'd heard some cheeping last week and went up to investigate. Found the nest. An untidy heap of twigs with three naked, pink, wide-beaked chicks. At that moment, the light from the hole was suddenly blocked. One of the parent birds, beak full of insects, had swooped in. Three heads swivelled round. Three beaks opened. Three larynxes screeched for attention. The parent bird, spotting me, backed out with a shrill tick of alarm.

'So, little fella, time to put you back with your nest mates,' I declared, looking down at the chick, still cuddled up in my hand.

'This should help,' said Maxeen, having found me a plastic food container to carry him in.

Once up in the loft, I sat a moment on the edge of the hatchway, to allow my eyes to adjust to the gloom. Whoever had installed the light up there had positioned it badly, the bulb being half-hidden behind the water tank, so throwing most of the loft into deep shadow. The nestling jerked awake and shuffled in the container.

'Okay, won't be long now,' I murmured and began to crawl from joist to joist, picking my way over the fibreglass insulation. The air was warm, musty. Broken cobwebs clogged with dust caught at my hair, one draped itself across my mouth. I jerked back, spitting it out and in the process rammed my head against a nail in a rafter. 'Bugger,' I said, feeling the warm ooze of blood trickle down the back of my neck.

To get anywhere near the nest, tucked right in under the eaves, I was forced to bend lower and lower until I was stretched out across the joists, inching along on toes and elbows, fibreglass sticking to my clothes, rasping my wrists and ankles, worming its way up my nose. But I still couldn't reach the nest and, in the end, was forced to slide the container as far as I could and tip it up. The chick sailed out, teetered on the edge of the nest and then toppled in. Job done.

My mood was one of relief once I had extricated myself from the confines of the eaves, crawled back across the loft space, lowered myself out and brushed off most of the dust and fibreglass splinters. I then gave myself a good wash, dabbing the blood off my neck. It was only as I was drying my face that I heard Maxeen calling from the garden.

'Malcolm, you'd better come down quick.'

'What now?' I muttered, as I stomped down the stairs, through the kitchen and out onto the patio.

Maxeen was standing front of the Spotted Laurel. 'That chick …' she said, pointing at the bush. 'The one you've just put it back in the nest.'

'Yes … So, what about it?'

'Well, it's in that bush again.'

'You sure?'

'Of course, I'm sure. Take a look for yourself.'

I did. She was right. A naked chick peered up at me as I parted the Laurel leaves. Bloody hell. I snatched him up as gently as my rising irritation allowed me to and hiked him back up into the loft in the plastic container. There I tossed him a little less carefully into the nest. Within 15 minutes he had reappeared in the Spotted Laurel.

Maxeen picked him up this time, crooning, 'Poor little thing, you're certainly being put through it,' before handing him over for me to attempt another re-nesting. That attempt also failed.

Maxeen was ready and waiting to pick him up. 'We can't keep putting you back can we? Diddums might hurt himself. Besides you must be starving by now. Don't you think, dear?'

Diddums I thought. Did I hear that right? Diddums? 'Well, yes, I'm sure he's hungry,' I said out loud.

'In that case we need to get you some food, precious.' Clutching the chick to her breast, Maxeen scurried indoors leaving me open-mouthed.

Not so the chick. His beak remained firmly closed.

But Maxeen was in one of her determined moods. Failure not an option. Minced beef was broken up, mixed with muesli and orange juice and then moulded into small balls. With the baby starling cocooned in cotton wool in a casserole dish, the next step was to get the youngster to take one of the balls. Maxeen waved one in front of him. His beak remained clenched shut. She tried gently prising his beak open to no avail.

She emitted a series of high pitched squeaks – a cross between a mouse being eviscerated and bagpipes being sat on. The effect on the baby starling was startling. His head jolted up, his beak tilted, the rubbery jaws stretched wide; and a yawning pink orifice was revealed. Into it, Maxeen popped a ball.

'There. Success,' she said. 'Well done, Diddums.'

The chick spat it out as she spoke.

Maxeen made another attempt with the use of a pair of forceps, which enabled the ball to be pushed further down the chick's gullet. That worked. After three balls had disappeared down his throat, the baby starling blinked rapidly, tucked his head under one of his tiny wings and fell asleep.

'He'll need proper sleeping quarters,' said Maxeen.

Under her strict instructions, a shoe box was lined with newspaper and cotton wool.

'It will need a cover,' she said. 'Don't trust Winnie or Judy.

Nor Queenie for that matter.' She had a point. So a chicken wire lid was constructed.

'How can we ensure he's warm enough?' was another question aimed at me.

'Er …' An infra-red lamp would have been the obvious answer. But we didn't have one: and the lamp over in the hospital was being used for a newly-whelped bitch's puppies.

'What about a hot water bottle?' said Maxeen. 'We must have got one somewhere.'

I pondered a moment. 'There may be one under the stairs.'

I was the one to find out whether there was. It involved worming my way past five litre cans of wood stain, several of tile polish, a pile of festering dog blankets and the two hideous pea-green vases shaped like frogs which Maxeen's mother had given us last Christmas. I located a pink, rubber water bottle of dubious age right at the back. On filling it with hot water, it leaked.

'We could make space in the airing cupboard,' suggested Maxeen.

We could. And we did. Or rather Maxeen did. Seemed she had opted to take control of proceedings. It was she who organised a routine for regular feeds. Feeds that she undertook to give.

And Diddums progressed well.

I did a search of the Internet to see how long it would be before a fledgling starling left its nest. At least 10 days. Those days passed. In that time Diddums had sprouted a mantle of grey feathers and was allowed to waddle round the kitchen, providing the dogs and cat were kept at bay. Only trouble was that he tended to blend in with the grey diamonds of the vinyl floor: especially if he decided to squat motionless in the middle of one, where he disappeared completely. I found myself kneeling down and peering across the floor before entering the kitchen rather than run the risk of walking in and squashing him underfoot: and incurring Maxeen's wrath in the process.

'This is nonsense,' I complained. 'You can't expect me to pray to Allah every time I want to go into the kitchen to make a cup of tea.' My pleas went unheeded.

The chick's home-base became a budgerigar cage from which he did his sorties. Some of which were now in the garden.

'Game little thing, isn't he?' I said, as Diddums plopped off the back of a sun lounger and tottered after Maxeen with a waddle like Charlie Chaplin; while Winnie, Judy and Queenie watched, eyes bulging, imprisoned behind the back door.

'A clever lad.' Maxeen bent down to allow Diddums to spring onto her finger where he perched, chest puffed out, as if knowing he had her wrapped round his little claw. 'You'll be wanting to fly off soon.'

'And we can help,' I said.

'We can?'

'We'll give him a few flying lessons.'

'We will?'

Within the hour we were on the back lawn. Me in full flying-instructor mode.

'Now what?' Maxeen said, as Diddums perched contentedly on her outstretched finger.

I took a deep breath. 'Throw him into the air.'

'What?'

'Throw him up.'

'But he might hurt himself.'

'Throw.'

'You sure?'

'I'm sure.' I marched over to Maxeen and yanked her arm up. With a squawk, Diddums shot off her finger, gave a feeble flutter and dive-bombed into the grass, beak first, wings tightly furled. I winced as he thudded onto the turf. Maxeen ran across, arms flailing as if it were her trying to get airborne, while Diddums hopped through the lank grass to huddle at her feet.

She scooped him up. 'There, there, Diddums, my love,' she crooned. 'We won't do that again.'

'Oh yes we will,' I said, marching over to her.

'He might break his neck.'

'He's got to learn.'

'Not if he breaks his neck.'

'He won't.'

'He might.'

'Give.' I clicked my fingers, hand outstretched.

'Oh, very well. If you say so.'

'I do.' Another click of the fingers: and the young starling was reluctantly handed over.

Without a pause, I tossed him into the air. Another cannonball landing ensued. I raced over to snatch him up before Maxeen could. A further throw. Higher this time. Up he sailed. Down he plummeted. Heading earthbound at a rate of knots. But a split second before plunging onto the lawn again, he flapped his tiny wings furiously. It was enough for him to suddenly swing to one side and soar up again. This time to crash-land on a branch of our ancient pear tree.

'See? He's made it,' I cried triumphantly.

'Oh no he hasn't,' said Maxeen, pointing. 'He's going to fall.'

Sure enough, Diddums tottered, teetered and lurched forward.

'Grip, you silly bugger,' I cried.

But gravity took over. With a final lurch, Diddums toppled off the branch and plunged into my newly planted rosemary bush below.

We both ran forward.

'Any damage? asked Maxeen.

'Seems okay,' I said, running my fingers through the bush seeking out any broken shoots.

'I mean to the bird,' Maxeen said, picking Diddums up to carry him indoors, reeking of rosemary.

It seems those few aerial excursions were enough to trigger Diddum's flying instincts since the next day he mastered the art of staying airborne in one fell swoop. As soon as he was let out of his cage. Whoosh. He was off round the kitchen: and then swooping into the living room, his every move radar-tracked by the dogs and cat.

With the extra freedom came the fledging's ability to start fending for himself. Tiny worms and beetles in the garden became part of his diet. Reducing the need to constantly offer him meat balls.

'Time he went,' I said, wiping away the trail-blazing deposits he'd dropped on his flight paths to and fro across the dining room table. That time came a few days later.

But not before an incident that left *us* speechless if not Diddums.

'Malcolm, come here quick.' Maxeen's voice rang out from the kitchen. 'You'll never believe what I've just heard.'

'What is it?' I said, striding into the kitchen.

'It's Diddums,' said Maxeen, grabbing my wrist and pulling me across to the budgerigar cage where the fledgling was on his perch, a beady eye on us. 'He's just spoken to me.'

'He's what?'

'You heard. He's spoken to me.'

'Dearest … I don't think …'

'He did. Honest.'

I tried not to sound too incredulous. 'And what did he say?'

'Diddums here.'

A smirk creased my face. 'Oh, really?'

'There. I knew you wouldn't believe me.'

'Diddums here.' We both reeled round on the cage. The words were repeated. Croaky. But distinct enough. 'Diddums here.' The young starling *had* spoken.

'See? What did I tell you?' trumpeted Maxeen. 'Now will you believe me?'

There was nothing more I could say.

But the young starling did. 'Diddums here.'

Diddums might have been there then. But two days later he wasn't.

He found the hall window open a fraction. A narrow gap sufficient for a fledgling starling to slip through. He duly obliged.

Maxeen was worried. 'Poor Diddums. Do you think he'll be able to cope?'

'He'll be fine,' I said, forcing my lips into a pretend smile as I thought of the potential tasty snack now on offer for Tammy, our neighbour's trophy-hunting tortoiseshell; the buzzard frequently perched on top of the telegraph pole in the neighbouring field ready to pounce on its next meal; the local fox often seen on the prowl around the village. 'Don't worry.'

Once he'd made his escape, we were never to see Diddums again. Not specifically.

But one summer's evening, a few weeks after he'd disappeared, we were out walking Judy and Winnie across the nearby cornfield which had just been cut. A flock of starlings swarmed from the stubble with much shrill burbling.

Maxeen stopped, put her hand on my arm. 'Malcolm, did you hear what I just heard? It sounded like …'

The starlings flew low over the cornfield and then soared up to settle noisily in a nearby oak tree. In the middle of their strident babbling, I heard, like my wife had done, two distinctive, very clearly enunciated words. Just those two words, 'Diddums here.'

11

Friday the 13th

The blackbird hopping about on the empty bird table just outside Willow Wren's kitchen window peered in at me and caught my eye with a beady look. With it being Friday the 13th, it could have been seen as an omen of doom since, according to those who believe in such superstitions, a stare from a blackbird can lead to an early death. I hoped it was just the fact I hadn't yet scattered any breakfast crumbs out for him. So I hastily crumbled half a loaf on the bread board, slid open the window and tossed it out onto the bird table. Well you can't be too careful, can you? Better be safe than sorry.

'Wimp,' was all Maxeen could say when she saw me doing it.

'Well it was stale anyway,' I retorted.

I don't regard myself as particularly superstitious. If I break a mirror, I don't get too cut up about it – no thoughts of seven years' bad luck – just annoyed at how clumsy I've been especially if I do slice myself on a shard.

As to walking under ladders, well it's common sense not to if there's a guy up there wobbling about with a dripping paint brush.

An umbrella being opened indoors? Sensible to check it's working okay in the dry rather than waiting to do so in the pouring rain and getting soaked in the process.

I'd have certainly got soaked doing so that morning.

It had been raining all night. And it still was, on and off. Loads of surface water on the drive into work over the Downs. The spray making visibility poor. Extra concentration required. Wipers at full pelt. Foul weather to make me feel foul. And it did.

My mood not helped when on arrival at the hospital, Jean's 'Good morning' was followed by, 'Did you see any magpies on the way over?' Her forehead creased like a child's paper fan.

'Er … what?' I said, perplexed.

'Magpies,' she repeated. 'You know, those black and white birds.'

Yes, Jean, I thought. I do know what magpies look like. But why mention them now?

'So, did you see one?' she went on.

I did as it happened, despite the atrocious weather. A rather bedraggled one, sheltering in a tree. Ah, yes. The lone bird. Of course. One for sorrow, two for joy … as the saying goes. I could see where Jean was coming from. I nodded. Anything to appease her.

'Was it circling Willow Wren, croaking?'

Now what was she wittering on about? 'No Jean, it wasn't.'

'Just as well then. That could have made it worse.'

'Worse?'

'Well, one on its own is a bad omen. But if it's circling

your home croaking then …' Jean paused and slid a finger dramatically across her neck, tut tutting. 'Could mean curtains for you. Death. Especially on a day like today. Friday the 13th.'

Oh, great, Jean. Seems I could croak even if a magpie didn't. Thanks for cheering me up.

There was more bad news to come.

It was via a phone call from a Mrs Hassett. Jean had been dealing with it, trying to persuade the lady to bring her cat in. But to no avail. Eventually the lady insisted she speak to a vet. I took the receiver Jean stretched out to me.

'Hello. Mr Welshman here.'

'Are you a vet?' The voice was a little tremulous. A little crackly. Partly due to the bad line but also, I suspected, partly due to Mrs Hassett – her voice sounded rather elderly.

I replied that I was indeed a vet and understood she had a problem with her cat but was unable to bring him into the surgery.

'No, I can't. I don't drive.'

'A neighbour perhaps?' A hopeful tone.

'He's away.'

'Taxi then?' A terse tone.

There was a pause. Several hisses. Mrs Hassett or the line? I couldn't be sure. 'Wellington's too shocked to be moved. I need you to visit.' A plaintive pitch ensued. 'Please. He's not looking too good.'

Click. No tone at all. The line had gone dead.

'She's bound to phone back,' said Jean, as I handed her the receiver.

'Tell her I'll call in later this morning then. As it's in Chawcombe I can pop home for lunch afterwards.'

'Watch out for magpies.' Now Jean was surely taking the mickey.

But I did keep a look-out for any as I sped back over the Downs later that morning. With fingers crossed that I hopefully wouldn't. Not that they would have been easy to spot. The sheets of rain making it almost impossible to see through the windscreen despite the manic to and fro of the wipers at full speed. Mrs Hassett's directions, when she had phoned back, had been clear enough though. 'Straight down Chawcombe's high street,' she'd said. 'Turn left by the Queen's Head into Mouse Lane. Cat's Cradle Cottage's on the left in a dip in the road.'

That dip seemed to be the reservoir for the whole of the South Downs. It was awash with water from the constant deluge we'd been having. And were still having. Arrows of rain lanced a murky, foamy whirlpool in which twigs and leaves swirled and in which, moments later, my boots churned and slipped as I waded across to the pavement and climbed the steps to Mrs Hassett's front door.

She opened it to give me a tight-lipped look as she took in my rain-drenched figure. She was in her sixties, slight of stature, her hair glacially-permed white, her eyes cold as blue-green water flowing under ice. 'You made it then,' she said, her voice equally frosty.

'Just about,' I muttered, through clenched teeth, fighting to remain civil. 'So where's the patient?' I added, as calmly as I could.

'Wellington's through here,' she replied, as we entered a low-beamed living-room with a log fire crackling in the hearth. The room was very hot. I began to steam. Not so, Mrs Hassett. She retained her ice-maiden manner. I looked round at the shabby furniture. A two-seater settee with an antimacassar. But no cat on it. A small fireside chair, a stool. Both cat-less.

'Well, he was here a moment ago,' said Mrs Hassett, her snowy cheeks quivering. 'He was lying in front of the fire, unable to move.' She must have seen the look in my eyes. Her frostiness began to thaw. 'Honest. And he did look in such a state,' she added.

I steamed a little more. It seemed Wellington had given himself the boot.

Mrs Hassett cracked her fingers together and eased her slight frame round the side of the settee. 'He may have slipped under the sideboard.' With great difficulty, she sank down and peered under. 'Ah, there you are, you naughty puss. Let's be having you.' Her arm swung under the sideboard and emerged with a large, limp cat attached to it. Like me, he was also steaming, his black fur in black strands, slicked against black flanks.

Ah, how prophetic today of all days. A black cat. Jean would have been delighted to tell me that in folklore traditions, contrary to the widely held belief that a black cat crossing your path bestows you with good fortune, the sighting of such a creature can mean impending death. A bad omen. Especially if the cat's seen from behind. Which is what I saw of Wellington as Mrs Hassett dragged him out. Great. Just what I needed to lift my spirits.

'He came in wet through and collapsed in front of the fire,' she explained.

I did wonder if he'd lain there with his back to the flames as that's a sign a storm's on its way. But the storm had already arrived so that seemed irrelevant. Likewise, a sneezing cat promises rain. The downpour had started hours ago, so again of no significance if he did sneeze now. Unless it meant he'd caught a cold. In which case if he then sneezed three times in a row, everyone around him would catch one as well. Mmm ... More good news? I think not.

Mrs Hassett sat down on the settee and cradled the soggy

cat in her arms. 'Thought maybe he'd been hit by a car.'

The same thought had struck me. Wellington was clearly shocked, his breathing rapid, his pupils dilated. But when I unsheathed his claws there was no evidence of shredding of the nails as so often happens when cats scrabble on the road after being hit by a car. As I straightened up, I noticed my fingertips were slightly blackened. There was similar smearing on Mrs Hassett's skirt where it was in contact with Wellington's fur. I ran my hand down the cat's back. More blackness. Soot.

When we began to gently dry Wellington with a towel it soon became obvious that his coat was singed. Somehow, he'd been too near a fire for his own good. Someone's bonfire perhaps? Having checked to make sure there were no actual burns, I gave Wellington an injection to counteract any shock and assured Mrs Hassett that he would make an uneventful recovery.

'Just think, Mr Welshman,' she said, showing me to the door, 'if it hadn't been for all this torrential rain, Wellington might have fared far worse.'

'Indeed yes,' I said to myself as I negotiated the puddled pavement back to my car. Some good had come of this downpour after all. The thought lifted my spirits somewhat. But not to the extent that I wanted to start dancing in the gutter like Gene Kelly. Besides which, what would I sing? *Singeing in the rain*?

Horses have a fair share of superstitions riding on their backs and have saddled me with many an ominous encounter. A white horse can warn of danger and live longer than a dark horse and is considered a living amulet against early death. Grey horses and those with four white socks are unlucky. The colour of Clementine, a bay-brown mare, wouldn't have given rise to an omen of doom. But her owners certainly did. George and Hilary Richardson. Doom-mongers of the highest order. So how appropriate they should loom large on Friday 13th. And how unfortunate.

I'd barely been back an hour from seeing Mrs Hassett's cat when Jean was searching me out down in the prep room where I was frantically trying to catch up on the morning's ops list.

'Sorry, Malcolm, I've had George Richardson on the phone.'

The mere mention of his name made me squeeze even harder on the cat's scrotal sac I had already slit open and from which I'd removed one testicle.

'He's demanding a visit ASAP.'

I curled my fingers round the second testicle and tightened my grip.

'I explained that it would have to be you as it was the partners' half-day.'

I pulled, stretching the scrotal cord, looping it in a knot round artery forceps to tie it and the testicle's blood supply off.

'He said you'd have to do then.'

I severed the testicle off and flicked it into the adjacent kidney dish to join its mate. Then steeled myself for the bollocking I was about to receive at the hands of George Richardson.

He and I had never hit it off even though I'd managed to deliver a handsome colt from Clementine in my early days at Prospect House. And that had been a breech birth. A big challenge. Seemed a second challenge was looming large.

According to what George told Jean, Clementine had gone down with colic. Very distressed. Danger of dying if not seen immediately.

Certainly, colic in a horse could be serious. Certainly, required attention. And certainly, I was likely to be on the sharp end of George's questioning in the process.

'I'll come with you, if you like,' Linda said, when she heard of my impending visit. It was accompanied by a shy, close-lipped smile. Linda was the junior nurse at the hospital. She was a quiet, unassuming girl of slight build. Fair hair fringed a freckled face with hydrangea-blue eyes. That face may not have been able to launch a thousand ships but could have easily floated a few boats. She'd been with me at the mare's foaling. Had been of great help in the handling of Clementine, the handling of the Richardsons: and indeed, in the handling of Malcolm Welshman – calming my nerves, assisting with the foaling. So, no problem with Linda coming along this time. In fact, I welcomed it.

Having driven back over the Downs yet again – no magpies in sight – we arrived at the Richardsons' farm to be met by a very agitated George, who immediately looked at his watch as we swept into the yard. As normal for George, he was immaculately attired in tweeds, shirt and tie, polished boots. Having bundled up our gear from the back of the car, we half-walked, half-ran across the puddled yard to follow him, as he dashed over to a line of loose boxes and disappeared into one of them.

Inside, we found both him and his wife standing next to Clementine. Hilary was clutching a lead rope attached to the mare's head collar, her pasty, white face creased with concern.

'You think Clementine's got colic,' I said, addressing both of them.

'We don't think, we know,' growled George. 'The signs are all there.'

Ah, here we go I thought. Nothing's changed. George still the prickly client. Put it down to nerves. Concern for Clementine.

But he was right. The signs were there. Dark, sweat-stained hair along Clementine's flanks and under her shoulders. Constant pawing at the ground. Sudden turning to look at her side. Tail swishing. All indications of pain. The classic signs of colic.

'How long's this been going on?' I asked.

'About an hour now,' said George.

'Has she rolled yet?'

'Twice.'

Hmm … Not a good sign I thought.

'I'll check her pulse.'

George grunted. 'It's bound to be high.'

It was. Over 50 per minute. Way above normal.

'And her mucous membranes.' I lifted the mare's lip and checked her gums.

'They'll be congested.' George was right.

Linda handed me my stethoscope. I ran it along the mare's flanks attempting to pick up gut sounds. Some tinkling. Some gurgling. The sloshing of fluids in the intestines. Indications of normal gut movement. If absent, we were going to be in trouble. Serious trouble. Or rather Clementine was. A blockage being likely.

'Already done that,' said George, waving his own stethoscope at me. 'Her guts are gurgling like mad.' They were indeed when I likewise listened. But at least they were working. Phew.

Without a word, Linda passed me a plastic glove. Here was something George wouldn't have been able to do. A rectal examination.

'Easy girl, easy,' I murmured, as with one hand on her rump, I slipped the sleeved one in. Clementine whickered quietly and shuffled a little. Nothing serious. But enough to make Hilary jump forward and cry, 'Oh my poor sweet, is he hurting you?'

An action which startled Clementine more than having a hand up her rectum: and which caused my arm to be violently squeezed. Ouch.

'Steady, steady,' said Linda, gently stroking the mare's neck.

I folded my hand into a small ball and continued to move further inside the mare. Cautiously done, as there was the danger of sticking a finger through the intestinal wall: and that would have been an unmitigated disaster leading to peritonitis and possible death.

'It's okay,' Linda whispered, while she caressed Clementine's forehead. Meanwhile, George continued to grip the head-collar's rope, staring intently at me. Questions lined up ready to be fired.

First of the salvo was, 'Is there an impaction?'

There wasn't. I hadn't felt any solid mass of matter indicative of an impacted gut.

'No twist?'

'Nope, thank goodness.'

'A build-up of gas then?

I nodded. 'Seems most likely.'

'Spasmodic colic?'

'Yes.'

'It's that new dietary supplement,' Hilary interjected. 'It's not suiting her. Upset her gut.'

'You'll give her an anti-spasmolytic injection to settle things down then?' George continued to stare hard at me.

'Just about to do so,' I said, sliding my hand out.

Linda handed me a syringeful of Buscopan she'd already drawn up. The exact dose I'd have given. Good girl. We were ahead of George for once. What a team. Instructing George to hold Clementine's head collar steady, I swabbed the skin of the mare's neck, put a thumb over the vein in the jugular groove to raise it, and gave the injection. She didn't flinch. Unlike George and Hilary. They both twitched and gave a sharp intake of breath.

'I assume this will work,' declared George, giving me another challenging look.

'It will,' I replied. 'It will.' Then gave what I hoped was a confident smile. The consequences of it not working didn't bear thinking about. A twisted gut. Death.

Which reminded me. Friday 13th hadn't finished yet.

Proof of that materialised when I got back to the hospital. Just in time to start evening surgery.

'Your list is pretty full, I'm afraid,' said Jean, as I slipped my white coat on ready for the impending onslaught. Shouldn't really be thinking in terms of 'onslaught' should I? Sounds as if I'm steeling myself for a whole load of trouble. Instead, I should be looking forward to the challenge of administering to the needs of sick pets. Doing my St Francis of Assisi bit. Caring. Compassionate. Soothing the brow of a fretful dog or cat. Stroking the wings of a poorly pigeon.

''It's that tarantula of his,' Jean was saying.

'What ... Sorry?' The saintly smile on my face vanished in the wink of a dove's eye. My beneficence banished. According to Asian cultures, if I were to have seen such a creature in the morning it would have brought me grief. In the afternoon, anxiety. And in the evening, bad luck with money. To my mind, it didn't matter what time I saw a spider, it was still going to give me the creeps.

Jean tutted. 'You weren't listening, Malcolm. I was saying that I've managed to squeeze in Mr Spencer's spider for you to see. His tarantula, Tammy.' Jean gave me one of her laser-looks. 'He did insist on you. You've seen Tammy before and apparently showed great empathy for him.'

Really? How on earth had I managed that? Tickled it under its fangs? Did a shake-a-paw with one of its eight legs? The mere thought made me bristle. Much like the tarantula had done when I first met it. Since I do remember Tammy only too well.

Mr Spencer had tipped Tammy out of his travelling box and it lay upside down, legs crossed over its bulbous abdomen, looking for all the world as if it was on its way out. At death's door. Turned out it was its exoskeleton that had been on the way out. Tammy was sloughing it rather than snuffing it. It's called ecdysis. Once we'd determined what was going on, it was just a matter of time before Tammy had shed that outer skeleton and was feeling right as rain. Bigger. Better. More beastly.

This time was a different story. Though same spider and just as beastly. It nestled in Mr Spencer's huge hand, its legs dangling over his fingers before it decided to crawl down onto the consulting table. In the process, making my skin crawl as well. We watched him move slowly across the surface.

'Did you know that when they walk, there are always four legs on the ground and four off it at any one time?' said Mr Spencer, nudging Tammy towards me. I used both my legs to jump back as one.

'What's the problem?' I said, at what I felt was a safe distance.

'He's developed some tiny white spots on his front there,' said Mr Spencer. 'Can you see?'

I couldn't without stepping in, which I did with great reluctance, bending down just as Mr Spencer poked Tammy. That made the spider lean back on his haunches, raise his head and legs, and expose long curved fangs.

'That's his attack mode,' explained Mr Spencer.

I retreated.

'Don't worry. He's quite affectionate. And it gives you a better view of the spots I've been talking about.'

I advanced.

'But some will turn their backs on you and squirt a nasty liquid in your face.'

I retreated again.

'Tammy doesn't.'

I went to move forward again.

'Well, not as a rule.'

I swayed on the spot.

Though I didn't know the precise trajectory Tammy's bodily fluids were capable of making, I stood at what I considered a safe distance away and made my diagnosis from there. 'Looks like a fungal infection to me,' I said.

Mr Spencer fished in his pocket and pulled out a crumpled sheet of paper which he smoothed out on the table. 'It's what it suggests on this print-out.'

He swung the page round and I leaned forward to scan it quickly before Tammy had a chance to swing round and do the same to me.

'Ah yes,' I declared. 'Gentian violet. Dab it on the spots. Just what I would have suggested.' True. I would have done had I known it was the treatment of choice.

'What's caused it?' asked Mr Spencer.

I glanced down at the page just as Tammy started to crawl across it. 'I … er … well …'

Mr Spencer pushed the spider off and picked up the print-out. 'Says here it's due to too damp an environment.'

I nodded. 'Well, if you remember, when Tammy had that problem with sloughing his exoskeleton, we decided that it may have been because his vivarium was too dry. And that he should have an area that was shady and a bit damper.'

'I did that. And yes, Tammy does now spend quite a bit of time in that corner. So, you think it's too damp and that's caused the infection?'

'Bit like mould in a bathroom,' I said, nodding.

Mr Spencer said he'd modify the vivarium's layout and monitor the temperature and humidity. Problem solved.

I breathed a sigh of relief since as the saying goes: 'If you wish to live and thrive, let the spider run alive.'

I might have been dead on my feet from the hectic day I'd had, but at least I was still alive. And what's more survived Friday 13th. Well almost. Only a few hours to go.

The drive home was uneventful and magpie-less.

The bird table blackbird-less.

Then a sparrow hopped onto it.

Oh dear. Hadn't I read somewhere that they carry the souls of the dead? I tapped the kitchen window sharply. Scram.

12

Battles with Brock

When I pulled back the bedroom curtains that autumn morning, I let out a groan.

'What's up?' queried Maxeen, stumbling out of bed to join me at the window overlooking Willow Wren's back garden.

'It's the mess down there, that's what,' I spluttered. 'Just look at the state of the lawn. Ruined.' I emitted another groan of anguish.

Actually, the term 'lawn' could no longer be applied to what lay below us. Gone was our neatly manicured grass. Replaced by a sea of churned up turves. Piles of them rolled back, leaving gaping patches of bare earth. It looked as if Ashton's junior football team had just finished a particularly mud-churning match.

I knew straightaway who the culprit was. A badger.

'I thought you liked badgers,' said Maxeen as I savagely

sliced the top off my boiled egg while bemoaning the fact I'd have to spend the morning trying to repair the damage that wretched creature had inflicted. 'After all, you used to spend many evenings watching them.' The crisp scrape of butter across her toast said it all. She'd never forgiven me for once clearing off across to the woods behind Ashton Manor where I'd discovered a badgers' sett. Probably from where this brock had come. It had been a bright, balmy early September evening. An evening perfect for settling down to wait for the badgers to appear from the sett. Only it was also the evening of Maxeen's birthday when I should have been settling down with her. Whoops.

But Maxeen is right. I do have a special fondness for *Meles meles*, the European badger, widely found throughout the British Isles. And widely recognised with its white head and conspicuous black stripes on either side.

I tried to remind myself of this after breakfast as I set to work with a trowel, on my knees, shuffling back and forth across our lawn, rolling back each uprooted sod and uttering similar in the 'You sod' said loudly, every few minutes, to vent my displeasure at the culprit.

My fondness for Brock goes back to school days in Bournemouth when I discovered one spring day a badgers' sett only a ten-minute cycle ride from where we lived. It was hidden in the dappled fringe of a wood where oak and hawthorn buds were unfurling, peppering the branches in green. Spring fever was at its highest pitch. Blackbirds in full voice. Singing in hedgerows and treetops. Blue tits flitting through white sprays of blackthorn. In the high canopy of an oak, a small olive-brown bird darted between the branches, its constant tic-tak call announcing the arrival of our first summer visitor. A chiffchaff.

Along the edge of the wood ran a path, muddy-yellow,

pitted by countless hooves. To one side, a field spread out – a green mist of emerging corn-blades. To the other, bordering the wood, a bank where sappy loops of bracken were beginning to uncoil, pushing through a carpet of last year's brittle, brown fronds. Scattered down that bank, a mound of sandy soil. Levering myself up using the exposed roots of an ancient beech, I was able to peer down into a gaping hole, an arm's length in diameter. Dark and dank. The entrance to a badgers' sett.

I revisited the wood one evening in May. The beeches were now a lacy cross-stitch of green. Beneath them, a misty carpet of bluebells, their delicate scent eddying with the breeze. I climbed into the crook of a heavy beech bough which overhung the bank and which gave me a bird's eye view of the sett, safe from noses scenting for danger. I waited.

The sun dipped below the tree line in a blaze of orange. A sylph-like form – a roebuck – slipped into the field and began to browse in the gathering grey. A blackbird zoomed into the holly thicket below me, clackering in alarm. Three woodpigeons crashed in to roost: then, having spotted me, whirled away in a frenzy of flapping wings. I fixed my eye on the sett's darkening entrance. It suddenly filled with a blur of black and white. A badger stood there, motionless, listening. Quietly, he slipped out and sniffed the air, paw raised. A smaller, slimmer badger appeared behind him. A sow. His mate. They touched noses and purred. Then the sow rolled over and, with both front paws, gave her belly a hearty scratch, lips curled back in a blissful grin.

It was June before I first saw their cubs. Four of them. And what fun it was to watch, as they played chase, fought mock battles, rolled over and over with each other, used the tangle of beech roots for king-of-the-castle; and, all the while, filling the warm, summer evening with a joyous cacophony of squeals and squeaks.

By the end of the summer, it was difficult to distinguish the growing cubs from their parents. Especially when other badgers came to visit. One evening, I counted eight bristle-grey animals hustling to and fro below me. Amongst them, an obvious newcomer. She was of slight build, with a sandy-brown tint to her coarse coat. The cubs gave her a friendly sniff. Their mother sent her packing with a brusque growl and a snap of sharp, white teeth.

The final watch of the year saw me shivering one crisp September evening while the sow, free from her pestering brood, began shunting in large bundles of dried grass and bracken. Fresh bedding for the winter months.

It was well into the following spring before I had a chance to revisit the sett. As I freewheeled down the lane from home, I noticed a grey mound, slumped in the side of the road. I hammered on the brakes, swerved to a halt and leapt off my bike. It was the body of a badger. A female. The mother of last year. Run over. Dead.

I still went on to visit the sett. But as the sky turned an inky blue and the birds turned quiet in their roosts, the bank below the beech tree remained deserted. Forlornly, I jumped down. As I landed, there was a grunt from behind a thicket of holly. I froze, still crouched. Then came the familiar sound of scratching. I crept forward and peered through the leaves. There was a new entrance. A face stared out. Sandy-coloured. The visiting sow of last year. She padded out and turned to softly purr. A small striped face appeared nervously at her side, joined moments later by another. Proudly, the sow began to lick and groom her offspring. Then a third cub bounded out, tripped and sprawled next to her. It was smaller than the other two, its coat yellow-flecked. A spitting image of mum. The new generation of badgers was complete. What joy.

No such joy as I continued to knee-shuffle across my mangled lawn. Many of the holes I was filling in were round, elliptical.

'They're called snuffle-holes,' I told Maxeen when she came out with a mug of coffee for me. 'It's where the badger has pushed his snout down into the ground so he can suck up a juicy worm without it snapping in two.'

I could also have told her that worms make up 50 per cent of a badger's diet. Other pests he'll seek out are cockchafers and leather jackets found in the roots of the grass, deftly pulled up and rolled back with the use of his razor-sharp long front claws.

I thumped a sod firmly back into place and remembered a similar thud back when I was 18. The thud of my head, snapping on to the bank after I'd fallen out of the beech tree while watching those badgers in Bournemouth. I remember as if it were yesterday.

It had been a disappointing evening for badger watching. I'd cycled down from home well in advance of sunset so that I could be up my usual beech tree before any badgers were likely to venture out. But for some reason, they didn't make an appearance. Though the branch I normally sat on was a good 15 feet above the sett, perhaps eddies of breeze were carrying my scent across to the bank and so alerting the brocks to my presence. I stayed huddled on that branch until it was too dark to see anything, willing a badger to emerge. But no. Nothing.

In the end, I decided it was time to make a move. Time to leave. I carefully levered myself off the branch to stand on the one below, ready to shuffled towards the trunk, side-stepping cautiously. And once reached, clamber down, using smaller branches as foot-holds. A manoeuvre I'd done heaps of times in the past. Only this time the manoeuvre failed dramatically. As I stood up, my legs a little shaky from having been curled up on the branch for over an hour, there was a loud crack. The splintering of wood. The branch snapped. Gave way under my weight. As did my legs. Helpless, I felt myself begin to slip down, plunging through lower, weaker branches and twigs, gathering speed until I was jettisoned onto the ground. My back was first to hit the bank. Thud. My head swiftly followed. It snapped back on the hard ground with a crunching crack. I stared up. Immobile. Petrified. Red and green stars danced before my eyes. Bloody hell. What had I gone and done?

I lay there, flat out, fearing to move. Indeed, fearful of not being able to move. I tentatively pushed my left foot sideways. It responded. So too did my right foot. I wriggled my fingers. Yes. Feeling was in them. Slowly, oh so slowly, I eased my legs up, bending them at the knees. Likewise, I pulled my right arm up until the elbow was digging into the soil. Then, with my left palm I pushed downwards in an attempt to lever myself onto my right. An agonising stab of pain seared down my neck as I did so. Gritting my teeth, I rolled onto my side, shifted into a sitting position, paused for breath, and then staggered to my feet. My heart was thumping. Head pounding. But I still had to get home. And I did so. On my bike. How I managed it I'll never know.

My parents had been out to their local pub that evening. They returned to find me slumped on the sofa in the living room.

'Malcolm, whatever's the matter?' cried Mother, seeing my collapsed state.

'I've had a bit of an accident,' I murmured, attempting to sit up. Then promptly vomited.

'Hospital for you lad,' declared Father.

Several hours and several X rays later, I was discharged from our local A and E department with my neck strapped in a supportive collar, the damage being torn ligaments. No break.

It happened to be the Easter weekend. The local paper got hold of the story – no doubt a reporter had been sifting through the admissions to the hospital. Here was a good story to fill the paper. Local vet student falls out of tree badger watching. The reporter came round and interviewed me while I was recouping in bed. The national papers picked up the piece.

'Well, who'd have thought,' said Mother, having bought three copies of the *Daily Mirror* in which I was featured.

I read the piece. Very tongue-in-cheek. 'Don't think it's that funny,' I said.

The next three days proved me right. Three excruciating days. Days in which I was comfortable enough sitting, my head held firmly in place by the collar. But when it came to lying down, the resulting efforts to get up again had me screaming out in pain. Was this really just torn ligaments?

'You'd best be seen again,' advised Father. 'I'll ring 999.'

'You sure? Bit dramatic isn't it?' I queried before another spear of pain coursing down my spine made me rapidly change my mind.

An ambulance duly arrived, siren sounding, lights flashing. Much careful shunting of me on a stretcher down our steep driveway had the neighbours' net curtains twitching in a frenzy.

It took five more X rays to actually pinpoint the problem. There was a fracture of the Axis – the second vertebra down the spine – which had been missed first time round.

'To put it bluntly, you've broken your neck,' said the consultant. 'A fraction of an inch more and your spinal cord would have been severed. You'd have been paralysed from the neck down. So consider yourself lucky.'

I tried reminding myself of that 'lucky break' time after time during the ensuing months. They put a strap under my chin weighed over the end of the bed where I was lying on my back. It was to restrain me. To ensure I didn't move. It didn't work. I moved. Well, my body did – my stomach emptying violently via projectile vomiting. The strap was replaced by sandbags either side of my head and my promise to keep as still as I could. A promise I kept for six weeks as I lay there, stretched out on my back. Towards the end of that period, two junior nurses attempted to give me a bed bath. One cupped my head in her hands. The other leaned across to grasp my shoulder. The idea was to turn me in unison. To both move at the same time. Only they didn't. One swung my shoulder over before the other had swivelled my head in the same direction. The result? A crack as my neck was wrenched.

'Bloody hell. What on earth do you think you're doing?' I screamed.

I was dropped like a sack of potatoes. The two nurses skipped out of the ward in a flurry of apologies. To later receive stern retribution from Sister. A further six weeks saw me encased in plaster from a collar moulded round my neck – Elizabethan style – that merged into a jacket of plaster that encircled my ribcage down to my waist. But it worked. The vertebra healed. And these days, only the occasional twinge reminds me of what could have happened.

This day was one of them as I stuck my neck out and continued my slug-like advance across Willow Wren's lawn. Which reminds me, slugs are another morsel relished by badgers – along with snails. They'll also take small mammals such as rats, mice rabbits and hedgehogs. But worms top their menu and our lawn must have been piled high with them to judge from the torn and shredded state of our grass.

As I toiled on, other memories came flooding back.

There was the time when a ball of grey fur shot out of the bushes, bounced down the bank and careered into my ankles. Shaken, two badger cubs sprang apart from the tussle they'd been having. Piggy black eyes blinked at me, puzzled. Moist grey nostrils quivered, pointing at me, uncertain. At the top of the bank, a striped black and white head appeared. There was a warning yelp. Alerted by their mother's call, the youngsters squeaked with alarm and bolted back to the safety of their sett.

I kept reminding myself of those more delightful experiences as I squeezed my fingers round another clod of earth before ramming back into place. 'This really is the pits,' I declared as I savagely bit into the biscuit I was having at coffee-break.

'Well, I'm sure there must be a way to stop it,' said Maxeen with a shrug.

Some hope.

Brock had found a rich supply of worms in our lawn. A yummy feeding area. Very yummy. I leapt out of bed earlier and earlier, dragging back the curtains to be confronted by yet another turf ravishing and yet another loud groan from me.

'Oh, for goodness sake,' growled Maxeen, burying her head back under the duvet, while I stomped out to don my wellingtons.

She later did an Internet search and came up with some possibilities on how to stop such badger incursions.

A variety of ultrasonic alarms are available on the market which emit a high-pitched sound – one not heard by humans – when they are triggered by the movement of an animal.

'One of those might work,' she said.

I shook my head. 'I very much doubt it. They might be okay

in deterring cats. But for the likes of Brock, I suspect he'd soon get used to one.'

Maxeen came up with another suggestion. 'Seems chilli peppers aren't liked by badgers. You chop them up finely and sprinkle them round the lawn.'

Again, I was sceptical. 'Can't see that working, either.'

'But worth a try, surely? You've nothing to lose.'

So I found myself buying up all the stock available at our local Tesco's, stripping the shelf and, at the same time, raising the eyebrows of the cashier at the checkout. 'It's for the badgers,' I said, sanguinely.

The cashier shook her head as she scanned the pile of peppers. 'I see,' she said. Though by the sad look she gave me as I paid for them, she clearly didn't.

My look was even sadder later when, having distributed the mashed peppers across the lawn, I stood back and, without thinking, rubbed my left eye. It was immediately set on fire from the juice left on my fingers.

It might have been a case of one in the eye for me. But not so for Brock. It didn't have the slightest effect in deterring him from another night-time invasion.

Not to be beaten, Maxeen trawled the Internet again and came up with soaking strips of cloth in Citronella or Olbas Oil and hanging them across the lawn. In trying that, we found the evening aroma that wafted over our lawn quite refreshing. So, it seemed, did Brock, as he commenced his turf tearing with fresh vigour that night.

There is no chemical which can be legally used as a badger deterrent. Using any chemical means you are at risk of committing an offence under the pesticide regulations or under wildlife protection laws. So I was a little wary when Maxeen discovered a rusty old tin of a badger deterrent called

Renardine – now banned – left by the previous owners in the back of the garage. Obviously, Brock must have been a problem in the past.

'So what do you think?'

I pulled a face. 'Worth a go, I suppose.'

It was difficult to decipher the worn instructions on the rusty tin but I managed to work out that I first needed to crisscross the lawns with strands of string raised about a foot off the ground. This I did with the help of pea sticks. With the lawn looking like a cat's cradle, it was time to daub the string with the Renardine.

'This lid's proving a bugger to get off,' I muttered. Eventually after more cursing, I managed to prise the can open; and instantly wished I hadn't. The smell. Boy, was it vile. Truly rancid. I felt as if I'd been hit in the face by the contents of a dog's suppurating anal glands.

'Well if that doesn't put the bleeding badgers off I don't know what will,' said Maxeen, her voice muffled by the tissue she had rammed over her nose. She watched at a distance as I painted the tarry deterrent over the lengths of string, holding my breath for as long as I could while I worked my way round the grass. It was extremely effective. It stopped Brock coming anywhere near our lawn. Trouble was it stopped us as well. Such was the rancidity of the deterrent it was like a barrel load of dead rats had been dumped in our garden. We couldn't venture outside. Even inside the cottage we couldn't escape the aroma of rotting flesh. Putrefaction stalked through our kitchen. Oozed up the stairs. Decaying fingers of flesh crept under our duvets and filled our mouths and nostrils with the cloying stench of death. Truly invasive. When it extended its range by drifting through the village we had neighbours phoning us wondering if we were having problems with our septic tank. And after a burial service in the graveyard of St Mary's opposite Willow Wren, Rev. James came hurrying over to inform us the relatives of the deceased were thinking of suing the undertakers for not providing a leak-proof coffin. So that strategy had to be abandoned.

Maxeen did some more digging on the Internet.

'I'm sure you know this, Malcolm ...'

I took a deep breath and waited.

'Badgers, it seems, are very cautious animals,' she went on.

'So?'

'So in theory they can be deterred by unusual objects – especially if they make a noise – or by changes to their surroundings.'

Uhm ... I had an inkling of what was coming next. And was right.

Maxeen reeled off a list of possibilities: a scarecrow wearing a rustling nylon mac, highly reflective strips of aluminised plastic, wind chimes, toy windmills. All intended to make Brock think twice about using our lawn as an eatery.

I still didn't think any of them would work.

One thing I did know. Being creatures of habit, badgers can be very determined in their efforts to keep to traditional pathways once they've been established.

I told Maxeen this. She glared at me. 'Well why don't you block his path into the garden,' she hissed as if that was the obvious thing to do and why hadn't I already tried it?

So I promptly did.

The track coming in from the field I plugged with plastic netting, weaving it through the base of the hedge.

Brock barged through it.

I replaced that with chicken wire.

It was bent and buckled.

Weld mesh with similar mesh laid flat to stop Brock digging under it was a further failure.

What was it with this brock? Did he have steel excavators for canines and claws?

I just couldn't see how we were going to put a stop to his incursions.

Maxeen and I were lying on the settee, watching a TV programme about dogs. Judy and Winnie were curled up between us, fast asleep, while we listened to the dulcet tones of the presenter telling us how a dog's sense of smell is so sensitive.

'We might be able to smell that there's a teaspoonful of sugar in our mug of coffee,' he was saying, 'but a dog can sense that teaspoonful in two Olympic-sized swimming pools.'

I wrinkled my nose, aware that a strong malodorous smell had drifted up between Maxeen and me that was decidedly unsugar–like. I sniffed and looked at my wife.

'Not me,' she said.

'Nor me.'

We both looked down at the two pooches.

The presenter continued to inform us. 'A dog's sense of smell can be up to 10,000,000 times more sensitive than a human's. And our canine chums have up to 300 million scent glands compared with our miserable five million.'

Clearly our dogs were not applying any of their 300 million as they continued to snooze on, oblivious to the obnoxious odours that were seeping from them.

'Bet badgers score highly in scent glands,' remarked Maxeen, waving a hand in front of her face and shifting away from the rear ends of the dogs. It was a throw-away remark of hers but a light-bulb one for me.

'Yes, of course. That's it.'

'What?'

'The answer. Well at least a possible one.'

I saw Maxeen's puzzled look. Clearly, I wasn't getting through to her. Maybe overcome by the silent deadlies leaking out of the dogs. But the more I thought about it, the more I became convinced I had an answer to our badger attacks. It was an answer that had been staring me in the face and yet I hadn't seen it. How many times had I gone badger watching, testing the wind direction before deciding where to sit? A finger moistened with saliva held up to feel the coolness of the breeze against my skin to ensure I positioned myself downwind of the sett. The slightest eddy of breeze wafting across to the sett entrance carrying my scent would be detected by a badger about to emerge and stop him from doing so. So my scent spread across the lawn could surely deter him from stepping on it?

I explained this to Maxeen.

She was sceptical. 'Just how do you propose to do that short of rolling round the lawn all night? Otherwise, your scent will soon disappear.'

'Not if it's strong enough, it won't.' I sat up, warming to my idea. 'We know badgers have a highly developed sense of smell. Right?'

'Yes.'

'And that they mark their territory with urine.'

'Er ... Yeess ...

'So what if I mark our lawn in similar fashion?'

'You mean ...'

'Piss on it, yes.'

Maxeen took a sharp intake of breath and then wished she hadn't as another rumble of rectal gas hissed out of Judy's anus. She quickly sat up. 'What if the neighbours see you wandering round the lawn squirting urine everywhere?'

'I can do it under the cover of night. And I'll fill one of our empty cleaner sprayers. That should do the job.' And that's what I did. Under the cover of dark, I sneaked round the back garden for a piss … piss here and a piss … piss there.

Drawing back the bedroom curtains the next morning, I let out a triumphant 'Yippie' when I saw the lawn had been left untouched.

Boy, was I relieved – in every sense of the word.

13

Monkey Business

I've always had a fascination with exotic animals. Ever since those days as an eight-year-old lad in Nigeria, when an ever-increasing number of unusual creatures filled our gidah and the adjacent outhouses and garage. My menagerie was encouraged by Father, who also had a passion for such animals. In addition to Poucher, Sooty and Polly, we acquired a baby duiker with a broken tibia; closely followed by a hawk with a damaged wing. Then, there was my own collection of tortoises, a chameleon called Chloe, bantams, ducks and a pair of geckos named Sid and Lawrence, that scuttled across the ceiling of my bedroom each night. But there was one creature we never did possess – a monkey. The idea never appealed because of a terrifying experience I had with a troop of them.

It occurred on one of our excursions to the River Ogan. This time it was during the dry season – in stark contrast to our previous visit which had been during the rainy season. Now, the river was a mere trickle.

It was a child's paradise. Certainly for me, it was heaven. To scramble across the gigantic grey boulders, shoulder high, between which flowed rivulets of water. The foaming splashes of miniature waterfalls murmuring down into swirling, warm pools. Pools in which I could paddle and wade, wriggling my toes in sharp sand. Deeper pockets of water, dark and sinister, sucked and gurgled through the exposed tangled roots of teak and mahogany trees that overhung the river's banks. Here were to be found shoals of mottled grey fish, trapped in those pockets until the next rains raised the level of the river. These fish proved a testing time for Father's rod. But once caught, made a delicious meal when cooked over a charcoal fire on the river's bank.

Mother and I left Father to catch our supper while we ventured upriver, with Poucher alongside us. We scrambled from one pool to another, enticed on by the sandy-fringed bays, the channels of white rapids, their spray dancing into the air, catching the sun in myriads of tiny rainbows, blue-red rays that shimmered and shifted in arcs across the ravine.

We trekked further than intended, caught up in the magic of the river. The thickly wooded gorge gave way to gentler slopes, still boulder-strewn but more open, the river bed more spread out.

It was here I spotted a blur of brown move high above us on top of a crag. I screwed my eyes up against the glare, attempting to make out what it was.

'Can you see it, Mum?' I said, pointing.

She raised a hand to her brow and scoured the hillside. 'No. Can't see anything.'

'There, look. It's jumped,' I exclaimed.

The creature had scrambled down a few feet and now, no longer silhouetted against the sky, was easier to see.

'Hey, it's a baboon,' I said, jumping up and down. 'Just wait 'til I tell Dad.'

Mother wasn't so enthusiastic. 'I think we ought to be getting back,' she faltered.

Meanwhile, Poucher had sprung up onto a rock and was staring in the direction of the baboon, hackles raised. The monkey bobbed its head up and down. Then disappeared.

'Come on, let's get going,' insisted Mother.

I turned away reluctantly. After all, it wasn't every day you saw a baboon.

Having gone a few yards, I couldn't resist the urge to look back.

'Hey, there it is again,' I yelled.

The baboon had reappeared halfway down the slope and hence much closer. He was leaning forward, knuckles resting on a rock, his shoulders hunched. He had a magnificent mane framing his head – thick, brown, flecked with black. Piggy, amber eyes stared intently down at us. He suddenly stood up, opened his mouth and exposed long, ivory-yellow fangs. He sprang forward. Stopped. Bent his head. Raised his rump. Then emitted a deep, menacing grunt.

My excitement instantly turned to fear. I'd read enough about baboons to know exactly what this fellow was telling us. And it wasn't good news.

It put an extra spring into my step as I hastily jumped from one boulder to another, attempting to catch Mother up who'd had the sense to keep going and not stop like I'd done.

The baboon's grunt now turned into a barrage of shrill, angry barks.

I was startled. So was Mother. She lost her footing. Slipped off a boulder. Careered down onto another one, her left leg buckling under her as she landed heavily on her side. She sat up with a groan. 'Damn,' she said, massaging her ankle, 'think I've sprained it.'

Another series of staccato barks echoed across the gorge. Closer. I looked round nervously. A baboon leapt into view only feet away from the river bank. Then another. And another. Well over a dozen or so. Brown heads bobbed. Menacing lips curled back exposing razor-sharp fangs. A very unfriendly troop had appeared, intent on defending their territory.

'We must get back, Mum,' I said, helping Mother to her feet.

We began the difficult task of edging our way downstream, navigating round the pools, Mother hobbling, clearly in pain. Every step seemed to be a signal for the baboons to follow. As the river bed narrowed, the ravine closing in, so too did the baboons. They loped nearer and nearer, urging themselves on with excited barks.

Until then, Poucher had kept close to our heels, every so often, pausing to turn her head and emit a low growl in the direction of the troop.

Then, Mother slumped down on a rock. 'It's no good. I'll have to rest a minute,' she gasped.

It seemed that the leader of the troop – the male we'd initially spotted – took this as a signal to launch an attack. He leapt from the bank, flying in a zigzag across the rocks, rapidly bearing down on us. The rest of the troop shot down the bank after him.

At that point, Poucher slipped away from us, heading straight for the baboons, hackles raised.

'No, Poucher. Come back,' I screamed. 'They'll tear you to pieces.'

My order was disobeyed.

Purposefully, Poucher stalked forward, head lowered, tail stretched out stiffly behind her. Each foreleg and opposite hind-leg slowly raised before being replaced on the rocks.

The leader of the troop halted. He postured. Body raised and lowered. Lips retracted in a demonic grin. Eyebrows repeatedly shooting up and down. He grunted, sticking his chin out.

But still Poucher moved forward stealthily, undeterred.

The distance between them narrowed.

Yards became feet.

The baboon faltered. Shuffled back a pace. Stopped.

Poucher stopped as well, her whole body rigid.

They were testing one another. Daring each other to make the next move. The baboon sat back on his rump. Then, sprang up with a defiant snarl, his eyebrows almost meeting the top of his forehead. It was a gesture meant to frighten. To intimidate.

But Poucher stood her ground. Never flinched.

The baboon faltered, twisting his head away. The rest of the troop had stopped on the river bank, awaiting his command. He turned back to face Poucher and with his mane fanned out by the breeze he seemed to double in size. Terrifying. Threatening.

Poucher's head suddenly shot up and a deep, rumbling growl welled up from her throat. The baboon squealed and took a flying leap back. Encouraged, Poucher padded forward, barking furiously.

That was enough. The troop leader turned and with a final grimace over his naked red rump, he tore back across the rocks and up onto the bank to join the other baboons before they all streamed off.

We were safe. All thanks to Poucher. What a dog.

That sort of encounter stays in one's mind no matter how long ago it occurred. So, when that morning at the hospital, Jean informed me I was to visit a monkey, my mind did briefly flash back 16 years to that troop of baboons in Nigeria. I saw her wait for my reaction. Would I throw a fit? Swing from the lights in panic? Beat my chest in fury?

'It's not too big a monkey,' she went on, as if that was reassurance for me. 'Nothing like King Kong.'

Oh, really, Jean? Thank you. Wind up time, here. My mind switched from baboons to the mighty King Kong stomping up the drive, reaching through the reception door to grab a squealing Jean in his hand. I smiled at the thought.

'Oh, so you're not daunted at the prospect then?' Jean said.

'What? Oh, no ... could be quite exciting.' King Kong had Carol gripped in his other hand, she using both of hers to pull down the hem of her ridden-up uniform, in a desperate attempt to retain a modicum of decorum. Typical of her.

'It's a squirrel monkey,' said Jean. 'Here's a picture of one I printed off the Internet for you.'

Hey, Jean, I thought. Surely, that's one step too far? The presumed lack of knowledge on my part. I saw King Kong's fingers begin to squeeze her even more tightly as she slid the printed page across to me.

I found myself looking down at a cute little monkey, crouched on a branch, staring out with big black-button eyes. He had yellow-brown fur with a black cap and white belly. A long, thin tail looped down under the branch, coiled like a clock spring.

'The one you're seeing is called Bimbo,' said Jean. 'His owner, Mrs Morello, is requesting a house visit as the monkey's quite poorly. It would be too distressing to come to the hospital. I said that wouldn't be a problem.'

King Kong began pulling Jean up towards his mouth, saliva

dripping from his open jaws.

'Oh, and you'd better take some stout gloves in case you have to catch Bimbo up. I'd hate to think you might get bitten.'

I considered that sound advice. King Kong gently lowered Jean to the ground and released her.

Later that morning, I found myself at Mrs Morello's house in a quiet suburban avenue in central Westcott, staring across a dining room table to where a squirrel monkey was curled up on the floor of a cage.

'Bimbo only goes in there to sleep,' said Mrs Morello, a woman of heavy build, whose slow movements as she lumbered across to the table had the plodding qualities of an ox of old, ploughing heavy soil. 'But he just hasn't wanted to come out for the past two days.' She leaned across the table and blew kisses at the monkey before pulling a gaudy silk handkerchief from the sleeve of her cardigan and dabbing her eyes. 'My sweet little Bimbo. You're proper poorly, aren't you?'

Even though I had no experience of dealing with sick monkeys, I could see this was an animal that wasn't feeling well. All the signs were there. He was huddled up, listless; that long tail of his curled over his back, wrapped round his body. The kisses blown by Mrs Morello made him look up briefly. Long enough for me to see the dullness in his black eyes. And, as if to accentuate his illness, he blinked and a large tear rolled down his cheek. That provoked more tears from Mrs Morello who used her hanky to wipe them away and blow her nose violently. She fluttered the sodden hanky at me in a theatrical gesture.

'He's been off his food for several days,' explained Mrs Morello, between sniffs. 'Even chocolate-coated peanuts which he usually adores.'

I could see a pile of them, untouched, inside the cage.

'I need to catch Bimbo up,' I warned Mrs Morello, as I

donned the stout pair of leather gloves that, on Jean's advice, I'd brought with me, Now, I wasn't too sure on how to approach this. Would Bimbo leap out as soon as I opened the cage door and tried to grab him? And how was I to grab him? A hand over his back? Round his shoulders? Over his hindquarters? Gingerly, I opened the cage door, inserted one gloved hand while barring the exit with the other just in case Bimbo was going to suddenly leap into action and shoot past me. But there was no such movement. No springing to the door. Only the merest chatter of protest as I grasped Bimbo round his shoulders and lifted him out, no resistance in his little body. Flicking off one glove, I levered up his tail and with the thermometer I'd already extracted from my black bag, took a rectal temperature. The reading was high. 40 C. The normal being around 38 C. Jean had Googled that for me before I'd left the practice. Good of her. Thus, King Kong had lumbered off into the sunset empty-handed.

I checked Bimbo's nostrils. Each was moist. Each had a clear discharge. Listening to his chest, I could hear a distinct wheeze. I caught hold of his legs which had been curled round my wrist and stretched him out. Red pin-points were visible in his armpits and groin. I was foxed. Mystified. No bells rang.

To be on the safe side, I decided a shot of antibiotic might be wise. At least it would provide some sort of cover. But here was a problem. I was holding on to Bimbo. I had no hands free.

'Here, let me,' said Mrs Morello, stuffing her hanky back up her sleeve to then gently prise Bimbo off me. He lay curled up in her cupped palms, staring up at her, his expression pitiful. Mrs Morello clucked and cooed as took off my gloves and drew up a syringeful of antibiotic. I was still uncertain of Bimbo's reaction to having an injection. It was going to sting a little. Would he swing round and try to bite? Couldn't risk it. So, I donned a glove on my left hand, eased it over his shoulders and covered his head, as I gave the injection in his thigh. He didn't flinch. No sound. Though Mrs Morello jolted and emitted a little squeak.

'What do you think's wrong with him?' she asked.

'Looks like he's caught a cold,' I said, though far from convinced of my diagnosis. 'Has anyone in the family got one?'

Mrs Morello shrugged. 'My Katie was a bit off colour this morning. But still went to school.' The front door banged. 'That will be her now.' She looked at her watch. 'Funny though, she's early.'

Her daughter walked in. 'They sent me home as I've come out in a rash,' she said.

Suddenly it dawned on me. The spots on Bimbo. A similar rash. I began to explain.

'Who'd have thought?' wailed Mrs Morello. 'My poor, poor Bimbo. Catching measles.' Out came the multi-coloured hanky again and another full-throttled nasal blast ensued.

'Who indeed?' echoed Jean when, on my return to the hospital, I told her about it.

Tony was listening in. 'Sounds as if that was a rash decision,' he said with a grin, wiggling his eyebrows at me.

Hey, careful with the puns, Tony. King Kong's got his hands free at the moment.

The next set of eyebrows to wiggle at me belonged to a woolly monkey.

'You'll never guess what,' Jean had said.

'What?' I replied, steeling myself for another of Jean's guessing games, a little habit of hers that I could never fathom. And which often irritated me.

But she got straight to the point. 'I've another monkey for

you to see.'

My turn for a wiggly eyebrow session. 'Really?'

Jean nodded. 'Apparently, it's a woolly monkey that's been a bit off-colour these last couple of days. Not wanting to eat anything.' She must have seen the look of panic that suddenly sprang on my face since she slid across a printed-off fact sheet about woolly monkeys and what they eat.

I scanned the facts. Seems they are omnivorous, eating meat, vegetables and fruit. In the description of the monkey, it did mention their prehensile tails and how they use them as a fifth limb.

I felt that tail wrap dexterously round my arm when the monkey was presented in my consulting room.

'Don't worry,' said Bill Sanderson, his owner, whistling through his teeth, while he scratched his stubbly chin. 'He won't harm you.'

All the same I was a bit apprehensive, as this monkey was a big, brown-furred fellow, his yellow eyes – below a fringe of hair – constantly darting round the room, while his tail kept me firmly in place next to him.

'What's his name?'

'Bolton.'

'Born there, was he?'

'No, he keeps bolting out of his pen. A right Houdini. Picks locks, undoes bolts. You name it, he can unlock it.' There was another whistle through Bill's teeth.

Uhm … funny guy here.

'I understand he's off his food,' I said.

'Yes. Very picky. Even turned his nose up at chocolate which he normally adores,' said Bill, his words punctuated with further whistles. 'And I reckon he's got a bit of tummy ache. He's a bit tucked up, don't you think?'

Bolton attempted to undo my watch strap, as I looked down, uncertain as to what a tucked-up monkey should look like.

'Do you think he'll allow me to palpate his abdomen?' I asked.

'No problem.' Bolton was now peering at the watch dial held in his hands, having successfully undone the strap. Distracted, he tolerated me gently sliding my hands down round his flanks to carefully probe his tummy. Never having palpated a monkey's abdomen before, I wasn't too sure of what to expect. But then everything we had, they had, more or less in the same position. Liver under rib cage. Kidneys to either side of lumbar spine. Spleen floating somewhere in the middle. All present and correct. Guts. Well there was a lot of gurgling as I massaged them. Gas build-up. Then, suddenly, I hit a tender spot. Bolton jerked up, dropped the watch and swung round, lips curled back, teeth bared. For a second, I thought I was going to get bitten. But it was a menacing threat rather than actual action. A sort of grin and bare.

'Hmm … You're right, sir. He has got tummy ache,' I said. 'And I think it's gut-related. Could he have possibly swallowed something?'

'Well, as I've mentioned, he's very clever at unpicking things.' Bill nodded at my watch. 'And several times has unpicked the lock on his pen. The key's now missing. You don't think …'

I did. And when we X-rayed Bolton, there it was, plain to see, lying in his stomach. The missing key.

It caused a buzz of excitement round the hospital when I announced I'd be doing a laparotomy on Bolton to extract the key. Though both Carol and Linda were a little nervous as to their involvement, particularly post-operatively when they would be responsible for the monkey's after-care. They proved right to show concern.

The operation went well, the key was extracted, and Bolton recovered smoothly from the anaesthetic down in one of the ward's kennels.

I strode down to the kennels the next morning to do my customary ward round, check the inpatients, and today, in particular, see how Bolton was faring. I discovered the door to his pen was open. No sign of the monkey. I swore, turned and raced up to the prep room where Carol and Linda were busy getting ready for the day's ops.

'Bolton's escaped,' I said, my voice full of panic. 'For goodness sake, drop everything. We need to find him.'

'Bloody hell, where on earth could he have got to?' exclaimed Carol.

A scream from up in reception gave us the answer.

We raced up to find a trembling Jean, backed in one corner, behind the reception desk.

'That monkey ... look ...' She pointed a trembling finger.

An inquisitive Bolton was sitting on her chair, rifling through her handbag.

'He's been at my lipstick ... the bugger ...'

Bolton looked across and pouted crimson-smeared lips at us. Similar smears of lipstick criss-crossed his cheeks.

'Now, look what he's doing,' wailed Jean.

Bolton had turned his attention to a packet of cigarettes he'd pulled out, deftly opening it to extract one. It now dangled from his mouth. Very Humphrey Bogart – Casablanca style. Just needed someone to give him a light. Jean, in Ingrid Bergman mode perhaps?

I felt a bubble of giggles rise in my throat. The same for Carol and Linda to judge from the knuckles they had rammed to their mouths.

Then, unbecoming of a Hollywood star, Bolton stood up on his hind legs, stretched to his full height, and relieved himself. His jet of urine sprayed up in an arc and splashed onto the floor, puddling at Jean's feet.

It was too much. I couldn't stop the snort of laughter exploding from my lips. 'Sorry, Jean,' I gasped, wiping away tears from my eyes.

Jean – still cowering in the corner – gave me a thunderous look. 'Well, don't just stand there like a wet blanket. Do something about it.'

It was Carol who came to the rescue. She'd disappeared and now reappeared waving a banana.

Bolton instantly dropped onto his haunches and grunted, his eyebrows wiggling with anticipation as Carol broke off a piece and handed it to him. More wiggles ensued as he followed her back down to the kennels, the remainder of the banana being waved in front of him.

Jean was instructed to get Bill Sanderson over to collect the monkey as soon as possible.

I just prayed Bolton wouldn't get so keyed up again.

14

A little Knowledge...

I can sympathise with the apprehension exhibited in dogs and cats when dragged to the vet's. Paws and claws skittering and skating reluctantly across the floor. Bodies all of a tremble. The sudden loss of bladder control resulting in the nervous piddle. I'm the same when I visit our health centre. Not exhibiting all of those symptoms of course. No nervous piddle. But nevertheless, a bag of nerves. On edge. Made worse by the waiting room's atmosphere. The harsh strip lighting that manages to make everyone look ill even if they aren't. And staff looking so depressed that whenever one leaves reception I wonder if they've gone out to shoot themselves. Then, there's the décor. A ghastly green that makes me feel bilious merely looking at it. And plastic chairs with high backs, no arms, that curve up at the front so I can see up the skirts of the old ladies sitting opposite me. There's a rack of pamphlets which advise you, amongst other things, on how to check your breasts for lumps and the symptoms which may indicate you have an enlarged prostate. Add to that, the posters lining the walls telling you about an alarming variety of diseases, the importance of personal hygiene and the dangers incurred from smoking. By the time I've read through that lot I feel worse than when I first arrived.

My current problem started some two months back. I'd settled on the bed for a Sunday afternoon nap. Yes, a snooze on a Sunday afternoon. Not something I normally do. And it made me feel a bit guilty. Especially as Maxeen was out in the garden, weeding. But then the likes of Winston Churchill and Margaret Thatcher used to have naps in the afternoon. Power naps they are called. Lasting about 20 minutes. So, wasn't I in good company for my 20 minutes' worth? I settled down and woke an hour later with a burning in my chest. It was like I was on fire. I abruptly sat up, as stomach acid filled my mouth. I swallowed quickly and raced down to get a glass of water.

'Ouch. That was a bit grim,' I muttered, taking a deep breath.

'Don't be such a namby-pamby. It's only a touch of heartburn,' said Maxeen, when I went out into the garden to tell her what had happened. 'Nothing to worry about.' She resumed her digging. My grave perhaps – the way I was feeling?

I decided to do my own digging and go on the Internet to find out more. Not that I considered myself a hypochondriac for doing so. I'm not one of those blokes who, when he catches a cold, says he's got flu which transmutes into double pneumonia and certainly – at the very least – will have tracked down onto his chest by the morning. Just seemed sensible to find out what was going on. Surely no harm there?

In doing so, I scared myself silly with worry. The symptoms

listed matched mine. Belching? Yes. Burping? Yes. Burning in the chest. A definite yes. Then, clearly I was suffering from GORD. Gastro-oesophageal reflux disease. It sounded serious.

'Common enough though. Millions get it,' said Maxeen. She'd taken a break from gardening and was now looking over my shoulder at the computer screen, her tone of voice decidedly unsympathetic. 'As it says there. Acid leaking from the stomach up into the oesophagus. Usually due to the ring of muscle at the base of the oesophagus weakening.'

She patted my shoulder. 'You just need to change your lifestyle. Alter your diet. Like it advises. Give up things that might stimulate acid production.'

I looked at the list on the screen.

Coffee. I relish my mid-morning latte. To be stopped.

Chocolate. The occasional bar of Milk and Nut a no-no.

Booze. A glass of chilled Prosecco of an evening. Out.

Cigarettes. Ah, that was okay. I don't smoke.

'But you do have a bad habit that won't help your condition,' Maxeen said.

'Really?' I mentally scanned through the habits that might be considered unsavoury. Picking my nose in a traffic jam? Using my little fingernail to pick out food wedged between my teeth after a meal? Scratching my backside when it was itching? Leaving the loo seat up?

Maxeen elaborated. 'Mastication.'

'Pardon?' I exclaimed, a little startled.

'You don't chew your food enough.'

'Ah, okay.'

She later printed off a couple of fact sheets from the Internet entitled 'Why Chewing Your Food Can Change Your Life' and thrust them in my hand.

I did try to follow the advice given together with a change

in diet. But the acid reflux, though less frequent, still occurred. So, I decided a visit to Graham Merriweather, my GP, was in order. Perhaps some prescribed medication could help?

Hence, I found myself sitting in that bilious-green painted waiting room, wondering what was wrong with the gentleman sporting a cluster of nasty red blotches on his face. To me, they looked catching. A similar view held by other patients, to judge from the fact they were all crammed at the other end of the waiting room, as far away from him as possible. There was also a woman, with a streaming cold, constantly coughing, her mouth wide open, sitting below a poster declaring that coughs and sneezes spread diseases. No doubt had she been at the animal hospital, she'd have been sitting below our poster declaring 'Has Your Dog Got Fleas?' with a dog frantically scratching itself next to her. I rapidly moved seats when the woman sneezed violently, jettisoning a virus-laden cloud across the room.

'Come in, come in,' said Graham when I was eventually summoned. He is a small, rotund man with shaggy brown hair and beard from which a triangular face with pointy chin peers out. Today, his eyes were leaden and red-rimmed; and when he spoke it was like his larynx had trawled through the bottom of a fish tank. 'Sorry, got a bit of a cold,' he said. 'Not surprising with all the bugs floating around in here.' He glanced down at his computer screen. 'Funny you should turn up today, Malcolm, as I've been meaning to get in touch about Mac and Tosh.' He was referring to his two pygmy goats that I'd treated in the past. He continued studying the screen. 'So, what can I do for you?'

I explained that I thought I'd developed GORD and wondered if I could have some medication to reduce acid production.

Graham seemed to half-listen, tapping on his keyboard, his attention still mostly on the screen. He eventually nodded.

'Mmm … I think it could be a case of SARA,' he croaked.

'Sorry?'

He looked up. 'Sub-acute ruminal acidosis. A digestive disorder.'

I shook my head, confused. This sounded far more serious than just acid reflux.

Graham tapped the computer screen and sniffed. 'Says here it can affect goats. So maybe that's what Mac and Tosh have got. Meanwhile, I'll give you some tablets to reduce your acid production and some oral stuff to take last thing which will coat the stomach lining. That should help calm things down a bit. And I'll make an appointment for you to see …' He paused a minute while printing off my prescription and handing it to me. '… Mac and Tosh.'

I smiled thinly, snatching the prescription from him. I don't know about his goats. But, oh my GORD, he'd certainly got mine.

The Internet is wonderful. A wealth of information at the click of a mouse. But often to excess. Too much knowledge becoming a dangerous thing. And a client armed with information as to the likely cause of his pet's illness then becomes a challenge. None more so when that client also happens to be your doctor. As illustrated by my dealings with Graham Merriweather.

The doctor and his wife and three children lived in the centre of Westcott with four cats, a Cavalier King Charles spaniel and two pygmy goats called Mac and Tosh. Whenever there was a problem with the goats, I'd get called out, arriving to find Graham with print-outs from the Internet of the likely conditions causing the problem and its diagnosis and treatment. He was often right. Irritatingly so.

A recent visit to check the two goats was a good example.

Brother and sister, black with white muzzles and white-capped heads, they lived in a sectioned-off area in the back garden. Tosh had developed an infection between her back claws.

The warning bells rang as soon as Graham said, '*Fusobacterium necrophorum*?' I knew straightaway he'd been Googling the condition – Scald.

I was able to swiftly counteract with, 'No sign of *Dichelobacter nodosus*, so it's not foot rot,' since I too had been on the Internet the night before, knowing I was going to be checking the goats' feet the following day. And I wanted to make sure I was on my toes even if the goats weren't due to lameness brought on by the infection.

'Good job, then,' said Graham, 'otherwise the horn could have been undermined and sloughed off. Then the whole foot could have swollen up.' My thoughts exactly. Seems he'd read the same article on the Internet as me.

When it came to Susie, the spaniel, a similar challenge occurred.

Jean forewarned me. 'I've booked an appointment for you to see Dr Merriweather. He thinks Susie might have got a loose tooth. She's been dribbling a lot in the past couple of days.'

Susie trotted into the consulting room quite bright-eyed and bushy-tailed. Though, once Graham had lifted her on to the table, I did notice the fur round her muzzle was wet, soaked with saliva.

'She won't let me open her mouth,' said Graham. 'So, obviously something's hurting her. And she's having difficulty eating her food.' He said that before I had a chance to ask him myself, adding, 'She's also pawing at her mouth. And the smell.' He leaned over her muzzle. 'Phew. There's quite a pong. And it's definitely coming from her mouth. Not very pleasant, is it?'

That was something I could certainly agree with. A

mere whiff was enough to make you think you'd trodden in something unpleasant on the way into the surgery. But just to be sure of its origins, I sniffed above, below and either side of her head. Yep. It was definitely coming from her mouth.

Graham went on, 'And there's been traces of blood-stained saliva by her food bowl. All points to a loose tooth.' He could have added, 'according to what it says on the Internet', as I had no doubt he'd looked up the symptoms. And most likely the treatment as well since he added, 'I expect you'll have her in to do a dental.'

Grr ... it made me grit my teeth. Very much in the manner that Susie was gritting hers. Though I wasn't salivating so much. And my saliva wasn't blood-tinged.

I have to admit Graham was right when he said Susie refused to open her mouth. 'Come on, girl, let me have a look.' I clamped one hand over the top of her muzzle, with finger and thumb of the other under her chin. But she just wriggled and shook her head, as I tried to prise her jaws apart. She even shied away when I attempted to raise her upper lip in the hope of glimpsing her teeth. Especially the back ones where build-up of tartar on the molars and subsequent gum disease can often result in the symptoms we were seeing in Susie. Then Graham would have been correct in his diagnosis. Clearly, something was upsetting Susie. But what?

'We'll have to have her in,' I said. 'Give her a quick anaesthetic and check her mouth out properly.'

'Just as I've suggested,' replied Graham.

I ground my teeth yet again.

Routine dentals are just that. A very standard procedure. Carol always ensured a sterilised pack of dental instruments was available. And that the dental machine with its scraper attached to a water jet was ready for use whenever necessary.

She tended to let Linda, being the junior nurse, help with such routine procedures. And today, Susie's dental was no exception.

'Seems rather young to be needing a dental,' Linda remarked, as the spaniel slipped into unconsciousness once I'd given the intravenous anaesthetic injection.

'I know ... I know ...' I remarked, a little impatiently. 'But since Susie wouldn't let me look in her mouth, I didn't have any choice in the matter.'

With the spaniel stretched out on the prep room table, I checked her reflexes, levering open her jaw to make sure she was anaesthetised enough. In doing so, the back of the dog's throat was instantly revealed. And wedged across the back, stuck between the molars on each side, was what looked like a piece of bone.

'Ha ... ha ... Methinks we've found the problem,' I chortled. Having prised it out with artery forceps, I held it up.

'The culprit,' I declared, waving a slimy, saliva-covered wedge of grey bone-like material at Linda.

'A bone then?' she said.

'Nope. It's hoof. And I bet you it's a bit of hoof I pared off Tosh's claws a couple of weeks back. So *not* a loose tooth as our dear doctor thought.'

Dr Merriweather and the Internet had been outwitted.

I was pleased as it meant I no longer felt fed up to the back teeth by it all. And certainly Susie, the spaniel, didn't.

Another client was to confront me with knowledge gleaned not from the Internet this time, but from her veterinary dictionary of diseases.

On the day in question, I'd driven over the Downs from Willow Wren, heading into work, full of the joys of spring – well, actually late spring early summer – as it was the beginning of June. But still I felt perky, singing a cheerful song, 'Morning Has Broken', which mentions a blackbird speaking. But having parked the car and bounded up the steps into Prospect House, it was more of a cantankerous crow than a blackbird I was confronted with, perched behind the reception desk. Shoulders hunched, cardigan draped loosely from them like folded wings, I got a beady look from Jean, that spelt 'Bad Mood' without a word being said. Oh dear. Jean in a bad mood? That *was* unusual.

'Miss Millichip's been on the phone, demanding a visit from you yet again,' she sighed.

Ah, so that was it. Mildred Millichip. The bane of my life; and Jean's. Her manner grated like nails down a blackboard. She was always demanding visits despite the practice policy of asking people to come in for an appointment. Miss Millichip could never be persuaded. It had to be a visit. And me, Malcolm Welshman, was the vet required to make that visit. Not one of the two partners, Tony or Clifford. Only me.

'I've booked you to go over this afternoon after you finish the morning ops' list,' said Jean. 'She'll expect you around 2.30.' Her tone was still grumpy, still clearly rattled by what I surmised had been an acrimonious exchange on the phone. Jean never did like being told what to do. Ditto, Mildred Millichip. So it was with some trepidation, I retraced my journey back over the Downs after lunch, in a far more sombre mood, wondering just what Mildred had in store for me.

She ran a sanctuary-cum-small holding near Ashton which comprised of a maze of sheds and outbuildings surrounding a bungalow – her HQ. The complex housed a variety of rescue animals; beagles, greyhounds, many cats. The nerve centre for this menagerie was the bungalow's kitchen, a room stuffed with growth charts, tattered farming journals and out-of-date text books lining one wall. Pots of tripe simmered on a range opposite. Alongside, a sink and draining board piled high with feed bowls. In between, a large pine table, its surface scratched and worn, black grime and matted hair impacted in its gaps. Here is where I found Mildred, my patient already wedged between her forearms on the table.

'It's Misty,' she exclaimed, after a cursory greeting. 'She's got flu. Needs you to give her some antibiotics.'

Wham. Bam. Straight to the point. No messing about with our Mildred Millichip.

'Yes, well, let's take a look first, shall we?' I said, fighting back the irritation that always threatened to bubble up whenever I was confronted by this woman. During my first encounter with her, she'd declared she'd always wanted to be a vet. And this was the ongoing problem I had with her. She self-diagnosed her animals' illnesses, telling me what was wrong. All spoken with conviction, a steely look in her torpedo-grey eyes and a toss of her scouring-pad of grey hair. She'd then often resort to old-fashioned remedies in an attempt to treat them. My battles with her had been many and frequent. It looked as if today would be no different.

Certainly Misty, a black and white cat, was snuffly and there was certainly a discharge from her right nostril. But only from that side; and her eyes were clear. Not typical symptoms of flu.

'I'll just check her chest,' I said, extracting my stethoscope from my black bag. 'Make sure her lungs are clear.'

'No need for that,' exclaimed Mildred, with a dismissive sniff. 'It's just an upper respiratory infection. Early signs of flu.'

Yes, well, I'm not so sure you're right there I thought while listening to Misty's chest. It was clear. And her temperature was normal when I checked it.

'You'll give her a course of tetracyline,' Mildred said bluntly, subjecting me to a further torpedo stare. 'Antibiotic to stop any secondary infection.'

I chose to ignore the question, asking instead whether any of her other cats were showing similar signs. After all, cat flu is very infectious and I would have expected some to be sneezing and have watery eyes.

Mildred shook her head vigorously. 'But then I did isolate Misty as soon as she started snuffling.' Another ballistic stare followed. 'So, … antibiotic?'

Unable to come up with any alternative diagnosis, I relented.

I gave Misty an injection of tetracyline and left a course of tablets, saying I'd pop out the following week to check the cat over.

'No need,' declared Mildred. 'She'll be on the mend soon.'

How wrong she proved to be. And even I was confounded when I eventually discovered what was causing Misty's problem.

'Something's on your mind,' said Maxeen, as we settled down that evening to watch TV. This is so typical of my wife. She is very intuitive, always able to sense if something is worrying me.

'So, what is it?' she persisted, turning to fix me with those glorious brown eyes of hers whilst pushing back a strand of dark hair.

'Well, I had to go and visit Mildred Millichip this afternoon,' I said. 'One of her cats was sick.'

'Ah, so that's it.' Maxeen held up a hand. 'Our Miss Millichip. Someone who always spells trouble.' Over the couple of years I'd been at Prospect House, Maxeen had got to know many of the clients and their foibles through my discussions about them. Mildred Millichip was no exception.

'Let me guess,' Maxeen went on. 'She told you what was

wrong with it and told you what treatment it should have.'

I nodded. 'Exactly.'

Maxeen put her hand gently on my shoulder. 'But you don't think she's right?'

'The symptoms aren't typical of cat flu.'

'But you went along with her diagnosis?'

'Well, you know what she's like.'

'Are you seeing the cat again?'

'I did suggest rechecking Misty in a week. But Mildred thought there wouldn't be any need.'

'Don't worry,' said Maxeen. 'From what you've told me about her, I've no doubt she'll be on the blower if things don't improve.'

How right she was.

Four days later, I found the phone in reception being shoved in my hand by Jean.

'It's her. Mildred Millchip,' she hissed. 'Misty's no better. She wants you to visit.'

I took a deep breath and allowed myself to be bombarded by Mildred's strident tones. 'Look,' I eventually managed to say, as forcefully as possible without appearing to be too impolite, 'I really don't think Misty has cat flu, as you keep saying.'

There was a momentary silence. 'So, what do you suggest we do?'

'I need to have her in for further investigation.'

'You'll collect her then?'

'No. You'll have to bring her in,' I insisted.

'But …'

'You can manage that, I'm sure.'

There was another silence before a curt, 'Oh very well then,' and the phone went dead.

'Let's hope it's not cat flu,' warned Jean. 'Otherwise you'll have every cat in the hospital at risk of catching it.'

'What's this about cat flu?' Tony had just walked into reception, his trousers flapping round his spindly legs, their waist band so high he could have kept his nipples warm in winter.

Before I could say a word, Jean remarked, 'One of Mildred Millichip's cats has cat flu. Or so she thinks. But Malcolm reckons it's something else.'

Tony raised his eyebrows, his forehead knotting in creases. 'Crikey, Malcolm, I hope you're right. We don't want cat flu in here thank you very much.'

'Hello, what's this I hear about cat flu?' Clifford, the other senior partner, had now joined us at the reception desk. He is a tall man, with dark hair streaked with silver, a fringe of which cuts across his forehead. Always well dressed in a tailored, tweed suit which gives him the quietly old-fashioned air of a man who has just stepped out of a Noel Coward play.

'One of Malcolm's patients,' chorused Tony and Jean. 'Mildred Millichip thinks it's cat flu. Malcolm doesn't.'

Clifford's gull-wing dark eyebrows knotted together. 'Well, hope Mildred's wrong,' he warned, waving a well-manicured hand at me. 'Cat flu in the hospital would be a disaster.'

All three of them stared intently at me.

Right. So, no pressure to find the correct diagnosis.

When Mildred Millichip turned up with Misty, I ensured she signed a consent form for anaesthesia, explaining that I might want to X-ray the cat as part of my investigation. 'Don't see the need,' said Mildred huffily. 'Still think it's cat flu.'

'We'll see,' I replied, biting my tongue.

An hour later, Misty was sedated and an X-ray taken of her head, prompted by the discovery there was still the discharge from her right nostril and now that side of her face was decidedly swollen.

The X-ray showed a distinct swirl of grey visible in the right nasal cavity which shouldn't have been there. With the aid of an auriscope, I peered up the nostril of the still-sedated cat and spotted something straw-coloured. Using crocodile forceps, I managed to grasp the end of it, gently teasing it out.

'Here's the culprit, look,' I yelped triumphantly, holding aloft the forceps. It was not cat flu that had caused Misty's snuffling, the sneezing, the discharge. But a grass seed lodged in her nose.

I placed the seed head in a plastic specimen pot and showed it to Mildred Millichip when she came to collect Misty later that day.

She was courteous enough and politely thanked me. But I sensed she was miffed that I'd been right and she'd been wrong. And that got up her nose without the need of a grass seed.

15

My Feelings for Felines

I am often asked whether I am a cat or dog person.

I confess that my answer rather depends on whether there's a Fido sitting on my consulting table or a Tibbles. But in reality, I have always preferred the company of dogs. There, I've said it. I can hear the raised hackles of the feline fraternity. Their hiss of contempt. Their unsheathed claws ready to dig in. Me, a vet. Not liking cats?

Whatever, a bubble of unease does tend to well up whenever I am confronted by a cat. Nothing too serious, mind you. Just a niggle. A twinge of uncertainty. Those who own cats – and there are 8.5 million in the UK – would say my fear is irrational, verging on a phobia – the technical term for which is ailurophobia. You would tell me cats are fascinating creatures with great characters and an independent streak to be much admired. You're right of course. Yet despite that, when I've tried to make friends with them over the years, I've failed miserably every time.

Trouble is the wretched beasts seem to sense my nervousness and as a result, I swear they deliberately try to provoke me.

Bobby, the black and white cat owned by my school pal, Terry, was a typical example. When I visited Terry, what did the wretched cat do? He fixed me with a penetrating stare and padded up, tail erect – a sign of greeting.

'See, he likes you,' said Terry.

Not reciprocated, I assure you, as Bobby then proceeded to rub his head against my leg, smearing me with his secretions – his way of telling me I smelt funny and needed to be marked by his own scent.

At Terry's insistence, I once allowed Bobby to leap onto my lap, where he promptly curled round and settled down.

'There. Friends at last,' declared Terry. 'Now give him a stroke.'

So as not to appear too much of a wuss, I tentatively ran my hand down the cat's back. I've read such action improves your immune system, your blood pressure goes down and your body halts production of stress-related hormones – making you a third less likely to suffer from heart disease. I should be so lucky. As my fingers caressed Bobby's fur, my hands shook and my heart pounded like a badly beaten bongo drum.

On another occasion, fortified by a couple of beers, I did try to make friends with Bobby by tickling his tummy. I got rewarded by my hand being snared in Bobby's claws, accompanied by the sinking of his teeth into my palm. Ouch.

An animal behaviourist would say, 'When a cat throws itself on its side and shows its belly, it's showing a greeting behaviour and showing trust. It is actually an abuse of that trust to stroke its belly.' Hence the claws and teeth.

Uhm … I'm not so sure. I swore it was just Bobby's excuse to have a go at me.

I've certainly not allowed him on my lap any more. Not since I read about the cat over in US that lived in a residential home. It used to curl up on the beds of those about to die. Was Bobby trying to warn me I'd go the same way unless I got a life?

There's only been one cat that I've felt really comfortable with. One that I knew wouldn't try savaging me. I'd just vaccinated the kitten belonging to a client, Ruth Frost, when she said, 'Let me show you something, Mr Welshman.' She reached into her holdall and eased out a white Persian cat, placing him gently on my consulting table where he sat very still, very upright.

'You do recognise Snowflake, don't you?' she queried, running a hand affectionately down the cat's back.

I did indeed. He'd been a good-looking cat. Long-flowing, thick, white coat. Very distinctive, almond-shaped eyes, the right being blue, the left copper. I'd put Snowflake to sleep two months back when he went into renal failure. Then he'd been an emaciated creature, a bag of skin and bones. Now he sat there, a picture of health. Plump, silky-haired, glassy-eyed and stuffed. An experienced taxidermist had transformed the cat back to the healthy feline he once had been. Even down to the colour if the eyes. Except now the right eye was copper and the left one blue. Everyone to their own.

Though Snowflake no longer had the ability to sense things, during life he would have done. Cats have a sixth sense.

Like Crackerjack, a feisty cat belonging to an elderly client of mine, Miss Jameson. Whenever I was due to make a home visit, the cat would disappear upstairs long before I arrived and hide under her large Victorian bedstead. Miss Jameson would usher me into the hallway and point up the stairs.

'I'm afraid Crackerjack's bolted under my bed again,' she'd say, apologetically. 'Seemed to sense you were on your way.'

The scenario that followed was worthy of a Feydeau farce with me crawling under the bed, Crackerjack, hissing and snarling before making his escape from the other end; leaving me similarly foul mouthed, spitting with rage under the bed springs.

That sense of anticipation can verge on the macabre.

Over coffee one morning in the back garden of the hospital, Jean recounted a story to illustrate the point.

'It was a Miss Jenkins, one of Clifford's clients. I don't think you ever met her. And you're not likely to now. She's dead.' Jean drew dramatically on her cigarette. 'Died of lung cancer. One ciggie too many.' She gave a rattling cough. By the sound of her, she'd be going the same way as Miss Jenkins if she wasn't too careful.

'Anyway, this lady used to walk her cat on a lead out from the bottom of her garden over to some woods each evening. But one day the cat refused to go.' Jean cocked her head to one side and gave me one of her nerve-numbing looks. 'Can you imagine? The cat sat down at the garden gate and simply wouldn't budge. What would you make of that?'

Lame maybe? I thought. Bladder full?

Jean told me the body of a young woman was found hanging from a tree the following day. Very spooky. The cat must have sensed what was going to happen. With such fine tuning is it any wonder cats can sense my fear even if it doesn't extend to tying a noose round my neck and dangling from a branch?

There are other attributes of cats to which I could attest.

A cat has the ability to fall from a great height, turning itself into a living parachute, spreading out all four legs to slow its fall. Then it manages to land on its feet, claws out. I've seen it happen for myself.

Our neighbour, Rita, called round in a panic to say Tammy, her tortoiseshell, had climbed the sycamore tree by Willow Wren and was now stuck up it.

'Can you do anything to get her down?' she asked.

I was certainly prepared to take a look. Even if a little unwillingly. As I peered up nervously from the base of the tree, Tammy decided she'd had enough, scrabbled along a branch and then took a flying leap. She careered downwards, her legs splayed out, to land on my head. And I can verify a cat does use its claws to ensure a grip when it lands. Tammy's claws searing into my scalp was proof of that.

It wasn't the first time I'd had a close encounter with Tammy. She was one of those cats who constantly brought home spoils of her hunting to deposit on Rita's back door mat. Mice, shrews, baby birds. Even a young grass snake. The list was endless. And a constant source of amusement for me. I'd hear Rita's agitated voice admonishing Tammy yet again for bringing in her latest offering. Whereupon, I'd pop my head over the garden fence and with a smirk on my face ask, 'What's Tammy brought in this time?'

'A chicken, would you believe,' declared Rita, one Sunday morning, holding up a mangled, plucked one.

My smirk was rapidly wiped off as I realised it was our Sunday-roast-to-be. Tammy had nicked it from our kitchen. Meanwhile, the cat was sitting on the patio, calmly washing her whiskers. When she did condescend to glance up at me, her look said it all. 'You're too chicken to mess with moggies.'

She was absolutely right of course.

The burgeoning population of mice in Willow Wren prompted the acquisition of Queenie, the chocolate and cream, long-haired Persian.

'Having her around the house will help you understand cats more,' said Maxeen. 'Just you wait and see.'

Bearing in mind my antipathy towards such creatures, I wasn't so sure. In the event, it worked out quite well. Queenie treated me with utter contempt. Regal distain, as befitted her name. To her, I was a mere underling not worthy of royal patronage. She kept her distance. I, mine. No problem. That all changed when Sabrina swirled in.

She was a large, middle-aged feline, green-eyed, with puffball white fur, pink nose and pink ears. A cuddly, dreamy-looking cat – the sort you'd associate with fairy castles and damsels in distress. Only, I discovered that lurking within all that puff was a deadly deviousness capable of making a damsel demented. As for me, in knightly terms, I found my armour sorely dented.

Despite her sugar-candy appearance, we'd been assured she was an excellent mouser; unlike Queenie, who we soon discovered had not the slightest interest in lifting a paw to help in rodent eradication. That was the reason Maxeen persuaded me to adopt Sabrina. Honourable intentions, for sure. Bless her.

By then, Willow Wren felt as if it had become an international centre for murine movements. It was heaving with mice. I swear there was a large contingency from France as our Camembert, Brie and Roquefort would disappear with great relish while the local Cheddar was never gorged. I began to dream of mice. There'd be one leaning against our pine dresser, a Gauloises stuck in the corner of his mouth, while his fellow compatriots, berets on their heads, played boules with peanuts across the kitchen floor. Ooh … la … la …

'I reckon they'll get along,' declared Maxeen, when Sabrina was first presented to Queenie. She was right. After a few introductory sniffs, a few wags of feathery tails swished from side to side like banners at a pageant, they got on fine. Royal assent had been granted. And before you could twitch a whisker, they'd started plotting. A certain member of the household was not to be trusted. Me. Though there was no Tower to dispatch me to, I could still be in for the chop. What lay ahead? I wondered. My head in a basket?

'Oh, come off it, you're just imagining things,' said Maxeen, when I first suggested that Sabrina was out to get me, alienating Queenie against me in the process. 'They're only cats, for heaven's sake.'

'But I swear Sabrina doesn't like me.'

'Only because she senses you're not keen on her. That you don't really like cats.'

'But I tolerate them,' I whinged. 'But Sabrina's really anti-me.' It was apparent within a few days of her setting paw in Willow Wren.

One of the first rules of the house – no pet allowed upstairs – was broken. Blatantly violated. I was undressing one evening, Maxeen already in bed, when a puff of white rolled into the room and floated up onto her side. There, it proceeded to wrap itself round her neck, lick her, rub noses, while giving vent to soft inarticulate cries of pleasure. As Sabrina's transports of affection subsided along with those she'd evoked in Maxeen, she cocooned herself at the end of the bed and fell fast asleep. Within days, Queenie was copying her.

There followed attempts to banish me from the bedroom. I was climbing our narrow staircase one evening, my head coming level with the landing, when I was suddenly aware of a silky, white paw flashing out between the rails above me.

'Ouch,' I roared as claws scraped across my scalp before disappearing back onto the landing.

There was no sympathy from Maxeen. 'It's just Sabrina playing games with you.' But when Queenie started to join in, it gave me claws for concern. Two sets of them.

Maxeen's solution was to throw a beanie at me. 'Here, wear this.'

Thanks, love.

The supposed 'games' continued when I attempted to lay a new stair carpet. I'd barely hammered in the top tread before Sabrina had ripped the bottom one out.

'She's just sharpening her claws,' said Maxeen. 'It's not deliberate sabotage.' I was unconvinced.

Then came the episode of the water butt. It was during a hosepipe ban. A common occurrence in this drought-stricken corner of West Sussex. I sneakily tried filling our water butt illicitly by snaking the hosepipe through the herbaceous border to the kitchen tap. So what did Sabrina do? She settled herself on the roof of the kitchen extension, peering down at the hosepipe trailing in through the window and proceeded to yowl. A spluttery caterwauling that, in my years as a vet, I've never experienced before. Her rendition had Rita dashing out to peer over the garden fence, bewilderment creased on her face. While Rev. James, busy in the vicarage garden across the way, dropped his shears and came running. As both spotted the now nearly full water butt, Sabrina stopped her caterwauling and proceeded to wash her paws. Job done. I'd been found out.

As for mouse hunting, no way was Sabrina going to oblige; and never did. I swear my continuing rant about the rodents was music to her ears. Every note a winning score. Grrrrrr ...

I thought I was having a nightmare. Claws were digging in my shoulder. The fetid, fishy breath of a feline was enveloped me. Strings of sticky saliva were dribbling across my cheeks. Eeek

… I woke with a start, feeling fur rubbing against my neck. A sing-song miaow echoed down my ear canal.

'What the hell are you up to?' I hissed as I opened my eyes to find them just inches away from Queenie's yellow ones. She was peering intently down at me while she continued to knead my shoulder. Maxeen, meanwhile, was still fast asleep.

'Bad puss,' I whispered crossly. 'You know you shouldn't be up here. Scram.'

Queenie sprang to the end of the bed and turned to look at me giving another plaintive miaow as she did so. Her message was clear. 'Follow me.' Her persistence was puzzling, as she normally kept her distance from me. And, why me for that matter? Why not Maxeen? But then she was a very sound sleeper. So perhaps Queenie had already attempted to wake her and failed. Whatever, I was wide awake now, Maxeen still breathing heavily in her sleep beside me. I slid out of bed, slipped on my dressing gown and tip-toed down the stairs behind Queenie. She gave one quick turn of her head to make sure I was behind her before disappearing through the cat flap.

'I hope you're not leading me up the garden path,' I groused as I unlocked the back door to discover she was doing precisely that. Up the garden path that led to the shed at the end of the garden. The door to it was open – its latch on my list to be mended. Queenie had already padded inside as I eased the door open and stepped in behind her, my eyes adjusting slowly to the faint light of an early September morning. She was nuzzling a black and white bundle in the far corner. That bundle suddenly hissed, making Queenie jump back, so allowing me to make a closer inspection of what had made the noise. It was a cat. A black cat with a white blaze on its chest and three white socks, one of which was soaked in blood. There was no attempt to move away. I suspected it couldn't even if it had wished to since the blood-soaked leg was sticking out at an awkward angle with a splinter of bone exposed above the knee. I noticed it was wearing a collar and tag. Kneeling down to gently ease the tag into view, I was just able to read the name. 'Lucky'.

'Hmm. Seems your luck's run out,' I said, suspecting the cat had had a run-in with a car. There was a phone number etched on the reverse of the tag. A local number. Once I'd eased Lucky into the cat basket I retrieved from the utility room, I called the number, even though it was barely 7.00am. The phone was answered immediately – almost as if someone had been waiting at the end of it. The relief in the man's voice when I explained the situation was clearly audible.

'Thank goodness you've found him,' said the gentleman. 'He's normally back indoors by now, waiting for his breakfast. My wife and I were so worried. Thinking he might have been hit by a car.'

I then had to further explain that this was the most likely cause of the cat's broken femur. 'And there might be other injuries,' I warned. 'But let me get him over to the hospital and make a better assessment.' I made a note of the gent's name and address, discovering it was a Mr and Mrs Compton, who lived the other side of Aston's recreation ground from us, in one of a small cul-de-sac of bungalows.

Later that day, the assessment wasn't good. No way could I save Lucky's right leg. Too smashed up.

'I'll have to amputate it,' I told Mr Compton. 'But, don't be too worried. You'll be surprised how well cats can manage on three legs.'

'Well please go ahead then,' instructed Mr Compton. 'At least he's lucky to be alive.'

The amputation went smoothly. Lucky was hobbling round on three legs in no time, rapidly adjusting to a new way of life.

And in more ways than one.

'He was extremely independent,' explained Mr Compton. 'Though we love him dearly we never saw much of him. Always out and about.'

'Just used us as a base really,' confessed his wife as I shared tea with them in their front room a few weeks after Lucky's operation. 'Now look at him.'

'A changed cat in every way,' said her husband, with a smile. 'Stays indoors more often now. Why, he's even commandeered one of our armchairs. Made it his favourite.'

Lucky was in it now, curled up, fast asleep.

'And he sleeps with us at night,' said Mrs Compton, 'Something he never used to do. But we enjoy having his company.'

At that moment, Lucky woke up, stretched contentedly in the armchair before getting to his paws – the three of them. He yawned, displaying a fine set of teeth. Then sprang down and started to hobble straight towards me, a glint in his eyes.

'There you go, my pet,' said Mrs Compton. 'Say "Hello" to your nice doctor.'

I decided to beat a hasty retreat. Before my luck ran out.

That experience with Queenie did change my perception of cats somewhat. Certainly, with regard to her. I felt nothing but admiration for the way she'd alerted me to the plight of Lucky. She'd dented my armour in a way that had been entirely unexpected. Almost pleasurable.

In much the same way that one of the practice's clients did, with her collection of cats.

Davinia Cresswell. The name rang a bell.

'She's a children's author,' Jean had informed me. 'Writes fantasy fiction based on the Arthurian legends. Princesseslocked-up-in-ivory-towers-rescued-by-knights sort of stuff. But a striking character in her own right.'

How true that turned out to be.

When Davinia Cresswell stepped into my consulting room that afternoon, it was as if she had stepped out of one of her Arthurian novels. Flaming ringlets of hair cascaded down over her shoulders. Fiery, emerald eyes blazed. And the swashbuckling demeanour in the way she carried herself, clad in tight crimson jeans and bodice-ripping blouse that plunged dangerously low over her cleavage. Wow. It was enough to light my fire. If she'd been a damsel in distress I'd have been cantering to her rescue in the wink of a dragon's eye. But somehow, I felt it would take a lot to get Davinia Cresswell distressed; and when it did, it would be due to a problem with one of her many cats since, unlike me, I discovered she was a confirmed cataholic.

On our first meeting, Davinia greeted me with, 'Allow me to introduce one of my merry band,' placing a cat basket on my consulting table. 'This little mite's just joined us. I'd like you to give him the once over. Make sure he's fit to join the clan.'

He was a small, timid creature, brindled, black and white, cowering in the bottom of the basket. As soon as Davinia eased him out, her manner changed. She cooed and clucked. Smoothed and cuddled. Reassured with sweet nothings in his ear. His right ear. The other one was missing. No doubt torn off in a fight. 'I've called him Tom Thumb,' she said. 'He was Arthur's court dwarf and honorary knight. And my own King Arthur has accepted him.'

'That's good,' I murmured absent-mindedly, still thinking of damsels in distress.

'Yes. He straightaway cleaned this mite's fur with his tongue. And then led him to his own dish of food and sat back allowing him to feed from his bowl. Amazing, don't you think?'

'Indeed,' I muttered. Still miles away. In Avalon in actual fact, climbing a turret.

When King Arthur finally made his appearance at the surgery some two months later, his name did indeed seem apt. He was a blue Persian. Long, flowing grey fur. Large, golden eyes and very aloof in the manner in which he padded round the consulting table, tail erect, swishing from side to side, its tip quivering. But that may have been due to the discomfort caused by an abscess under his tail for which he was admitted, sedated and the abscess lanced. He made several more appearances over the months with battle wounds that needed treatment.

'Perhaps he should have been called Lancelot,' said Carol, as I reached for a scalpel blade yet again.

'Ha, ha, very funny,' I muttered, plunging the scalpel blade into the swollen lump on his flank, dodging the stream of green pus that shot up in the air and splattered over my gloves.

I was subsequently to meet many more members of King Arthur's Round Table. Galahad, Lancelot Geraint, Lamorak. And a few ladies of the Court – Brangaine, Celia and Guinevere. A mixed collection of stray and rescue cats that seemed to live together with only the occasional warring whenever a new member was introduced. Each spat deftly dealt with by King Arthur or one of his cohorts.

Of the group, Dagonet was the funniest character.

'Well, he was Arthur's court jester,' explained Davinia, with a toss of those wonderful ringlets of hers. 'And he certainly makes me laugh with the pranks he gets up to.' She parted her full, ruby lips and gave me a dazzling smile.

Mmm … I felt I could play games with her any day.

One such prank of Dagonet's involved the central heating in Davinia's home – aptly called 'Camelot Cottage'.

'I woke up one night very hot,' she told me. 'And had to

throw back my duvet. Can you imagine?'

I could. All too clearly. Got me hot and very bothered.

She went on, 'Even though I'd taken my nightie off. I needed to cool off a bit more.'

So do I … So do I … I thought.

'So I went down to the kitchen to get a drink,' she went on.

Yes … Yes … And?

'Can you picture it?'

I could … I could … And? I swallowed the saliva building up in my mouth.

'There were all the cats in the front room watching TV, warm as toast, spoils of a midnight feast scattered over the sofa and armchairs. Can you imagine how I felt?'

All too vividly.

Davinia paused. 'Mr Welshman, are you feeling all right?'

I nodded weakly.

She continued. 'Dagonet was to blame. I discovered he'd jumped up on top of the washing machine and reached across to flick on the central heating switch. Same with the TV switch.'

Seems he was also responsible for raiding the fridge. Clever little fella. I managed to compose myself sufficiently to give him his annual booster.

When Davinia's latest Arthurian adventure was published she left us a complimentary copy. Maxeen tried reading it but gave up.

'I don't go for imaginary knights saving damsels in distress,' she said that evening with a yawn, snapping the book closed. 'Especially as I have my own knight.' She looked up and gave me a wink. 'Time to head up to bed.'

Indeed, yes. And time for me to show her my amour. It might have been bashed about a bit, but it was still serviceable.

16

Parrots on Parade

I'm not too sure how I came to be the parrot man at Prospect House. Perhaps it was something to do with the fact that I'd often talked about dear Polly, the African grey parrot we had acquired when I was growing up in Nigeria.

Anyway, whenever there was a consultation involving a parrot Jean was sure to send it flying my way.

I was to discover that the vicar of St Augustine's over in Chawcombe, the other side of the Downs, was parrot-mad as indeed was his wife, Maureen. In fact, she more than him when it came to rescuing forlorn-looking parrots from pet shops.

It started with Titch. He was the first of their parrots to be acquired. An African grey. But as his name suggests, he was titchy. Far smaller in size than the average African grey.

'We don't know much about parrots,' said Maureen as her husband heaved the enormous cage containing Titch onto my consulting table.

Puffing slightly, Rev. Charles stood back. He clasped his bony hands together and smiled benevolently, head tilted to one side.

'Titch seems to be somewhat on the small size. Wouldn't you agree?' The reverend's chin worked methodically up and down when he spoke as if being manipulated like a ventriloquist's dummy; the jaw chomping movement accentuated by the deep line that ran down each side of his mouth.

'Er … yes,' I said, nodding meekly, not wishing to confess my knowledge of parrots wasn't that vast and merely stretched to what lay between the pages of a slim volume called *Parrots for Dummies*.

But even to the uninitiated in parrot matters, Titch did seem undersized. He viewed me suspiciously through the bars. He still had the pale-grey eyes of a juvenile. The dark-grey plumage of the adult bird was only just growing through; and the striking vermilion tail, so characteristic of African greys, was a mere stubble of red.

'We'll take a look, shall we?' I said as confidently as I could.

'Yes, please do,' urged Maureen. 'But don't get bitten.' The reverend crossed and uncrossed his hands rapidly behind her.

There was growl as I lowered Titch off his perch in the folds of a towel. He hissed, his black beak yawning wide.

'Thanks for the good view,' I chuckled, peering into his mouth. All looked well. I felt his chest. There wasn't much muscle. But otherwise he seemed sound. 'He just needs fattening up,' I said as Titch scrambled back onto his perch. 'The usual parrot diet. Sunflower seed, millet, peanuts, a variety of fruit, even the occasional titbit such as bread and butter or a choc drop.'

Rev. Charles extracted a notebook from the folds of his

voluminous cassock and methodically wrote everything down.

Over the ensuing months, Titch matured into a handsome, plump bird.

Beaky appeared next. A Quaker parrot. He should have been called Peaky instead of Beaky as he was such a moth-eaten specimen. Poor soul. He had chewed away most of his chest feathers. Plucked bare. Pimply grey skin exposed. Almost oven-ready. As if to demonstrate his skill at feather plucking, Beaky yanked at a mutilated wing feather, nearly pulling himself off the perch in the process.

'We rescued him from a pet shop,' said Maureen. 'He seemed so sad, just sitting there, pulling out his feathers. We thought he'd be company for Titch.'

'And we pray it might stop his feather pulling,' added Rev. Charles. 'You know, company for him. A distraction.'

I agreed that it could help to take his mind of mutilating himself in due course. But now he had savaged himself so much and was persisting in doing so, we had to find a means to stop him.

'A collar might do the trick,' I explained.

'What, like mine?' said Rev. Charles, running a finger along the inside edge of his dog collar.

'Not quite. More like a cone. Looped round Beaky's neck to stop him getting to his feathers.'

'What's left of them,' murmured Maureen, gazing sadly at the semi-naked bird with his array of mashed stumps.

I constructed the collar out of a slice of X-ray sheet. He didn't take kindly to wearing it.

'We all have our crosses to bear,' observed Rev. Charles as we watched Beaky throw himself around his cage, bashing into the bars. He was more than a little cross.

But the collar did give new feathers a chance to grow

through. And that helped to break the cycle of feather plucking.

Beaky and Titch got on so well together that when the collar was eventually removed Beaky didn't start feather pecking again; and his sleek new plumage continued to grow unscathed.

The Red-browed Amazon appeared six months later. A smart, apple-green parrot with splashes of yellow and red on his head.

I raised my eyebrows at this ever-increasing menagerie.

Rev. Charles gave an embarrassed cough and glanced at his wife.

'My fault, yes,' Maureen confessed. 'The poor bird was in this pet shop …'

I smiled. 'What's he called?'

'Nick!' said Rev. Charles, holding up a hand, three fingers of which were bandaged.

'He's a bit of a devil,' admitted Maureen. 'He doesn't seem to like my husband.'

I was lucky to complete my examination of Nick unscathed. There was some overgrowth of his beak which I trimmed back amid a babble of shrieks and squawks.

'He'll need a beak trim every six weeks or so,' I yelled above the racket.

Dozy was the last parrot to be acquired. Another African grey. Another rescue.

'They're asking for a visit this time,' said Jean. As Rev. Charles had explained to her on the phone, with such a menagerie it would be easier all round if I could pop over to the rectory. 'Do you know where it is?' Jean added.

I didn't but surmised it must be near the church. And I knew where that was. In the centre of Chawcombe, just off the high street.

I found the rectory easily enough. It was tucked behind

St Augustine's. Up a small lane called Church Lane, surprise, surprise.

The rectory was an elegant, stone-built Georgian house typical of its type – stone-tiled and pillared porch, tall sash windows symmetrically placed to either side, matched by similar above: and a carved-pillared balustrade to the roof edge, running the entire length of the front.

When I arrived, the reverend and his wife showed me through to their drawing room. Wax-polished floors gleamed. An eye-catching stone fireplace, with fluted pilasters to each side of the hearth. And arranged on four identical dark-oak occasional tables, four steel parrot cages. From each cage, a parrot stared out.

'Our little flock,' said Rev. Charles. 'Such chatterboxes. Well, as a rule they are.' He spread his arms with a flourish. Four pairs of beady, yellow eyes watched me intently. Each bird silent. Not a sound. No movement.

Maureen voiced her concern. 'Dozy's eating and drinking okay. But ever since he arrived he's been so quiet. We're wondering if he's lost his voice.'

I gingerly placed my medical bag on a sofa. The eerie silence was unsettling. Not a bird stirred. They were like stuffed specimens. I tiptoed across to Dozy's cage, reached in and scooped him up in the towel that Maureen had thoughtfully put by the cage. He remained mute as I gently prised open his beak with a pair of forceps. I peered down his throat.

'Nothing wrong there as far as I can see,' I said.

Dozy remained passive in my hands, breathing a little rapidly, but no protestations. Not a squawk. Not a screech. When I released him, he scrambled back onto his perch, ruffled but silent.

I was about to speak when suddenly he swung round,

cocked his head to one side, and blew a large raspberry.

There was a pause. Maureen went pink, Rev. Charles a shade darker.

'Er, yes, well ...' he spluttered. 'At least he's found his voice.'

We all burst out laughing. And all four parrots joined in.

Jean went into charades-mode at tea-break one day. Why, oh, why she chose to have these funny little sessions, I could never fathom. A little idiosyncrasy of hers I suppose. It just so happened that on this occasion, Tony and Clifford were in the office at the same time.

'We've a rather special guest appearing this afternoon,' she said proudly, clapping her hands with glee.

We three vets eyed each other and pulled faces. All three of us glee-less.

'Yes, indeed,' she went on. 'I did have to persuade her to come in. Reassure her that we had the expertise to deal with her pet.' She scrutinised each of us in turn, making sure she had our full attention, before continuing. 'And, I can tell you it's a very special pet. In the Guinness Book of Records. Been on TV. Known the world over.' She stepped to the centre of the office.

Here we go I thought. Another guessing game about to start.

Jean raised a hand. Clifford immediately jumped to his feet.

'Sorry, Jean, but I must just pop down to the ward and check the pinning I did this morning is okay. So, if you don't mind.' With a flick of his grey fringe, he was gone.

'That just leaves us two,' whispered Tony, surreptitiously looking at his watch, before giving a quick grimace in my direction. 'I've ... er ... appointments to see,' he said, addressing Jean as he attempted to get up from his chair.

'They don't start for another 10 minutes,' snapped Jean.

Tony slumped down again.

Clearly, it wasn't wise for me to try and make a move as well.

'So,' Jean clapped her hands again, 'here we go.' She smartly brought her feet together and hopped forward.

'A rabbit?' suggested Tony, giving her a quizzical look.

Jean shook her head and waved a finger from side to side at him.

'Uhm … not a rabbit, then,' he said, with a shrug of his shoulders.

Jean placed her hands on her hips and jerked her elbows back and forth.

'A bat, perhaps?' said Tony, after a moment's reflection.

I looked at him in surprise. A bat? His smirk made me realise he was having Jean on.

Jean gave him a suspicious look and wagged her finger at him again.

'So, not a bat,' he sighed.

Jean started to flap her arms.

'A bird?' I said, hoping I was right so that this silly charade could be over quickly. Jean nodded. Phew. I was right. With a sigh of relief, I made to get up.

Jean waved me back down in my chair. She crooked a forefinger, raised her eyebrows and tilted her head to one side.

'A bird with a brain injury?' said Tony.

Jean glared at him.

We watched as she stuck her finger and thumb out, tapping them against each other.

'A bird eating a worm?' That was Tony again, his voice so innocent.

Careful Tony, you could be walking into a minefield here.

'Could it be a talking bird?' I suggested.

Jean's face lit up. She nodded.

'A budgie then?' Tony volunteered. Wrong.

'A mynah?' I suggested. Wrong again.

'Ah, I know what it could be,' I exclaimed. And was just about to say when there was the ring on the reception bell and a shrill woman's voice called out, 'Has anyone seen my knickers?'

'That will be the patient in question,' Jean blurted out. 'Go and see what he wants.'

'Besides her knickers,' added Tony, with a loud guffaw.

When I strode into reception, I was greeted by two sets of beady eyes, both of which stared intently at me. One was grey-green, fronted by spectacles in gold frames, belonging to a petite, silver-haired lady. She was smartly dressed in a 1970s-style pale lemon trouser suit and matching jacket. The other pair of eyes – piercing yellow – belonged to an African grey parrot which was perched on the lady's shoulder.

'Who are *you*?' screeched the parrot in a lilting Scottish accent, raising his head questioningly.

'Now then, Hamish, mind your manners,' said the lady, in a similar Scottish accent, turning her head to give the bird a wag of her finger.

'Mind *your* manners,' echoed the bird, bobbing his head up and down, adding another, 'Who are you?' as Jean hove into view behind her computer.

'Well, we all know who you are,' said Jean, glancing over at the parrot.

'My name's Hamish,' declared the parrot, ruffling its feathers.

'And I'm Amy MacTaggart,' said his owner, introducing herself to me. Once in the consulting room, she went on to explain that there was nothing actually wrong with her parrot.

'Fit as a fiddle,' Hamish interjected, puffing up what was

a rather moth-eaten chest of feathers. Several clumps were missing, allowing pimply grey skin to peep through.

It turned out that Amy was hoping to go away for a few days. Visit her sister up in Scotland. And needed somewhere to leave Hamish. Somewhere safe and with someone knowledgeable about parrots. She was a friend of Maureen Charles, the wife of the vicar of St Augustine's over in Chawcombe.

'Oh, yes. They own four parrots,' I said.

Amy nodded. 'Maureen suggested I asked you whether you'd be willing to let Hamish stay here for a few days while I'm away.'

I hesitated. 'Well we don't usually board pets in the hospital.'

Amy's face dropped. 'I understand you used to own an African grey and that you're very knowledgeable about them. And I'd feel far happier if I knew he was in expert hands.'

'Hands off,' squawked Hamish.

'Now, now,' reprimanded Amy. 'You don't really mean that.'

'Who says?' the parrot replied, far too defiantly for my liking. Mmm … If I did offer to board Hamish for a few days it seemed likely we'd have our hands full. Very full indeed.

'He can speak well over 800 words,' Jean informed me when Amy and her parrot departed, having finally persuaded me to board Hamish the following week while she went up to Scotland. 'And he's won the National Cage and Aviary Birds' Championship for best speaking parrot in the world 12 times in a row. Imagine! 12 times. Quite an achievement, don't you think?'

I had to agree, it was quite impressive.

When Hamish arrived for his stay, Jean was delighted to rub shoulders with him, chattering to the parrot constantly as they sat alongside each other on their respective perches in reception each day. But the bird's constant babbling proved a problem, particularly when directed at incoming clients.

A prim, brittle-mannered spinster had been standing in reception, complaining about the cost of her vet bill.

'Bugger off, then,' declared Hamish.

'Well really,' she retorted, exiting with great haste.

During the course of the next few days, Hamish's outpourings got worse. More and more obscenities rent the air, turning it blue. A repertoire of swear words and curses that any sailor would have been proud of. All spoken in Amy's lilting Scottish brogue.

'It's no good, he can't stay here,' Jean eventually admitted. 'He's offending too many clients.'

Maxeen thought it all a bit of a laugh when I told her. 'Why not let him stay with us for the last couple of days?' she suggested.

So, Hamish came back to Willow Wren from the Wednesday through to the following Monday when he was going to be picked up by Amy at the hospital.

During that time, we fussed around him at every opportunity possible. Plenty of chatter. Lots of different things for him to eat. Taken from the list Amy had provided. The usual parrot-mix supplemented with a variety of fruit, walnuts, almonds, peanuts in their shells. He was utterly spoilt. Accompanied with constant chatter on our part. From 'How are you, Hamish?' first thing. To 'Good night, sleep tight, Hamish' last thing. And masses in between. Especially over the weekend. A non-stop stream of chatter. Problem was he didn't respond in kind. The incessant out-pouring of words in the hospital dried up. Nothing said from the moment we carried his cage over the threshold of the cottage.

'Perhaps he's pining for Amy?' said Maxeen.

I shrugged. 'Maybe. Though he's eating okay.'

And he certainly continued to take an interest in his surroundings. Watching what was going on with those beady eyes of his. All in all, he seemed perfectly healthy. So it was a bit puzzling.

Monday morning, I went down to the lounge and took the cover off his cage, announcing that, today, Amy was back. Guess he'd be pleased. Hoped he'd enjoyed his stay. We'd been delighted with his company. Blah. Blah. Blah. On and on I babbled. Only when I paused for breath did he speak for the first time since he'd arrived. Turning his head to give me a beady look, he screamed in Amy's voice, 'For Christ sake, *shut up.*'

'I do hope Hamish behaved himself,' said Amy, on her return from Scotland.

'Of course I did,' he shrilled.

I didn't say a word.

It was many months later before we were to meet again.

One afternoon, up in reception, a loud 'Don't get your knickers in a twist' rang out. Very precise. Very clear. Even though announced in a Scottish burr.

'Ah,' exclaimed Jean, finishing the remains of her mug of tea. 'That will be your next appointment, Malcolm. You know who that is, don't you?'

I must have looked puzzled for a moment, briefly searching my mind for the connection.

'Knickers,' hissed Jean, in enigmatic mode. Something she could do at the drop of a hat if not at the drop of her own undergarment.

Then the penny dropped. Of course. Hamish. The African grey parrot, owned by Amy MacTaggart. The bird who had boarded with us when she went away for a short break.

As I ushered them into my consulting room, I asked, 'So,

how are we?' looking at Miss MacTaggart.

'She's fine,' said Hamish, looking at me.

'He's not though,' said Miss MacTaggart, looking at Hamish, perched on her shoulder.

I had to agree. The parrot's plumage, light-grey in colour, was ragged and ruffled. His claws far too long. Beak overgrown. And the striking vermilion tail he should have been sporting, just a clump of chewed barbs. He looked as if he'd flown through a hedge backwards.

I hesitated, not wishing to offend Miss MacTaggart and ruffle her feathers.

'You don't have to tell me,' she said. 'He's in rotten shape.'

'Speak for yourself,' said Hamish, with a swift bob of his head.

I had to prevent myself from correcting the parrot. Miss MacTaggart looked in peak condition. Well groomed. Positively bouncing with health. Her hair colour-matched that of Hamish's plumage. Grey, bordering on silver. Swept back into the perfect chignon. Had she sported feathers, not one would have been out of place.

'I want a clean bill of health,' she declared.

'You'd be certain to get one,' I nearly said, for a brief moment thinking she was referring to herself. But, of course, she was referring to Hamish.

'You know his background, don't you?' she went on.

Yes, I did know. We'd been given his full history when he was boarding with us. 'He can speak 800 words.'

'A lot of words,' shrilled Hamish, puffing up his chest.

'Indeed,' I said.

'He's in the Guinness Book of Records,' Miss MacTaggart reminded me, her chest also puffing up.

What for? I wondered. Tattiest tail? Parrot with the longest claws? Hamish opened his beak and hissed at me, as if reading my thoughts.

'Get me out of here,' he said.

'Most certainly not,' declared Miss MacTaggart. 'I need Mr Welshman to put you right. Get you shipshape.' She went on to explain that the BBC was doing a feature on intelligent birds. Crows. budgies, mynahs.

'And me,' butted in Hamish.

'Well, parrots certainly. And African greys in particular. After all, they're known to be the most intelligent of all the parrot family.'

Her parrot nodded his head vigorously. 'Clever Hamish,' he said.

'Yes, we know you are,' said Miss MacTaggart, with obvious pride in her voice. 'And now you're going to be on TV. A star.'

'Big star,' said Hamish.

'Big head,' I was tempted to say.

'But not looking a mess like you do.' Miss MacTaggart turned to me and asked if I could give Hamish a beak trim and nail pedicure. This I did with Hamish bundled up in a towel. And at the same time I had a look at his tail end. There was a muffled 'Do you mind' from Hamish as I examined his bottom.

I found a small cyst just below his preening gland. The area was sufficiently inflamed to have made him nibble at it and excessively tweak some of his tail feathers. Hence their mashed appearance. I pulled out the worst stumps amid several 'Leave off darlings' from him.

Once back in his cage, Miss MacTaggart told him to say, 'Thank you.'

He glared at me. 'Not on your Nellie,' was his response.

Uhm. That's gratitude for you, I thought.

A course of an antibiotic in the drinking water was

prescribed to treat any infection in the inflamed area. I reassured Miss MacTaggart that it should all settle down before he made his TV appearance.

'Fat chance,' growled Hamish.

A couple of weeks later, Miss MacTaggart phoned to say Hamish was going to be on the Meridian show that night.

'We'll have to watch it,' said Maxeen.

'Don't see why I should bother,' I said, rather churlishly, remembering Hamish's ungrateful comments. They still rankled.

But, nevertheless, curiosity overcame me and I did watch the show.

Hamish looked well, sporting a fine set of new red tail feathers. And he spoke well. When the presenter commented on his sleek appearance, Hamish turned to the camera and said clearly, 'All thanks to my vet.'

On hearing that you could have knocked me down with a feather. One of Hamish's naturally.

17

Snakes Alive

I remember the time as a lad in Nigeria when six feet of cobra weaved its way past me while I was in the bathroom. A sight to guarantee a rapid cure for constipation.

That bathroom was a separate building, linked to the rest of the gidah by a covered walkway. A walkway festooned with bougainvillea. The bathroom itself was surrounded by creamy-flowered, heavily scented frangipani and hibiscus. These, combined with the drainpipes and soakaway, made an ideal habitat for snakes. No surprise then that while we were making calls on Nature, Nature often made calls on us. That visit by the cobra was a good example.

The snake had slithered in through a drainage hole, possibly heading for the comforts of the laundry basket. I saw the latter move first, stepped out of the shower to investigate, spotted the cobra – a long, slate-grey creature – and hastily stepped back in again.

'Help,' I cried feebly, my voice a mere squeak. Despite the steamy atmosphere, my mouth was dry, parched with fear. I took a deep breath and tried again. 'Help.' The word came out like the croak of a dying frog. A third 'Help' was even more strangulated.

But Poucher heard me. There was the scrabble of paws at the door. A whine. I peered out from behind the shower curtain. No sign of the cobra. But it could have been coiled up behind the laundry basket. I shivered despite the heat. No way could I risk crossing the bathroom in case it lashed out.

'Poucher,' I whispered. The dog worried the door even more. 'Good girl, good girl,' I encouraged. Poucher's whine turned to a furious bark, sufficient to alert my parents. I heard Father run down the walkway.

'Don't come in,' I yelled. 'Snake.'

There was a hurried discussion outside. I recognised the voices of the houseboys. The door opened a fraction, sufficient for Yusefu's head to peep round, eyes wide open.

'Where's dat snake?' he whispered.

I pointed at the laundry basket. Yusefu edged in, a hand clamped tightly round a broom handle. He gingerly stretched out his arm and jabbed the basket. There was a rattling hiss and the cobra sprang into view. Yusefu disappeared behind the door. I disappeared behind the shower curtain. The snake disappeared out of the drainage hole that led to the soakaway outside. Moments later, I cautiously emerged, a towel wrapped round my waist, and scooted out onto the veranda. There, I was joined by Mother.

'That snake has to go before I do,' she declared, her face flushed, legs crossed, obviously desperate for a pee.

'I'm not going either,' I added, determined to hold out in

sympathy. Neither of use relished the idea of sitting on the wooden thunder box, not knowing where the cobra might strike next. A buttock-clenching thought.

Meanwhile, Poucher had slunk away and was sniffing the entrance to the soakaway, her nose twitching, her ears pricked. We guessed the snake must have disappeared down there.

It was Father who came to our relief.

'Now then,' he declared, 'we need a precise plan of action. Everyone wait here a moment.' With that, he hurried indoors, to reappear carrying a small metal cannister, grey-green, stencilled in white. A smoke-bomb. 'We'll smoke the blighter out,' he said. 'That should do the trick.' In brisk, military fashion, he organised the two houseboys, lining them up, one each side of the soakaway, with machete and knobkerrie clutched in their hands.

'Poucher, out of the way,' ordered Father, shooing the dog from the soakaway's entrance. 'Match, please.' He snapped his fingers. Mother hurried over with a lighter. Father lit the fuse on the smoke-bomb and tossed it down the hole.

'Stand back,' he ordered, waving his arms. 'Stand back.'

But the command was unnecessary. Thick, black smoke poured out of the hole. A billowing cloud that forced us to retreat, coughing, eyes streaming, Father and I as black as the boys.

'Masa ... Masa ...' they chorused, doing a nervous war dance on the spot. They pointed to the hole. The smoky entrance framed a large, whiskery snout. With a shrill squeak, out shot an enormous rat, equal in size to Sooty, our cat.

Poucher gave an excited yelp and sprang forward.

'Poucher ... don't,' I yelled. But it was too late. There was a scuffle of whirling fur and legs. A shriek of pain from the rat. With a final vigorous shake, it was all over. One dead rat.

Poucher trotted over and proudly deposited her trophy at my feet.

''Uggh ...' muttered Mother, stepping back from the rodent, which lay, convulsing slightly, eyes glazed, blood oozing from its open mouth.

Then she screamed. Startled, I looked at her. She was gesticulating. A finger pointing at the entrance to the soakaway. 'Look, there. See?' she blabbered.

I turned. And did see. All too clearly. The cobra had appeared. Foot after foot of sinewy grey whipped out of the hole to weave swiftly across the path.

'Attack,' roared Father. 'Get in there.'

The two houseboys, jolted out of their petrified stance, moved in. The snake reared up, inflated its hood and swung round on them. The machete-carrier lost his nerve and leapt back as the cobra lashed out. and struck his blade with a loud *ping.*

It was left to Yusefu to confront the creature. Gripping the handle of his knobkerrie tightly in his right hand, the head of it balanced in his left one, he tiptoed forward, weaving from side to side in time with the snake. Hissing loudly, the cobra raised itself up, stretching into a gigantic S shape, ready to strike with all the venom it could muster. With a tribal bellow to steel his nerves, Yusefu swung out his arm. The knobkerrie whistled through the air as the snake lunged forward. Its cranium was no match for the hard wood of the knobkerrie. There was a sickening crunch and the splat of mashed brain as the two met. The cobra dropped to the ground, pole-axed. Dead.

Father posed for a photograph with his spoils of war; rat by the tail in one hand, arm held high to dangle the six-foot snake in the other.

Poucher was given her bounty; and spent a happy bone-splintering hour devouring the rat.

I blamed Mother for the fact we seemed to have more than our fair share of snakes in and around the gidah.

She liked rockeries and had insisted on having two great piles of boulders heaped each side of the veranda; the gaps between them filled with soil and planted with clumps of dense ivy, zinnias and tufts of spiky lemon grass. These rockeries presented bold splashes of red, orange and yellow against a jumbled mass of greenery. Much admired by visitors. And much adored by snakes. The word must have gone out to the local snake fraternity. Hey mates, head over to the Welshmans' place. Plenty of shrubs to slither through. Great boulders to burrow under. And you can sun yourselves to your hearts' content on top of them. A real treat's guaranteed.

As a result, we were inundated with the wretched creatures. It made sitting on the veranda a somewhat unnerving experience since it was the inter-connecting highway between the two rockeries. You might try to laze in an armchair, feet up on a pouffe, but could never completely relax as, in the back of your mind, you couldn't help wondering what green, black or spotted-brown scaly creature might be gliding beneath you.

One morning, Mother was doing some weeding before the sun got too savage, pulling out errant clumps of lemon grass from one of the rockeries. From the deep shade under a tangle of purple bougainvillea, I sat watching iridescent weaver birds flit from bloom to bloom. Mother's scream shattered the peace.

She, in pulling up a bundle of grass, had also pulled up a green mamba, tightly coiled through the coarse strands and brilliantly camouflaged.

'Ugh,' she shrieked. 'A snake.' And in a display worthy of a mountain goat, she sprang from rock to rock to veranda in a series of flying leaps. The mamba remained entwined in the grass, glistening, emerald-scaled, unable to move or strike as its poisonous fangs were embedded in a large, partially-devoured toad. Meanwhile, Mother collapsed, quaking in an armchair. A shriek from her brought the houseboys running out, machetes flashing in the sun. 'No worry, madam,' they shouted. 'We dun kill dat snake.' And with much whooping and yelling, it took only seconds for them to winkle out the snake and slice off its head. The toad, reprieved from its venomous digestion, stepped out of the predatory jaws and crawled under a boulder.

The armchair into which Mother had collapsed was instrumental in a trick I played on her a few months later; and it involved another snake.

By then, I had a tree house. It started out as just a platform some 30 feet up a pine tree in the bottom of the compound. But I fancied turning it into a proper little house.

'Dad. Can I have some walls and a roof?'

Wooden walls and a roof were built.

Mother's turn next.

'Mum. Can I have some curtains and cushions?'

Curtains and cushions were made.

So I ended up with a very smart chalet up in the shade of the pine tree's needles, supported on a platform lashed across two sturdy boughs. Here, I could retreat from the heat of the day, fanned by the breeze, listening to it sighing through the needles while I gazed across to the red rusty-roofed town of Ibadan, a shimmering blur on the sun-scorched hills across the valley.

During a particularly severe tropical storm at the start of the rainy season, my little house collapsed in on itself. Only when the storm had passed, did I venture back up. The platform, still solid, was to be cleared. Over went the wooden walls, crashing down through the branches. Down cascaded the remains of the roof. I picked up the soggy cushions, tossed them over the edge. I picked up the bundle of curtains. Out fell a snake – a small, mottled brown viper. It hit the floor with a thud, hissed angrily and rapidly wound into a coil, mouth open, ready to strike.

I screamed and stepped back – into empty air. Only a wild dive at an overhanging branch prevented me from toppling over to join the cushions and timber splattered on the lawn below me. And there I remained, suspended like a hammock, arms round the branch, heels resting on the edge of the platform. At the slightest movement, the snake hissed and lashed out.

'Help!' My cry emerged as a mere whimper. But the houseboys had heard my initial scream.

'Coming, master,' they cried and swooped across the compound. One boy shinned up the tree. His fuzzy brown head cautiously slid into view at the other end of the platform. The whites of his eyes gleamed. 'Where dat snake?' he whispered.

'In that pile of curtains,' I hissed, unable to point.

A broom was slowly levered into view. With a deft flick, the bundle of material was swept off. The snake shot out, bounced down through the branches to be met with a sharp blow from the boy on the lawn. I hoisted myself back onto the platform and scrambled down to examine the lifeless creature. Prising open its mouth, I was fascinated by the array of backward pointing needle-sharp teeth, the tiny tubular forked tongue.

Then my schoolboy sense of humour overcame my zoological interest. I decided to play a joke on Mother. I carried the viper up to the veranda and coiled it under one of the two armchairs there. I sat in the other one, waiting. Mother had gone shopping in the market; and I knew that on her return she'd sit and cool off over some iced lemonade.

She duly returned, handing her bags of shopping from the jeep to one of the houseboys. Her face was pricked with beads of perspiration. Her cotton frock stuck to her in limp, wet folds. Up on the veranda, she collapsed in the armchair opposite me. 'Phew, that's better,' she said, having taken a gulp of the iced lemonade that had been placed on the small table next to her. 'So what have you been up to, dear?'

I told her I'd been clearing the debris from the treehouse. No mention of the snake. Not until I'd taken several sips of my lemonade. 'Er, Mum,' I said, in a voice that I hoped expressed concern, even if it wasn't genuine. 'There's a snake under your chair.'

Mother calmly continued to sip her lemonade. No frantic response as I'd anticipated. Strange.

I tried again. 'Mum … There's a snake under your chair.'

Still no reaction, other than a smile. 'Yusefu warned me you'd coiled a dead snake under my chair.'

At that moment, the snake started to move. Hell's bells. It hadn't been dead after all. Just unconscious. My voice immediately became strident. 'But Mum … that snake … it's alive.' I flapped my arms and pointed.

Mother continued to smile. 'My, my, Malcom, you're so convincing. You'd go down a storm in the local amateur dramatic society.'

At that moment, the snake uncurled itself and slowly slithered forward, over Mother's left open-toed sandal. Startled, she looked down. At which point, all hell broke loose. She leapt to her feet, knocking both the chair and table over. Lemonade showered in all directions. Her screams rent the air. The two houseboys raced out, each waving a machete. The snake didn't stand a chance, despatched in seconds. I too was despatched – to my bedroom for the rest of the day.

*   *   *

I'd related that tale to Jean over coffee one morning. A mistake. As ever since then, whenever there's been a snake to be seen, I've been the one to see it. As if paying penance for that trick I'd played on my mother all those years ago.

There was the young anaconda that had a 13 amp plug sticking out of its mouth. I was shocked. So was the snake. Sid had swallowed the heating pad on which he'd been sleeping. I'd have to pull out all the stops to save him. Well, at least the heating pad.

'We'd better get an X-ray just to see what's going on,' I said to his owner.

'More like what's going through, eh?' joked Mr Patel, a turban-headed young gentleman, who I half-expected to entice the anaconda from the wicker basket in which it had been brought in by means of some deft flute playing.

I dragged the wicker basket containing the anaconda down the corridor. Sid hissed and thrashed about inside. Uhm ... rather too lively, I thought. He needs cooling down. With that in mind I decided to stick him in the fridge for a while. So I cleared a space, hauled the snake out and squeezed him between the cartons of milk before returning to the office.

Only I forgot to tell Jean. Come tea-time, there was this loud scream when she went to the fridge for the semi-skimmed. She rushed into the office, trembling like jelly, and collapsed in a chair rather like Mother had done all those years back in Nigeria. As for Sid, while Jean remained hot and flushed, he had chilled out.

I hiked the anaconda's coils out of the fridge and arranged them in a heap on the X-ray table. It was all a bit hit-and-miss as to which parts I chose to X ray; and it took three plates before the heating pad was eventually highlighted.

I was tempted to operate to remove it but as it seemed to be slowly passing through I decided to try helping it on its way with some liquid paraffin.

Down in the prep room I prised open Sid's jaws and inserted a stomach tube down the sleepy snake's oesophagus. I then syringed in 10 millilitres of liquid paraffin.

A three-day wait followed. I felt the strain and I'm sure Sid did as well – especially when he passed the heating pad. Within 24 hours his appetite had returned and a rat had been devoured. Mr Patel was over the moon.

'And guess what, mate,' he exclaimed. 'I tried putting another plug on the heating pad ... just on the off-chance.'

'And ...?'

'It still works.'

It was over a year before Sid turned up again.

Waves of unease surged through me as I ushered Mr Patel into my consulting room, dragging the large Ali Baba basket behind him. Was it my imagination, or was this basket bigger than last time? Did that mean it held a bigger snake?

The turban-headed Mr Patel gave me a dazzling smile.

'Want me to do the honours, mate?' he said and without waiting for my reply, lifted the lid off the basket. There was a hiss from deep inside echoed by a ping in my guts.

Mr Patel leaned over the basket and inserted both arms. The basket started to heave. The hissing got louder, more threatening.

'Sid's in a bit of a strop,' declared Mr Patel as he started to pull out coil after coil of snake. 'Can't blame him though. Must be scared to death.'

He's not the only one, I thought as I watched the coils loop onto the consulting table. The anaconda's green, black-spotted flanks gleamed, the muscles rippling beneath the scales. I'd been correct about the size of him. He had got bigger. Much bigger. Sid zigzagged towards me and nearly slithered over the edge of the table. Mr Patel yanked him back in the nick of time. 'Steady on, lad. Steady on,' he gasped. 'He can't see,' he went on. 'He's become disorientated.'

Disorientated or not, Sid was still able to feel his way up his owner's arm where he wrapped himself round and round it as he inched up his shoulder. But I could see the cause of Mr Patel's concern. Each of Sid's eyes was covered by opaque white crusts, blinding him to his surroundings.

'It happened after his last moult,' explained Mr Patel. 'I looked it up on the Internet. It's what's called retained eye caps.'

Good lad. Least that saved me doing the same. Meant I could just nod sagely. Which I did.

'So what can you do about it?' he went on.

'Er ...' I stopped nodding.

Fortunately, the Internet had provided the answer which Mr Patel proceeded to tell me. I started nodding again. Seems we were going to have to soften up the remnants of the moulted material stuck over Sid's eyes. More precisely I – rather than we – was going to have to attempt that since the Internet stated it required expert veterinary treatment to ensure no damage was done to the corneas of the eyes. Thank you, Internet.

Hence 10 minutes later, having sent Mr Patel home, I found myself hauling the Ali Baba basket down the corridor leading to the prep room. It heaved. It wobbled. It hissed. Inside, one very angry snake. Outside, one very worried vet.

Now I was having to deal with a snake many times larger than last time. And full of life. The basket jerked from side to side. Sid was clearly as anxious to get out as I was anxious to keep him in. I would definitely need some help. But the hospital had suddenly become like the *Mary Celeste*. All personnel had mysteriously evaporated. No sign of Jean. Well, no surprise there. She's no doubt scuttled out for a fag to calm her nerves. As for the two nurses, Carol and Linda, they should have been around to lend a hand. But no. No sign of them either.

I'd already decided that eye ointment would be the best softening agent to remove the offending eye caps. But no way could I apply it to a snake that was too powerful to restrain by myself.

In a fit of petulance, I yanked the basket into the prep room and stormed off to the ward assuming one or both of the nurses were hiding down there somewhere. Nope. Empty.

'Where's everyone when I need some help?' I yelled, causing a couple of in-patient dogs to cower back in their pens.

I angrily retraced my steps to the prep room half-hoping someone might have appeared by now. But that room was still empty. But emptier than it should have been since the Ali Baba basket was now on its side, the lid off, and no sign of Sid. He too had vanished. Heaven knows what an angry blind snake in unfamiliar surroundings was likely to do. Wherever those surroundings were likely to be.

A scream from Jean out in the garden gave me a clue.

Okay. Another dose of mayhem now loomed. We had a rather large, rather angry, blind anaconda having made its escape from the confines of the Ali Baba basket: and to judge from the scream that had erupted in the garden, Sid had weaved his way out there. I tore out to discover Jean standing on the rickety garden bench, one hand clutching a fag, the other clutching her bosom, her face as ashen as the tip of her cigarette.

'Malcolm,' she spluttered, 'a huge snake's just slithered under the bench and disappeared over there.' She gesticulated wildly towards the end of the lawn where it merged into a dense thicket of rhododendrons.

I groaned. Of all places for the anaconda to head, this had to be the worst. A tangled mass of bushes – the overgrown remains of a Victorian shrubbery – which stretched down each side of a densely shaded path that led out onto the Green.

'I'll have to get some help to find him,' I said, pulling Jean off the bench. Whereupon, she scuttled across the lawn like a demented crab and disappeared into the hospital, me following closely behind.

As we reached reception, Tony bowled in from the carpark, having just returned from a visit. At the same moment Clifford appeared from his consulting room, escorting out his last client, an elderly lady clutching a tiny Chihuahua.

'What's all the fuss about?' demanded Clifford, looking at me, his eyebrows arched.

'It's Malcolm's last patient,' intervened Jean before I could reply. 'An anaconda. It's escaped.'

At which point, the lady with the Chihuahua fainted. While Jean attempted to revive the client with smelling salts, Tony and I dashed back down the corridor and headed out into the garden.

'Where do you think it went?' said Tony.

I pointed to the rhododendrons. 'Jean saw in slither in there.'

'Oh boy, we've got our work cut out to find it then. Could be anywhere.' Tony ran a hand through his wisps of hair. 'Tell you what, let's start from the road end and work our way back up.' He sprinted smartly over to the tunnel of rhododendrons. I followed closely behind. We were both like jellies on sticks, aware of the seriousness of the situation. Why, the snake could even now be working its way across the Green, leaving a trail of dazed and collapsed elderly folk in its wake. That's if it hadn't already squeezed one to death first. As we entered the dense shade of the overhanging bushes, a figure with a walking stick hobbled into view at the far end, haloed by the bright sunshine beyond. There was a small terrier on a lead next to it. As the distance between us narrowed, the figure materialised into that of Major Fitzherbert, a client of mine. No mistaking the hooded, blue eyes, white mane of hair swept back from the high forehead and the twitching white, caterpillar eyebrows matching the white of his bristly moustache.

'Ha … Mr Welshman …' he cried, waving his stick in the air. 'Was just coming up to get some worm tablets for Carruthers here.' He yanked at the terrier, a Jack Russell, next to him. The major's eyes darted between the two of us. I suddenly realised we must have looked rather odd. Two breathless, figures racing down the path from the hospital.

He was quick to grasp the situation, having witnessed a similar situation with a python last year. 'Don't tell me, laddie, you've had another escapee.'

I nodded sheepishly. 'An anaconda.'

'Streuth. That's some snake. And you think it's in these rhodies here?' The major whirled his walking stick round. Tony and I nodded. 'Tell you what, let's see if Carruthers can track him down.'

I felt an ice pick of fear stab my chest. I really didn't think that was a good idea. What if Sid decided the Jack Russell could make a tasty snack? But Major Fitzherbert had already let Carruthers off his lead and the dog had immediately darted into the bushes to the right, stopped in the middle of them and began barking.

'Ah, there we go,' boomed the major. 'Bet you he's found your snake already.' Without further ado, he plunged into the bushes and within minutes had reappeared, Sid draped over his shoulder. 'Guess this is your patient, eh, laddie?' he said with a deep chuckle.

I was dumbstruck.

'Nothing to it,' he went on. 'Had many such encounters with pythons during my time in East Africa. Nothing here I couldn't handle. Now let's get the beast back up to the hospital.'

It was a relief to see Sid once more ensconced in his basket. What's more, the jaunt through the undergrowth had remedied his problem. It had rubbed off his retained eye caps. That was certainly a sight for sore eyes. Both his and mine.

There was another client who had no qualms about handling her own snakes. She was my 4.10 appointment one afternoon. A new client. Jean did warn me it was a python I would be seeing. But couldn't have predicted what else would come under scrutiny at the same time. Oh, boy.

Miss Lillywhite was certainly a striking lady to look at. Of medium height, straight, glossy, black hair scissored in a fashionable short bob with heavy fringe; her slim figure complemented by a belted black pencil-skirt and red blazer; and a white shirt unbuttoned at the collar from which hung a loosely knotted tie in bold red and black stripes. The overall effect was that of a well-manicured, seductive-looking pupil from St Trinian's ready to spank rather than be spanked. From her right arm hung a large crocodile-leather holdall which she slid off onto the consulting table. I assumed, quite rightly as it turned out, that my patient – the python – would be inside.

'I'm worried about Monty,' she purred. 'Shall I get him out for you?'

There was a flicker of her long, dark eyelashes.

'Er ... Please do.'

Miss Lillywhite grasped the tag on the holdall between long, red-lacquered thumb and fingernails and gently eased the zip back.

The head of a python appeared. A tongue flickered out. Then, with alarming speed, the whole python seemed to ooze out of the holdall until every centimetre of its glistening, olive-brown diamond-patterned body had slid into view. It's amazing how snakes move. Their bendy backbones allow then to wriggle their bodies in the shape of a wave; and they push themselves along using muscles joined to their ribs. This python was using those features to great effect. Weaving its bendy backbone across the table straight at me.

'Naughty, naughty, Monty,' said Miss Lillywhite, reaching over to grasp the python's tail and slide him back towards her. He swung round and quickly slithered over her forearm, encircling it in several coils while continuing to employ his bendy backbone to advance up her shirt front. He only stopped moving when his head was nestling in her cleavage, level with the open top button. 'He's developed these two large bumps behind his head.' Miss Lillywhite thrust her bosoms towards me. 'Can you see them?'

I felt myself beginning to shake a little. Yes. I did have a fear of snakes. But this trembling was due to a little more than that. In fact, far more. And they were leaning over the table, willing me to take a good look at them.

'So, what do you think these bumps are then?' queried Miss Lillywhite.

I actually did know and told her. ''You've got some big ticks there, Miss Lillywhite.'

She pulled back, her glossy lips widening in astonishment. 'Mr Welshman … really!'

'*Ticks*,' I enunciated more clearly. 'On Monty.'

'Oh. For a moment I thought you said …'

'Yes, yes.' I knew exactly what she thought I'd said. But I had been referring to the two raised areas of scales on the python's neck where a couple of ticks had penetrated between the scales, started sucking blood and then swollen up.

'Oh, my poor Monty,' crooned Miss Lillywhite, stroking his head before running a finger delicately down his bendy backbone while my backbone straightened. 'Is there anything you can do about it?' she went on.

Stop doing that for a start, I thought as my backbone stiffened even more.

Treatment for the ticks was relatively straightforward. A Diclorvos strip in a jam-jar with holes in its lid was to be put in Monty's living quarters for three to four hours twice a week for three weeks. The insecticide would ensure any mites on Monty or in his environment would be killed off.

Miss Lillywhite was profuse in her thanks. She bundled Monty back in her holdall and deftly zipped him in. 'I had been worried it was something I could have caught as Monty's part of my act. I work at the Rocarno Club over in Brigstock. A members-only club. Very exclusive. But if you'd like to pop over one evening I'm sure I could squeeze you in.'

She picked up her holdall, pouted an air kiss at me and wiggled out.

It was highly unlikely that I'd ever visit that strip club. Besides which, in time, I imagined Monty would grow too big for Miss Lillywhite to handle. When mature, Burmese pythons can reach twenty feet. At that length, Miss Lillywhite would be completely out-stripped.

18

Beside the Seaside

I went to Bournemouth Grammar School back in the 1960s and when in the sixth form, ran a club called RAM – standing for Reptiles Amphibians and Mammals. I'd organise day trips out to the New Forest or along the coast from Swanage in the Purbecks. That Dorset coastline, in particular, with its limestone strata upended in a ragged toothcomb of grey cliffs, riddled with the skeletal workings of disused quarries, has given me a treasure chest of memories.

A typical day out for a small group of us boys – usually five at the most – would involve a bus trip one Saturday in late March. With the dawn a mere slit of red, we'd rattle out of Bournemouth. Once across the ferry at the entrance to Poole harbour, the green bus gear-crashed up the chalk slopes of Ballard Down and rumbled in twisting descent to Swanage. Bleary-eyed and yawning, we braced ourselves for the hike up the steep hill to Durlston Head and the Globe. Hewn from

Purbeck stone, the Globe stands in the grounds of Durlston Head Castle. Here, once steaming cups of coffee from the thermos flasks in our knapsacks had revived us, the day started in earnest.

A flurry of notepads would appear.

'Sorry, sir ...' faltered Pink Jim. He always looked flustered and blushed easily. Hence his nickname. He'd mislaid his notebook yet again.

We jotted down date, place, time of arrival, leaving the rest of the page blank in anticipation of the day's sightings.

From the Globe, the path winds along the precipitous cliff edge, safety ensured by a solid limestone wall. That wall was a constant source of irritation to the 11-year-olds. I, a gangling youth of 16, was tall enough to peer over. They weren't. In the wall there is a rock on which, by carefully placing a foot, each lad could gain those important extra inches. But it caused squabbles.

'My turn.'

''tisn't.'

''tis.'

'You've had long enough.'

Meanwhile, I was lost in the dizzy world below.

A world of sheer grey cliffs, pocketed with tussocks of pink sea thrift, that plunge down into a gently undulating quilt of blue and green. A sea flecked with white on breezy days. Black-headed gulls whirl and plummet in the gullies. Their raucous cries echo against the rocks, blending with the pounding surf far below.

I often brought a bag of stale bread to entice the gulls into a frenzy of aerial acrobatics. Sometimes, lunchtime sandwiches, if not to one's taste, were pulled apart and tossed out to snap-happy beaks.

'Got him,' cried Pink Jim, chuckling as he hit a gull squarely on the head with a Hovis bullet. Both gull and I gave him a beady look.

I would stretch over that wall, feeling its warmth on my belly, the breeze funnelling up to brine-kiss my cheeks. Kittiwakes and fulmars sail past you at eye-level, stiff-winged in the eddies of air channelling up the cliff face. Below them, dinner-jacketed guillemots and razorbills hurl themselves out to skim the surface of the sea and land in bubbles of white.

On good days, another jewel could flash into view. The comical puffin. Resplendent with its black and white plumage, white cheeks and orange-red bill, it always took pride of place at the top of our notebooks.

Skirting the old quarries of Tilly Whim caves, their entrances round, black, like the orbs of a skull, we'd slip-slide down a steep valley, haul ourselves up past the white-washed lighthouse and set out along the coastal path to Dancing Ledge, our destination for lunch.

There were many distractions along the way.

Grassy slopes fold back onto farmland half a mile inland. Those slopes are criss-crossed with dry-stone walls. Some have toppled over, their limestone slabs fanning out down the hill like scattered packs of cards. There are pockets of hidden blackthorn and secretive muddy pools. As we scrambled into view, young heifers would snort with alarm and plough away through the brambles, leaving us the acrid smell of cowpats, the rasping drone of horseflies.

One such spot we'd visit each spring. Here was a haven for adders just out of hibernation. Often, we'd come across half a dozen snakes in the space of a few yards. Mostly the dull browns of the females, occasionally the handsome zigzags of a black and white male.

'Look, there … see?' I once whispered, motionless for fear of disturbing a basking snake only inches from my boot.

'Where, sir?' Pink Jim exclaimed, rattling across the limestone slabs. I shrugged in exasperation as the adder swiftly glided back into the brambles.

Time flew.

Suddenly it was a, 'Come on, lads, we'd better hurry.'

A route march ensued.

We scrambled over stiles. We pounded the short turf, home of the rare spider orchid. We zigzagged through clouds of marble white butterflies that drifted over the grass. Our strides got longer. Our faces redder. Our welly-booted feet more squelchy.

'Made it,' I gasped as we finally clambered down the rocks onto Dancing Ledge. We were one short. Pink Jim. Still a crimson blob on the skyline.

Dancing Ledge is a dimpled, wave-worn promenade of rock that juts into the sea: its centre carved out as a man-made swimming pool the local school used to use. We were grateful to paddle and cool off. Sheer bliss. Until one lad spotted a dark green shore crab scuttle into the depths.

'Sir, it was the size of a dinner plate,' he cried. All feet got rapidly withdrawn.

But it was still fascinating to stare down into a world of darting prawns, pink shrimps, lumbering hermit crabs and tentacle-waving cream, orange and blue sea anemones.

Then overcome with hunger, we raided our rucksacks. Out came the plastic boxes, levered open to reveal piles of squashed sandwiches.

Discussions followed as to what each had as filler.

'Ham and tomato.'

'Cheese and pickle in mine.'

'I've got peanut butter. Scrummy.'

Pink Jim would look on in silence having eaten most of his along the way.

On the return hike, we scaled the higher slopes. There was always something new to discover. Something new to delight. Butter-splashed pockets of primroses. Banks of snow-blossomed blackthorn, its scent vinegar-sharp. Yellow spikes of gorse, drone-heavy with bees.

'Uhm … Coconuts,' I'd say, inhaling the scent of the warm, perfumed flowers.

'My mum's cakes,' said one lad, nose in the gorse, sniffing.

'Honey,' said another sniffing lad.

Pink Jim also sniffed. But said nothing. His hay fever had started. His eyes were streaming, nose blocked. He couldn't smell a thing.

And the birds. The speckled-brown of a spotted flycatcher. The snap of its beak, an insect caught mid-wing. The burble of a willow warbler, newly arrived from Africa. The scythe-flight of grey cutting across the fields. Puzzlement for a moment. Recognition when the familiar cu-coo rang out.

There was always that extra slab of limestone to look under. Another adder maybe. Snails banded in black and white. Red slugs. Ants in a swarming frenzy of egg-carrying once disturbed. And many, many slow-worms.

We once did a survey of these wriggling reptiles. A line of us stretched up the slopes, advancing slowly forwards, looking under every likely stone. Our notebooks recorded 25 that day. A record number.

We drank the remaining dregs of our coffee suspended between the azure of sky-larked heaven and the glint of a diamond-speckled sea. Bewitched, we'd drowse in the pollen-clouded grass, lulled by the murmur of the distant waves. Only a glance at my watch would break the magic.

'Crikey, we'll miss the bus.'

A headlong flight would hastily ensue. Across the grassy slopes. Down, down, down the long hill to Swanage. The green bus rumbling in readiness.

And on the journey home, time for notes to be compared. Who spotted what and where.

Pink Jim's stoat that nobody else saw.

'Honest, it dashed under a wall.'

'Oh yes?' we'd chorus, flicking our notebooks firmly shut.

Another outing over.

Another storehouse of memories made. Bringing sunshine into our minds. Filling our hearts with joy.

My early days as a vet saw me in a different seaside environment. That of the pebbly coastline along which Westcott-on-Sea sprawls.

The town has a 1950s feel about it. A faded gentility encapsulated by its wide promenade, white-painted pier with its mock neo-classical pavilion built in 1862 and mile-long stretch of pleasure gardens – the planting of which echoes that of the Green further inland – rather unimaginative alternate beds of red geraniums and white geraniums, each bordered by a single strand of silver cineraria.

In the 18th century Westcott did briefly become a fashionable resort to travel down to from London, 50 miles away: following in the wake of the Prince Regent whenever he desired to pleasure himself by dipping his oar in the sea over at Brigstock. By contrast, Westcott was the watering hole of Princess Amelia, daughter of King George III – the town deemed a little less risqué than Brigstock for her more refined visit. In 1798 she descended on Westcott for a spot of sea bathing in the hope it would aid in her recovery from tuberculosis. And people have been coming ever since. To relax. Take a dip. Stroll along the promenade. Be invigorated by breathing in the bracing sea air.

Unfortunately, that air is not always as bracing as one could wish for. The intake of air not as invigorating as one would hope. This is on account of banks of dark green bladder wrack that can build up along the shore. At low tide, these then dry out to fester in the sun. To these banks, swarms of black flies are attracted. The stench from the banks drifts through the town on the sea breeze, to mix with that of fish and chips, kebabs and burgers. A heinous foul blend which triggers many nostrils to twitch in disgust; and arouse suspicions that the public conveniences have become blocked. Even at Prospect House, two miles inland from the coast, its presence could be smelt. Jean was constantly on the go spraying the premises with cloying blasts of *Summer Bouquet* making it feel like some seedy brothel rather than a hospital for treating sick pets. The seaweed had another attribute, a lethal one, far more serious than its onslaught on our olfactory senses. It was one that I'd never experienced before. But that all changed one summer Bank Holiday Saturday.

The weather was kind. Cloudless skies. Plenty of sun. For Westcott-on-Sea, like the other resorts along the Sussex coast, this was good news. It meant an extra surge of trippers to its Victorian promenade and pebbly beach.

Mr and Mrs Symonds were two such trippers. They arrived for an out-of-hours appointment during the afternoon, having returned from the beach with a very poorly dog.

'We're staying at the Hotel Apollo,' said Mr Symonds, when Carol, the duty nurse at the time, asked them for their details.

'Down for a long weekend,' added Mrs Symonds.

Both she and her husband were in holiday attire. He wore

baggy white shorts to his knees topped by a vivid green and red Hawaiian-style, short-sleeved shirt, the outfit completed by Panama hat and sandals. Mrs Symonds was more simply dressed in a loose-fitting, cream cotton dress, pink straw hat and flip flops. Both wore dark glasses which they took off in reception. Though in holiday gear, they were certainly not in holiday mood. Far from it. The cause of their concern crouched on the floor between them – Bertie, their four-year-old Border terrier.

'Bring him through,' I said, having introduced myself as the vet on emergency duty. Mr Symonds picked Bertie up and carried him into the consulting room where he lowered him gently onto the table. The dog lay there, listless.

'This isn't like Bertie,' said Mrs Symonds. 'He's usually so bouncy.'

'And he was perfectly all right when we went down to the beach this morning,' said Mr Symonds. 'Wasn't he, luv?'

His wife nodded. 'We're wondering if he's suffering from a bit of sun stroke. It *was* very hot down there.'

'Mind you,' said Mr Symonds, 'we did have an umbrella. And a bottle of water and a bowl for him.'

'And he did drink lots,' interrupted Mrs Symonds quickly, as if fearing I might accuse them of letting Bertie get dehydrated. It had crossed my mind.

'Well, little fella, let's see what's going on,' I said, patting Bertie gently on the head. He felt hot. A temperature check verified his temperature was a little on the high side but nothing too serious. Certainly nothing like the high readings seen in dogs suffering from heat stroke. I raised the skin on his scruff. It settled back quickly which wouldn't have happened if he'd been dehydrated. Bertie turned and gave my hand a feeble lick.

Mrs Symonds gave a little sob. 'That's so typical of him. He loves everyone.'

I ran my hands down his flanks. His tummy felt somewhat distended. Quite bloated in fact. I gently palpated him. That elicited a moan. 'Sorry little 'un,' I murmured. 'Just trying to find out what's wrong.' It was just then a gust of hot air bowled in through the consulting room's small upper window which I had open as it was so stifling in there. Immediately the stink of rotting seaweed filled the room.

Mr Symonds wrinkled his nose. So did his wife.

'It's quite bad down there today,' he said. 'Shame really as it rather spoils being on the beach.'

'Though Bertie loves it,' said Mrs Symonds. 'Typical terrier. Goes for anything smelly.'

That's when the symptoms clicked into place. 'Do you think Bertie might have eaten some seaweed?' I asked.

'Well he was certainly rummaging through a pile of the stuff,' said Mr Symonds. 'Though I can't swear he actually ate any.'

However, I had a strong hunch this was likely to be the cause of Bertie's symptoms. I admitted him for X-ray, warning the Symonds that should I see anything suspicious then I might have to open him up. In the event that's what happened. I found and extracted several strands of ingested seaweed that were swelling up and causing a blockage – likely to expand further and rupture his intestines had they not been removed.

Bertie had a lucky escape thanks to the prompt action of the Symonds. They still liked to be beside the seaside but decided the sands of Bournemouth were a safer bet for Bertie in future forays onto the beach. Especially as there'd be nothing on those sands to raise a stink.

What a contrast is a wintery scene on Westcott's beach. Gone are the trippers. A few brave souls bowl along the promenade, bent over in their waterproofs, battling against the wind whipping in from the white-flecked surf. The banks of seaweed have been washed out, to be replaced by a tide-line littered with flotsam: blocks of shredded white polystyrene, dented plastic bottles, strands of blue nylon rope and many other dubious cast-offs bobbing in the surf – including the odd shoe. But one late autumn day, something got washed up that was a real surprise to me; and of great interest.

It was in a large cardboard box that was slid across my consulting table by two lads, both around 12 years of age. Both were wearing T-shirts emblazoned with 'May the Force be with you' and both sported baseball caps indicating their allegiance to the Jedi.

The lads looked vaguely familiar. 'Haven't I seen you before?' I queried as they peered across the table at me.

'We brought in a bearded dragon which someone had left on a bus,' said one lad. 'The number 10.'

'The one that goes to Westcott pier,' said the other earnestly, as if thinking the direction in which the dragon was heading could have given me total recall. But though the 'Force' wasn't entirely with me, I did remember the dragon. 'Dino' I think it was called.

'So what have you brought in today?' I said, staring down at the cardboard box, its top stuck down with Sellotape. 'Not a lizard this time, I take it?'

One of the lads, with black-framed spectacles and freckled face, shook his head vigorously. 'Not unless you can get a lizard with a beak.'

'And webbed feet,' added his friend, giggling.

'And feathers,' said the first lad, starting to giggle as well.

'Right. A bird then,' I said, my voice clipped. 'We'll take a look shall we?' I began unpeeling the sticky tape securing the top flaps of the box.

'We found it down by the pier,' said the bespectacled lad.

'Where the number 10 bus stops,' said his friend.

'But it wasn't on the bus.'

'Didn't say it was.' The friend glared at his mate and then pulled his cap off to scratch his head. 'It was on the beach.'

Pushing his spectacles up the bridge of his nose, the first lad said, 'We think it's a sea bird cos it was on the beach. Not in a bus.'

I sighed. Having established the bird had *not* arrived on the beach courtesy of National Express Coach Services, I levered open the lid and peered inside. I'd already thought of possible seabirds. Cormorant. Puffin. Guillemot. Gull. But was completely floored by the bird I found myself looking down on. For a start, it was far larger than I expected. The size and appearance of a gannet, but with a brown and white belly, rump and tail. And red legs and feet.

I lifted the bird out of the box and lowered it onto the consulting table. It remained where I placed it, huddled, neck tucked in. But it did wag its tail to relieve itself on the surface.

'Poo ... ee ...' chorused the lads. 'Gross.'

The bird, whatever species it was, looked decidedly bedraggled and had certainly felt light when I'd lifted it out of the box. Dehydrated. Definitely in need of fluids and feeding.

There was one man well qualified to do that. Mike Masters. Chief executive of WARS – Westcott Avian Rescue Society. He, of all people, should also be able to identify it. I sent the lads packing, explaining what I intended doing; and promised to let them know what happened to the bird.

Mike Masters was a retired RSPCA inspector who had moved to Westcott-on-Sea with his wife, Debbie, and set up

WARS as a sanctuary and rescue centre for birds. Everything about Mike shouted 'professional'. Always immaculately turned out. Dark blue uniform with gleaming buttons. Shoes with shiny toecaps. And the WARS van he drove, always spotless. Never a bird dropping on it. Or in it, if Mike had his way.

'So, Malcolm, you've got me a bit of a challenge, Jean told me on the phone,' said Mike. It was later that afternoon, Mike and I in the hospital prep room. The cardboard box, bird inside, between us on the prep table. 'Found down on the beach, you say? Storm Lorna gave us quite a battering earlier in the week. So we've had quite a few exhausted seabirds in these last couple of days.' He folded down the flaps of the box. 'Now let's see what we've got here. Ah …' His voice trailed off … Followed by 'Mmm … well I never,' as he lifted the bird out.

Holding the bird cupped between his hands, he turned to me. 'We've a first here, Malcolm. It's a red-footed booby.'

Mike went on to explain. It was a white-tailed brown variety. Usually found over in the Caribbean. So it was 4000 miles off course. Possibly came over on a ship, exhausted.

'But no problem getting him shipshape again. Stomach tube him with some food. And when he's got his strength back, plenty of handfed sprats should do the trick.'

In Mike's expert hands the booby did recover well.

The lads came in for an update a week later.

'So where's he now?' queried one.

'In the Caribbean.' I went on to tell them the bird had been transported by charter plane to join a flock of boobies on the Cayman Islands.

The boys looked at each other in amazement. 'Better than Westcott pier,' said one.

'By number 10 bus,' piped up the other.

19

Taking Stock of the Stockwells

Gizelle, despite her name conjuring up some sylph-like bovine, was a mean cow. A bony beast covered in body-bruising projections encased in untanned armour. And definitely not dainty on her hooves. Especially today when she was holding up her left hind leg.

It was Jean who'd booked her in.

'Guess what,' she'd said that Monday.

'Mmm ... what?' I murmured, preoccupied with the morning's op list I was running a finger down. A bitch spay. A couple of dentals.

'You've a visit later on.'

'Yes, right ...' Three dog castrates. Four cat castrates.

'To the Stockwells.'

My attention immediately snapped from pairs of testicles to a pair of twins. The Stockwell twins. Yes. Yorkshire lasses who had moved down to West Sussex some 30 years back. They owned 50 acres or so over the other side of the Downs. Their farm, Hawkshill, just a few miles from Ashton, approached up a rutted chalk track; a rickety five-bar gate to be opened before you could drive on down into the valley and to their farmhouse.

The view seen from that gate gives the sense that you are about to step into a Hardy novel. The farm, red roofed, tile hung, small-paned windows, wisteria draped over a red-tiled porch. Only this was West Sussex not Dorset, and the inhabitants of the farm, Madge and Rosie Stockwell, not the likes of Bathsheba Everdene in *Far from the Madding Crowd*. Even so, there was an idyllic, rustic feel to this corner of the Downs where I always felt the pace of life slowed as soon as I opened that gate and drove down the rutted track to the farmyard. And it was never helped by the twins who conducted themselves in an unhurried manner and considered me as always being 'vet in a hurry'.

Gizelle was one of their 12 Jerseys. These and a small flock of sheep were the only livestock they kept. In the past year I'd been called out twice. Once to a cow with bloat. That had been something of an emergency requiring quite a dramatic intervention, with me stabbing the side of the cow to release gas from her grossly dilated rumen – one of her four stomachs. The second visit was to a cow which was calving. Or trying to. Another dramatic intervention was needed. That time a caesarean section and the delivery of a healthy calf.

Half an hour after lunch saw me stopping at their gate to let myself through – a gate still as rickety as last time. No repairs had been attempted. Just the four bars instead of five; and that fourth bar just about serviceable, tied into its bracket by baler twine secured to the upright. And like on the previous occasions, I had the gate drop down on me as I prised the latch open. 'When will they ever learn?' I muttered to myself as I lifted it up and dragged it across the chalky track.

Driving on down, I slid to a halt in the middle of the yard, jumped out of the car and bellowed 'Hello?' in the hope someone would appear. A diminutive figure in green overalls and wellies slowly ambled out of the main barn. Tomato-soup complexion, hooked nose, hair with pudding basin cut squashed under a green woollen beanie, it was either Rosie or Madge. I could never tell them apart despite having visited them several times.

'Rosie, vet's here,' the twin called out over her shoulder.

An identical version shuffled out, to halt next to her sister and declare, 'So I see.'

'You've come to see Gizelle,' they chorused.

'Yes ... Yes ...' I said, glancing furtively at my watch. I had appointments starting at 2 o'clock and time was ticking on.

'Well, let's be showing you then,' said one twin. Was that Madge?

'Good idea,' said the other. Rosie? 'She's in the barn.'

The building she was referring to was a classic oak tithe barn with exposed beams, infilled with knapped grey flint, linked to the farmhouse by a row of stables, their walls of similar flint construction. It was the picture-perfect setting for two comely young milkmaids in mop caps to swish through the yellow straw that could have carpeted the yard; yokes straddling their shoulders, from which could have swung pails of rich, creamy milk. Instead, I was subjected to the sight of the dumpy twins, waddling like a pair of beanie-headed bantams between the dry, crusty cow pats that polka-dotted the yard, heading for the barn. I yanked on my wellingtons, threw on a brown coat, snatched my black bag from the boot of the car and hop, skipped and jumped over the cow pats to follow them. But

I missed my footing, landed on a fresher, still semi-liquid pat and skidded.

'Doesn't do for vet to be in hurry,' chorused the twins, turning to see me land on my bum in an even fresher pat.

Once inside the barn, I was confronted with my patient. Gizelle.

'Nice name, that,' I said.

'Nice name, yes,' said one twin.

'Not nice-natured though,' said the other.

'A bit of a bugger,' they said as one.

Turned out they were right.

'She's lame,' remarked a twin as the two of them watched me cautiously sidle up to where Gizelle was tethered to a post via a rope and halter. The only means of restraint. No kick bar to clip over her haunches and immobilise a kicking foot to make it safer to examine her hooves. Mmm ... The two sisters seemed to sense my unease.

'I'll keep check on her head,' said one.

'You do that, Madge,' said the other who, by elimination, must have been Rosie. 'And I'll pull her tail round and wedge her against the wall.'

'Fine.' That was Madge.

'We're ready when you are, veterinary.' That was both of them, now stationed at their allotted positions.

'Okay.' That was me. Speaking in a rather uneasy tone of voice. My unease due to being left to deal with a leg liable to swing out and deliver a swingeing blow to my nether regions.

But it seemed I had no choice. So I pulled a hoof knife from my bag and stepped forward. Gizelle promptly stepped to one side, swung her back-end round, dragging a twin with her and coughed. An action which forced a stream of liquid dung to be excreted at high velocity – a brown watery arc that shot over my head. I got splattered.

'One of Gizelle's little tricks,' said the front twin as I wiped my face.

Suddenly, the Jersey lashed out with her raised leg, clipping my right shin.

'And that's another,' said the back twin as I rubbed my leg.

'Any more?' I queried, having run out of hands to apply to my splattered and battered body parts.

'Yes, she's liable to ...' The twins' voices were drowned by a loud moo from Gizelle as she dropped like a stone between them. This caused her bladder to contract and allow a fountain of urine to cascade out like an erupting sulphur spring and pour into my boots. But at least she was down. And, if not out for the count, sufficiently constrained with Rosie and Madge on top of her to allow me to anchor her ankle between my legs and examine the inside edges of her two claws.

'Madge reckons it's foot rot,' said one twin who must have been Rosie.

'I do,' said the other, who had to be Madge.

'She does,' said Rosie or Madge.

'Do you?' said both.

I did actually. Infection and inflammation of the hoof causing the pain and lameness. I pared away the affected tissue where possible and sprayed the area with an antibiotic aerosol.

I left instructions to repeat the spraying daily, hoping they could cope.

'Don't worry. We'll manage,' said Rosie.

Or was it Madge?

The Stockwells' rickety gate was to blame for what happened the following weekend. Something I'd predicted could have happened but not in the way it did happen. Over Sunday lunch.

Maxeen and I had been invited for a meal with Sarah and Jordan Ledbetter, clients of the practice, who owned several cats – or rather the cats owned them. Over the course of the year since I started at Prospect House, we'd become friends. And as they lived just a mile down the road from us in Ashton, it made it easier to meet up for the occasional meal or a drink down at the local. Their bungalow was one of three that edged a busy section of the A283 from Ashton through to Chawcombe. Though their situation meant there was a constant background murmur of traffic to the front, the backs of all three bungalows looked south with stunning views up sloping fields to the Downs; and all three had long stretches of garden backing onto those fields. Fields which were part and parcel of the Stockwells' land; and used for grazing the twins' cows and sheep. Indeed, the entrance to the track running up to that rickety gate of the Stockwells lay right next to Sarah and Jordan's property.

Maxeen and I were in their lounge enjoying a pre-Sunday lunch drink. The smell of roast lamb was wafting from the kitchen when suddenly it was joined by a chorus of baas and the crash of chairs tumbling to the floor. It sounded as someone was wrecking the joint – and I'm not talking roast here.

Jordan leapt to his feet. 'What the heck?'

Both he and Sarah dashed through to the kitchen, Maxeen and I closely following. There we were confronted by a sheep standing behind the breakfast bar. She gave us a bright, yellow-eyed stare and wagged her tail. A pile of droppings showered onto the floor. But that wasn't our main concern. It was the 50 or so other sheep crowded round the open back door, many also wagging their tails, their droppings beginning to blacken the Ledbetters' patio.

The sheep in the kitchen gave another plaintive baa and twitched her ears – actually just the one ear, her right one. The left was missing. And that gave me the clue to her identity.

'I think she's Esther,' I declared. 'One of the Stockwells' pet sheep.'

'I don't care who she is, let's get her out of here,' said Jordan, grabbing a fistful of wool on the sheep's neck and attempting to drag her towards the back door. She skated reluctantly forward across the tiled floor. With me tugging her tail, we eventually managed to manoeuvre her outdoors. That caused the rest of the flock to back away and turn to trample through Sarah's carefully cultivated herbaceous borders, liberally fertilising them at the same time. Ouch.

If she was Esther – and I was pretty certain she was – then she and I had met up a fair number of times in her short life.

I'd been at her birth – in the back of the Stockwells' Land Rover, one wild March night, the previous year. She was a breech presentation that I had to turn around in her mother's womb to get her out. It had left mum exhausted, unable to suckle. Even at that tender age, Esther knew how to get to grips with things. Especially if it was a nice, soft teat attached to a large bottle of milk. There was no bleating about the bush for that little lamb.

As a consequence, she grew into a plump yearling blessed with her mother's looks: a black face with white freckles, startling yellow-ochre eyes, black-tipped ears – well, one ear – a thick, curly coat and a tail that was forever wagging.

It wagged now as Madge and Rosie Stockwell came into sight, making slow progress as they plodded in zigzag fashion down the field. Why didn't their lack of speed surprise me?

They eventually made it down onto the track alongside the Ledbetters' bungalow and halted at the gate into their back garden – the one Esther must have nudged open to allow her pals to flock in.

'So sorry,' said one twin. (Madge?)

'We got here as quick as we could,' said the other. (Rosie?)
No comment. (Me.)

'Esther's up to her old tricks again, I see.' (Your guess.)

'Always escaping. Making a nuisance of herself.' (Don't bother.)

The two of them began to shuffle round, shunting the sheep through the gate onto the track back up to Hawkshill Farm.

Esther was not with them. Oh no. She'd skedaddled round the corner – perhaps sensing that the roast-lamb smell was too close to home for comfort. She was now methodically stripping Sarah's roses of their new spring growth.

One of the twins sighed and pulled a head collar and rope from the pocket of her dungarees. 'I guess we'll have to lead her back, Rosie.'

'Looks that way,' said her sister.

'It does.'

'Well lead the way, then.'

'Will do.'

They did, dragging the errant sheep behind them.

Esther went on to become a real escape artiste.

Her Houdini capabilities grew in line with her quest to seek pastures new. Everything seemed greener on the other side of the fence. And if there was the smallest of holes in that fence, Esther was sure to find it and wriggle through. The two bungalows next to the Ledbetters' suffered from her incursions.

Esther, having had a taste of Sarah and Jordan's patch, decided the two others were worth exploring.

The first gave her neat rows of spinach, cabbage and sprouts to chew over. The second, blocks of ornamental grasses and bonsai trees to be stripped bare – so adding to the minimalist nature of the plot.

However, Esther hadn't anticipated that minimalist garden was also the territory of a far from minimalist dog. One of large proportions. A very big, and very muscular Alsatian. It seems that as her tongue curled round the last clump of ornamental grass in that garden, the Alsatian appeared and saw her more as lamb chops than a woolly friend. A badly mauled sheep was salvaged from amongst the pagodas and wind chimes; and driven in by the twins to the hospital. Once in my surgery, Esther lay on the consulting table, her yellow eyes glazed, her chest heaving like bellows. Very shocked.

'Don't hold out much chance for her,' I said.

'You don't?' said one twin.

'He doesn't,' said the other.

I didn't.

But I did my best and got to work, stitching up the large gash in her flank. As this was Esther we were talking about, there was no holding this sheep down for long. And sure enough, she was up on her trotters in no time.

The next thing I knew she'd trotted over a main road, down a track to one of the disused gravel pits in the area, lost her footing and toppled in. I was presented with a very wet, very sandy-coloured sheep whose back leg stuck out at a very funny angle.

'Might prove difficult to mend,' I murmured.

But of course, this was Esther. Within days she was hobbling about with the aid of two metal splints and plenty of supportive bandage. And was soon on the look-out for her next adventure.

But she hadn't reckoned on Rambo.

'Who?' I queried, when one twin mentioned him.

'Our ram,' said the other twin.

'He'll soon sort her out,' said the first one.

'He knows what's what,' said the second.

Better than me then, I thought. Not knowing who was who.

It seems Rambo did a good job as by the following spring Esther was waddling around with an expectant air.

I might have guessed she'd choose a bitterly cold evening in April to go into labour. A night when I was on duty. There was a call from Carol at the hospital to inform me Esther had been straining for over two hours. Nothing had happened. Could the twins bring her in? They'd be there as soon as possible. Oh yes? Really?

I'd driven over from Ashton and had been waiting half an hour before I heard a car drive into the hospital's carpark.

The two twins slowly eased themselves out of the Land Rover as I raced out.

'She's in the back,' said one.

'We'll open up,' said the other.

'Otherwise you won't be able to see her.'

'And that wouldn't be much good.'

'No, it wouldn't.'

'No good at all.'

'Complete waste of time coming then.'

'Yes, it would.'

'Course it would.'

'Wouldn't you agree?' Both twins looked at me, blinking in the glare of the outside light flooding the carpark.

'Yes … Yes … I do,' I spluttered, hopping from one foot to another as the twins painfully edged round to the back of the Land Rover and swung the back down.

I scrambled in, straining to see Esther huddled in semi-darkness, hidden in a mound of straw, only her head visible.

'Hello, Esther … we meet again. Always in trouble, eh?'

She stared at me with those yellow eyes of hers and then

gave a bleat. It was echoed by several high-pitched bleats alongside her.

As my eyes became accustomed to the gloom, I saw two tiny dark-coloured heads buried in the straw next to her – two tiny Esther look-a-likes. She had given birth during the drive in.

I breathed a sigh of relief. No breech. No caesarean required.

Thanks to the slowness of the Stockwells she'd had extra time in which to have her lambs.

Fingers crossed she'd have more good times ahead – albeit unhurried ones – with both sets of twins – her own and Madge and Rosie.

But that wasn't the last I'd hear of the Stockwells

The call came through just after I'd finished morning surgery.

'It's the Stockwell sisters,' hissed Jean, one hand over the receiver, the other gesticulating at me. 'They're in a bit of a fix. Want you to visit.' She handed over the receiver.

'Is that the veterinary?' enquired the voice at the other end.

'Malcolm Welshman, yes.'

'We need you to come out and see to Daphne, one of our Jerseys.'

'What's the problem?'

'She's stuck.'

Mmm … in the mud … in a cow stall … I wondered before venturing to ask what she was stuck in.

'A tree.'

'A tree?'

'Yes, a tree.' There was a pause, a distant muffled murmuring before the voice returned. 'Madge says it's an oak tree, if that's of any help.'

Nope, that didn't help. If the cow was stuck, it was stuck.

The variety of tree wouldn't make the slightest difference.

After a few words of reassurance, I promised to be over within the next half an hour, curious to discover how a cow had landed up in a tree, be it oak, ash, beech or whatever.

'Could have been worse,' Jean commented.

'It could?' A tree-bound bovine sounded bad enough to me.

'Yes. It might have been a yew tree.'

'So?'

'Well, they're poisonous. She might have eaten some and be dead by now.'

'Well it wasn't. It was an oak tree.'

'But aren't acorns poisonous to cattle? You still might have a dead cow on your hands.'

Thanks, Jean. You give a guy such confidence.

The view of Hawkshill Farm tucked down in the valley was usually pleasing. Today, once I'd driven down into the farmyard, the view at close quarters wasn't so pleasing due to the heavy rain we'd had over the past few days. The yard was a morass of cow dung, puddled and odorous. A sea of slurry. And sunk in it, up to their welly-booted calves, waiting for me, were Madge and Rosie. Both attired in mud-splattered green overalls. Both, as usual, indistinguishable from each other.

'You've arrived then,' said one.

'Come to rescue Daphne,' said the other.

'Well, if possible,' I said, having donned my own boots to join them in the middle of the yard's lagoon of bovine excrement.

'Anything's possible,' chorused the twins.

'Well, let's get cracking. Lead the way,' I said, anxious to see this arboreal cow.

'You want to take him, Madge,' said Rosie to Madge, 'while

I fetch bow saw and shears?'

'Or I can get them, Rosie, while you take him,' said Madge.

I eventually found myself wading out of the yard being led by one of them, though I didn't know which one. We slipped and slithered along a hoof-pitted track round the back of the farm complex until we reached a wooden five-bar gate, tied shut with a piece of orange baler twine.

'Best climb over,' said Madge/Rosie. Ahead, stretched into the distance up a slope, was a wide meadow, much of the grass eaten down, the results of its digestion scattered in piles as far as the eye could see. Almost central to that meadow was a solitary tree. House-high. Dead. Its branches bleached and ridged by countless storms and summer sun. About shoulder height, there was a natural bifurcation of the trunk into two limbs. Weathering over the years had caused a split between those limbs. The result was a crack which had spiralled down to open up in the bole of the tree as an ovoid cavity of decayed wood, large enough to be filled by a Jersey cow's head.

'There's the oak,' said the twin, pointing at the tree unnecessarily. 'And that's Daphne stuck in it,' she added, even more unnecessarily. 'See?'

Of course, I could see. What did she take me for? A fool? But when I said, 'Least she's not dead.' (I'd been thinking yew, oak trees and acorns courtesy of Jean) I got a look from the twin that clearly suggested I was one.

Daphne's head was currently entrenched in that tree's bole, out of sight. On approaching her, I could see the rest of the Jersey looked remarkably calm. Regular movements of her rib cage as she breathed. Otherwise stock still, only the occasional swish of her tail.

Several of the other Jerseys had gathered round, curious as to what had happened. Madge/Rosie shooed them away while

I put my black bag down and bit my lip, wondering what to do. I felt I was in as deep a hole as Daphne. Not helped when the other twin turned up with the bow saw and a claw hammer. The tree was far too big to hack any of the tree's two limbs away from the cow's head. But it gave me an idea.

I walked round to the other side of the trunk and tapped it. As hoped, it sounded hollow.

'Let's try chipping the trunk away here,' I said, giving my reasons why.

'Veterinary wants a hole,' said Madge to Rosie. Or was it Rosie to Madge?

Within 15 minutes, we'd succeeded in making a large enough aperture for us to see Daphne peering through at us from inside.

'Right, now let's see if we can shoo her backwards,' I declared. 'Make a bit of a song and dance.'

'Veterinary wants a song and dance,' said one twin, turning to her sister.

'Would a waltz do?' said the sister.

'Or perhaps you'd prefer a foxtrot?' said the other.

'I don't mind what you do,' I shouted, jumping up and down in frustration.

'A bit of hokey cokey might be fun,' they chorused together.

So Rosie and Madge put their left arms in, their left arms out, in out, in out, they shook them all about. They did the hokey cokey and then turned around, yelling, 'That's what it's all about.'

There was no stopping them now.

At full throttle, they roared:

'Whoa, the hokey cokey.

Whoa, the hokey cokey.

Knees bend, arms stretch

Rah, rah, RAH.'

At that final RAH, they lunged forward and slammed the palms of their hands against the tree. There was a petrified moo from within the trunk and then a scrabbling of hooves as a startled Daphne backed away from the sight of the twirling twins and freed herself.

Phew. What a relief. Daphne had got herself out of a hole.

And I had done likewise. Hoo … RAH … RAH … RAH.

20

Always Good for a Laugh

I've always had a rather juvenile sense of humour. I can trace it back to when I was around seven years old – a year before our move out to Africa and when we were still living in Bournemouth. It was then I first discovered the joy of jokes.

My parents had made friends with a couple who had a daughter around the same age as me. Christine and I hit it off immediately, especially when we discovered a mutual interest in playing jokes on our parents. Oh boy, did they suffer as a consequence. Two incidents, in particular, are indelibly fixed in my mind.

The first involved a picnic outing. A drive out to the New Forest. The two sets of parents had organised the food between them. Christine told me her mum was bringing some hard-boiled eggs as part of their contribution. That gave me the idea for a joke.

We were breezing along the A31, all crowded into my father's old estate car, me and Christine squashed in the back with her parents, when I broke the seal on the glass stink bomb I'd hidden in my pocket. The smell of badly rotting eggs began to odorously engulf the car.

There was a sniff from my mother. 'Phew,' she gasped.

A fanning of the face from Christine's mum. 'What a pong,' her response.

Christine's dad pinched his nostrils between finger and thumb without saying a word.

Father, who was driving, was less subtle. 'Bloody hell. Who's farted?' he demanded, winding down his window.

By which time, Christine and I had been reduced to giggling heaps, rocking backwards and forwards, tears streaming down our faces, gasping for air.

'Oh, you poor dears,' exclaimed Christine's mum, leaning over to fan our faces. 'It must be the eggs.' Which made us convulse even more.

'Better stop then,' said my mother. 'Get some fresh air.'

'Too damned right,' muttered Father, swerving into the next layby he spotted. Here, we all piled out, Christine and I staggering round in exaggerated circles, screwing up our faces, flapping our arms wildly, milking the scene for all it was worth; while Christine's mum wrenched open the hamper and tossed the suspect eggs into a nearby hedge.

Then there was the incident of the smashed crockery. My parents and I had been invited over for afternoon tea. Nothing too grand but nevertheless a traditional tea with the best china, a range of finely cut sandwiches, a cake-stand of freshly baked scones, homemade strawberry jam and clotted cream. All very scrumptious.

Christine and I planned a prank. I'd already bought a joke package consisting of a tiny pile of thin metal sheets looped together, which, according to the instructions, if dropped on a hard surface sounded like crockery smashing. What could be better than an afternoon tea to try it out?

We could barely wait to put our plan into action.

With tea finished, I stood up. 'Can I take the plates out?' Christine's mum had started to pile them up on a tray, going from armchair to armchair where we had been sitting.

'Why that's very kind of you, Malcolm. Thanks.'

I tried to hide a smirk as I looked across at Christine who was gathering up the teacups, making a pile of the saucers and placing them on the tray.

'Make sure it's not too heavy for you, dear,' said Christine's mum, looking a little concerned as more and more of her best china got stacked on the tray.

'Don't worry, I'll be really careful,' I reassured her, lifting the tray up; and with Christine opening the living room door for me, walked slowly out of the room and down the hallway to the kitchen.

'Right,' I whispered as she joined me. 'Here goes.' I put the tray down on the kitchen table, slipped the packet of metal plates out of my pocket, held them up; and then dropped them.

I must say the sound of them hitting the tiled floor sounded very realistic. An explosion of breaking crockery. Absolutely smashing.

As rehearsed, Christine cried out, 'Oh, Malcolm, just look what you've done.'

''I couldn't help it. It was an accident,' I replied at the top of my voice; following it with a very life-like wail which I'd practised to perfection.

We both ran quickly into the living room before anyone had a chance to come out and see what had happened. The sound of those metal plates crashing to the floor must have sounded convincing. That, coupled with our melodramatics, would have accounted for the looks expressed on our parents' faces. Horror on my mother's, her mouth open, cheeks white. Fury on my father's, cheeks burning. Confusion and concern making Christine's parents' cheeks a motley mix of red and white blotches.

'Never mind, dear,' stuttered Christine's mum, clearly struggling to mask her despair at having her precious tea set smashed. 'Accidents will happen.' She patted my arm. 'They can always be replaced.'

Christine tittered.

Her dad rebuked her. 'It's no laughing matter.'

That started me off. I sniggered. Mother and Father tutted and shook their heads. 'We'll pay for the damage,' Father volunteered.

A loud guffaw exploded from me. 'No damage done, Dad,' I gasped. 'It was a joke.'

'I don't think it's funny,' he said when I explained.

'Nor do I,' said Mother, with a loud sniff.

Which made it all the funnier for Christine and me.

I still get the giggles thinking about it.

Christmas at Prospect House gave me the excuse to come up with another wheeze.

The plastic Father Christmas that I carried into reception was attired as one would expect. Red tunic trimmed in white, red hat with bell, brown sack on his back. He was of medium height, sporting long flowing white locks and beard. His smile looked fixed as did the glazed look in his eyes. He shuddered into life as Tony opened the front door into reception, rocking backwards and forwards while emitting a croaky Ho … Ho … Ho … reminiscent of a grasshopper being eviscerated.

'What the heck …?' he exclaimed, looking at the Santa with the wide-eyed wonder of an alien from outer space, his jaw almost hitting the floor as it finally subsided into silence.

Jean, perched uncomfortably on her stool the other side of the reception desk, fiddled nervously with her pearls. 'Nothing to do with me. It's Malcolm's idea.' She nodded in my direction.

'A car-boot find of mine last Sunday,' I explained. 'He's wired to the front door. Thought it would give the hospital a bit of extra cheer.'

The Santa suddenly erupted into another spasm of jerks and Ho … Ho … Ho … s as Mrs Paget, a client of mine, entered with a toy poodle. The little dog took one look at the rocking Santa, raised his hackles and with a high-pitched growl, shot under a chair. Mrs Paget, having registered her arrival, scooped the dog up, muttering reassurances to him as she quickly disappeared into the waiting room.

Tony scratched his chin dubiously. 'Well, maybe it's better than that Christmas tree of yours last year.'

Ah, yes. My tree. I had indeed tried to get in the spirit of things last Christmas by suggesting the hospital had a real tree in the waiting room. Carol had been dead against it, she being very strict about keeping the hospital spick and span. 'All those dropping needles, Malcolm. Could get very messy.' In the end, Tony and Clifford let me have my way. After all, being the new boy and on duty over the Christmas period, they felt it was the least they could do. Carol and Linda did eventually get into the festive mood and set about decorating the tree once I'd potted it up and dragged it into the waiting room. They festooned it with cheap Poundshop buys: lurid purple and emerald glass balls; red shapeless plastic figures which could have been Victorian carol singers or Darth Vaders from *Star Wars* depending on how you viewed them. But no lights.

'Definitely out,' declared Clifford. 'We don't want anyone's pooch chewing the wires and electrocuting themselves, do we?'

No … No … No … I thought.

When I eventually got to see Mrs Paget, I was confronted with her toy poodle shaking his head. His topknot was tied up with a red ribbon and some tiny Christmas bells so that he was ringing all the way through to the consulting room.

Ding-a-ling. Ding-a-ling.

'He's been doing it for a couple of days now,' she said. 'I've tried to stop him and told him off several times.'

Told or tolled? I wondered.

Ho … Ho … Ho … went Santa down the corridor.

'Just hold his head while I have a look down his ear canal,' I instructed. With the cone of my auriscope gently eased down the poodle's ear, I could see the cause. A pine needle. I inserted the tip of some crocodile forceps through the cone and was able to grasp the needle and pull it out.

'Good boy, Tinkerbell,' said Mrs Paget with a sigh of relief. The poodle, true to his name gave a final ring of his head.

Ho … Ho … Ho …

There were more appointments to come. Many more. Oh … Oh … Oh …

A first vaccination. The puppy cowered on the table and piddled. 'There, that wasn't so bad was it?' I finished injecting him in the scruff and rewarded him with a doggie choc drop. He gave me an enormous slobbery lick, wagged his tail, hunched his back and jettisoned a solid sausage of faeces over the edge of the table. Thanks, matey.

Terry, an Airedale, plodded in for his monthly check-up. I was wondering if the change in digoxin dosage for his heart was suiting him.

'He chased a cat down the garden,' his owner proudly informed me.

An overweight, rheumy-eyed spaniel waddled in. He'd been rubbing his head along the edge of the owner's settee. Turned out he had a wart growing on the edge of his upper right eyelid causing irritation. Hence the rubbing. An op was booked in to have the wart removed.

A peke with severe halitosis was next. He reeked. 'Ming's teeth do need a good clean-up,' I explained to the owner, as three plaque-encrusted, yellow lower incisors fell out between my fingers when I prised open the dog's jaws to take a look.

'Providing there's any left,' said his owner, huffily.

Dexter, a young black Labrador, was next. He'd presented a couple of days back. Dejected. Off his food – usually had the typical eagerness for food exhibited by most Labradors i.e. an absolute piglet. No normal bowel actions. I was worried I was seeing a foreign-body case. Symptoms were similar. Though no history of him having swallowed anything untoward. At that first examination, I'd poked and prodded his abdomen and not got any reaction. No indication of pain. Even so, I gave Dexter a shot of antibiotic and anti-inflammatory – more as a precautionary measure; and I did warn that we might have to have him in for an X-ray if there was no improvement. 'Meanwhile, keep a watch-out in case he passes something,' I instructed.

There was clearly a much-improved dog when Dexter bounded in full of tail-wag.

'I kept a careful eye on him as you instructed,' said his owner. 'And he did pass something this morning.' He rummaged in a carrier bag and pulled out a rectangular white tab. 'I have cleaned it up,' he added as he passed it to me. 'Rather appropriate for the time of year, don't you think?'

I found myself looking at a plastic cake decoration. The red lettering on this one spelt out 'Merry Christmas'.

Ho ... Ho ... Ho ... went my Santa down the corridor.

By the time I'd finished afternoon surgery, I was feeling quite frazzled. The wretched Ho ... Ho ... ing constantly echoing up from reception, contrary to filling me with Christmas spirit, had had the opposite effect. I now felt quite hostile to the Santa.

'You worn out as well?' I said to Jean as she switched off the computer, ready to go home.

'I coped. But can't say the same for him.' She nodded at the Father Christmas. There were yellow stains up his trousers where I was told several dogs had cocked their legs. The long scratches down his tunic were due to a cat that had clawed him. And the green droppings that hung from his hair and beard were from an escaped budgie.

Jean and I looked at each other and grinned.

And, no joke, our mutual 'Hee ... Hee ... Hee...s' rang out as we slammed the reception door shut.

I'm not sure religion and practical jokes go together but I've experienced occasions when the two have interacted.

One involved another of my pranks – that leg-pulling phase when I was an eight-year-old still going strong when I was a 15-year-old. Oh dear. Seems I never grew up.

It all started when I discovered the art of paper folding – the fascination of origami. I began with simple folds, but rapidly progressed to more complicated shapes. I ended up creating a massive spider. A gigantic tarantula which I covered in black gloss paint and added two large, menacing red eyes and a sharp, red beak. A splendid creation of which I was duly proud. I'm not too sure how the practical joke evolved but having taken the spider to school with a ball of thin twine attached, I clearly had something in mind. And it involved our divinity teacher. A mild-mannered man, of even disposition and serious intent. He was certainly passionate about his beliefs and the teaching of them. And it showed. Godliness oozed from every pore. Though no reason to subject him to the joke I was to play on him. But then God works in mysterious ways. And this was one of those ways.

Before the start of class, I threaded the ball of twine up through the catch of the upper casement window of the classroom and lowered the attached spider outside until it disappeared below the sill. I then unwound enough thread to stretch across to the desk where I was sitting. So far, so good.

In marched Mr Longfellow, the sleeves of his black gown flapping from his shoulders, a sheaf of papers and a large red Bible under one arm. 'Good afternoon, boys,' he said serenely, placing his papers on the desk to the side of the blackboard while holding on to the Bible, opening it at one of many pages marked by a folded slip.

'Good afternoon, sir,' we obediently replied in unison. Several faces had barely suppressed smirks on them, anticipating what was to come.

Mr Longfellow smiled benignly. 'Today we're going to cover the topic of "Forgiveness" and how the Bible can teach us to do just that.' He turned to the blackboard and chalked up the words 'What is forgiveness?' in his large spider-like scrawl. I tensed my fingers over the twine wrapped round them, jerked the string a little, testing.

Mr Longfellow swung back to face us again and glanced down at the Bible open in his left hand. 'Ecclesiastes 7:9. Do not be quick to take offence, for the taking of offence is the mark of a fool,' he quoted, gazing round the classroom with another benign smile on his face. 'And I'm sure none of us would want to feel a fool, would we, boys?'

'No, sir,' we murmured.

'No, of course not.' Mr Longfellow raised his Bible up. 'Now I'm going to give you five points taken from the Bible here. These will show you how to forgive someone.' He turned to the blackboard and started to scribble the first point – about remembering what forgiveness involved.

Cue for me to pull on the thread. Up rose the spider to loom large above the windowsill. A ripple of mirth swept across the room. Mr Longfellow paused in his chalking and turned sharply.

At the same time, I released the tension on the thread and the spider dropped rapidly out of sight.

If Mr Longfellow was puzzled he didn't show it. He thumbed through to another marker in his Bible, turned back and continued to write.

Second point: to recognise the benefits of forgiving. Matthew 6:14,15.

Cue spider's ascent. More titters.

Mr Longfellow twisted round in mid-sentence.

Cue spider's descent.

Back to the blackboard. Third point: be empathetic Matthew 7:12.

Giggles as spider's legs swirled in the breeze halfway up the window.

Mr Longfellow's benign smile turned into a semi-grimace as he spun round to peer at the class.

Fourth point scribbled up. Be reasonable. Colossians 3:13.

Another arachnoid appearance. A wave of laughter washed

across the room. A full-blown grimace from Mr Longfellow ensued.

Fifth point. Act quickly. Work to forgive as soon as you can rather than letting your anger fester. Ephesians 4:26, 27.

Point five ignored as in full fury, Mr Longfellow roared, 'Welshman, haul that thing in at once.'

I hadn't been quick enough during point five and the spider had still been dangling by its thread in full view of everyone.

I did as instructed, sincerely hoping that Mr Longfellow would abide by the forgiveness points he'd outlined on the blackboard. No such luck. Not one of the five were forthcoming. So, no practising what you preach then.

Instead, my spider was wrenched from my hands, and trembling, Mr Longfellow wound the remains of the thread round my neck to allow the spider to dangle down my chest. 'Go stand in there,' he seethed, pointing to the waste paper basket.

He saw my questioning look.

'Yes, in that basket where you belong,' he hissed, his features twitching as he fought to control his feelings.

So, with spider attached, I found myself standing in the waste paper basket for the rest of the lesson. That certainly taught me one.

There was one client who'd have had a good chuckle if I'd told him about my spider joke. He saw the world as a place to have a laugh. Rev. Sidney Jolie. He was a travelling rector, based in Westcott, who spread the gospel round the churches of West Sussex and beyond while imbuing his preaching with humour.

He'd recently paid a visit to St Mary's across the way from Willow Wren in Ashton. I'd been passing the vicarage on my way over to the rec with Judy and Winnie when Rev. James collared me by beckoning from over his garden wall. I glanced at my watch. Did I have half an hour spare for a 'quick' chat I wondered, knowing Rev. James' tendency to drone on and on? There was a further wave of his hand, so I was clearly being summoned. No choice then.

'Ah, Malcolm, I've been meaning to have a word,' he began (a word ... one word? No way was that possible with you all week), 'but with time fugit as it does then the minutes tick by and before you know it the time's passed, hasn't it?'

It does if one gets cornered by you, I thought.

'It's just that this coming Sunday we're having a special service conducted by Rev. Sidney Jolie who I understand from my conversations with him over the phone, is a client of yours?'

I nodded and opened my mouth to speak.

But not quick enough. Rev. James had stepped up a gear and was in full throttle. I was regaled with the Rev. Sidney's CV – much of which I already knew. How he'd become interested in clowning at the age of eight. Read theology at Bristol. Was a vicar in Bermondsey. But resigned to attend the Fool Time circus school. Since when, he'd travelled all over the country juggling and playing the fool in churches, rugby clubs, hospitals, even prisons. 'And now he's coming here,' Rev. James concluded, 'to St Mary's next Sunday. Hope you and Maxeen can come along, should you have the time to do so, bearing in mind your other obligations. Apparently, his services can be very entertaining.'

'Sounds as if it could be fun,' I said, my curiosity aroused. 'We'll certainly pop over.'

And it was certainly fun. Dressed in an outsized dog collar, size 18 red boots and a large red nose, Rev. Sidney proceeded down the nave mounted on a unicycle. Several times during his sermon he stopped to blow bubbles above the pulpit. 'God's promises,' he declared. 'Now let us pray.' For a finale, he clomped down from the pulpit to where a slack wire hung across the aisle attached to two poles. I had been wondering what it was there for all the way through the sermon. And now I was to find out.

'This is my slack rope of faith,' he announced before lifting himself onto it from a pew. 'It demonstrates the wobbliness of faith,' he continued, flailing his arms while the wire swung backwards and forwards, threatening to topple him off into the adjacent font. During this time, Rev. James was biting his lip and crossing himself fervently, lost for words. A first for him.

It was Rev. Sidney's little Cairn terrier that brought him to Prospect House. A dark brindle by the name of Toto. 'After Dorothy's in *The Wizard of Oz*,' I heard him explain to Jean as she took his particulars. 'I just adore that film. Don't you?' There was no reply from her. I imagined the sight of him in his full clown regalia, with white-painted face, vermilion nose and cheeks, was giving her plenty to think about without conjuring up munchkins skipping along a yellow brick road.

When he klick-klacked into my consulting room wearing his 18-size red boots and cuddling Toto, he was humming 'Somewhere Over the Rainbow'.

I remarked on the Sunday sermon we'd attended, and how much Maxeen and I had enjoyed it.

'Why, thank you, thank you. Most kind.' He gave a little bow. 'I like to instil a bit of fun. Perform a bit of slapstick. A few tricks. Helps to spread the message more. And Lord knows, we do need to have our spirits lifted whenever possible. Talking of which, my precious little Toto seems lacking in spirits at the moment. A bit down in the dumps. Aren't you, sweetie.' The reverend kissed the dog on her nose. She responded with a lick on his lips. 'Just hope it's nothing too serious.'

With Toto gently eased onto the table, I started a general check-over while asking some questions.

'How's her appetite?'

'A bit off her food. Getting picky. Usually woofs it down.'

'Any sickness?'

Rev. Sidney shook his head.

'And are her motions okay?'

The reverend nodded. 'Fine.'

I took the Cairn's temperature. Normal.

Rev. Sidney went on, 'I have noticed the occasional cough. Especially after she's been for a walk. Thought perhaps it was her pulling on her lead too much.'

I listened to Toto's chest with my stethoscope. Checked her heart at the same time. Both seemed okay. Then, I gently palpated her abdomen. All the while, she patiently stood on the table and let me do it without a murmur. Only when I was pressing her mid-abdominal area and felt a lump, did she let out a little squeak. 'Sorry, pet, did that hurt?'

The clinical examination completed, I turned to Rev. Sidney. 'I think we should have Toto in and get her tummy X-rayed. There's something there that's a bit of a worry. And we'll get some blood tests done at the same time.'

I'm sure Rev. Sidney's face blanched under all that white paint. His quavering voice said it all. 'She will be all right? She's my life.'

My worst fears were confirmed when X-rays taken of Toto showed a large white mass in her abdomen; and with petechia in her liver and lungs. Cancer. Lymphosarcoma most likely. And it had spread to other organs. The prognosis was poor.

Rev. Sidney listened while I told him the bad news, his hand constantly ruffling Toto's neck. 'How long have we got left?' he whispered, hugging her to his chest.

That was always going to be a difficult question. Maybe a week or so. Depended on how Toto's quality of life deteriorated.

'I wouldn't want her to suffer,' Rev. Sidney murmured.

The decision was made 10 days later. 'The time has come,' said the reverend, taking a deep breath as he gently laid Toto on my consulting table. 'Can I stay with her?'

'No question. Of course,' I replied.

Rev. Sidney gathered the little dog in his arms, hugging her close, his cheek brushing hers. She licked his hand, seeming to sense she was leaving him – this to be her last good-bye. As I slipped the lethal injection into the Cairn's vein, her black-button eyes slowly sank down; and with a final big sigh and a twitch of her paws, she passed away. 'Bye … bye … my precious,' the reverend murmured as his red-clown lips quivered and tears coursed down his white-painted cheeks.

On my drive home across the Downs that evening, the sky was grey-lilac, low, rain-packed. A heavy April shower swept ahead of me. The setting sun caught the cloud burst. As it did, a rainbow suddenly shimmered across the sky, arching over the pewter clouds in a glowing kaleidoscope of blue, red, yellow and green.

It was a sign. I was sure of it.

Toto was happy in heaven.

Somewhere over that rainbow.

Now joining those precious pets of mine that have passed over. None of which will ever be forgotten.

Loyal, sweet-natured Poucher. Cheeky, chirpy Polly with her 'Wotcher mates'. And of course, Nigel the newt in his little box. Priceless? Maybe not. But he was certainly matchless.

They, and others, have coloured my life in much the same way the rainbow ahead now coloured the sky. All of them a treasure. Far better than any pot at the end of a rainbow. Truly worth their weight in gold.

28091717R00165

Printed in Great Britain
by Amazon